# Cambridge Theology in the Nineteenth Century

## Enquiry, Controversy and Truth

DAVID M. THOMPSON
*University of Cambridge, UK*

ASHGATE

© David M. Thompson 2008

David M. Thompson has asserted his moral right under the Copyright, Designs and Patents Act, 1988, to be identified as the author of this work.

Published by
Ashgate Publishing Limited
Gower House
Croft Road
Aldershot
Hampshire GU11 3HR
England

Ashgate Publishing Company
Suite 420
101 Cherry Street
Burlington, VT 05401-4405
USA

Ashgate website: http://www.ashgate.com

**British Library Cataloguing in Publication Data**
Thompson, David M.
  Cambridge theology in the nineteenth century : enquiry, controversy and truth
  1. Church of England – Doctrines – History – 19th century
  2. Theology, Doctrinal – England – Cambridge – History –
  19th century
  I. Title
  230.3'42659'09034

**Library of Congress Cataloging-in-Publication Data**
Thompson, David M.
  Cambridge theology in the nineteenth century : enquiry, controversy, and truth / David M. Thompson.
    p. cm.
  Includes bibliographical references and index.
  ISBN 978-0-7546-5624-1 (hardcover : alk. paper) 1. Theology—Study and teaching—England—Cambridge—History—19th century. 2. University of Cambridge—History—19th century. 3. England—Church history—19th century.
  I. Title.

  BT30.G7T46 2007
  230.0942'09034—dc22

                                                                      2007029144

ISBN 978-0-7546-5624-1

Printed and bound in Great Britain by TJ International Ltd, Padstow, Cornwall.

# CAMBRIDGE THEOLOGY IN THE NINETEENTH CENTURY

Many books have been written about nineteenth-century Oxford theology, but what was happening in Cambridge? This book provides the first continuous account of what might be called 'the Cambridge theological tradition', by discussing its leading figures from Richard Watson and William Paley, through Herbert Marsh and Julius Hare, to the trio of Lightfoot, Westcott and Hort. It also includes a chapter on nonconformists such as Robertson Smith, P.T. Forsyth and T.R. Glover. The analysis is organised around the defences that were offered for the credibility of Christianity in response to hostile and friendly critics. In this period the study of theology was not yet divided into its modern self-contained areas. A critical approach to scripture was taken for granted, and its implications for ecclesiology, the understanding of salvation and the social implications of the Gospel were teased out (in Hort's phrase) through enquiry and controversy as a way to discover truth. Cambridge both engaged with German theology and responded positively to the nineteenth-century 'crisis of faith'.

*For much of the twentieth century, especially in the thirty years after the end of the Second World War, Cambridge theology was no mere academic ghetto. David Thompson himself recalls the intellectual excitement of the early 1960s, when the questions raised by the Cambridge theologians – and their manner of raising them – were able to capture the minds and imaginations of a generation about to transform British society. As an historian, Thompson knows that such moments do not arrive from nowhere, and that to understand the story and the significance of Cambridge theology in the twentieth century, one has to go back to the nineteenth. As might be expected, the great trio of Westcott, Lightfoot, and Hort feature prominently in his groundbreaking study, but their work too is contextualised by a series of figures and debates reaching back to the eighteenth century. A story that weaves its way through so many shifting and interrelated currents in national, Church, and university life, as well as touching on private histories of faith and loss of faith is not easy to summarise, but Thompson brings the passion of his protagonists to life. Cambridge theology itself emerges as equally hard to summarise: 'broad', tolerant, questioning, difficult, attentive to the validity of science and to the demands of new historical criticism – certainly; but, at the same time, often all too 'establishment' (until the arrival in the late-nineteenth century of the nonconformists); and, then again, repeatedly courageous in breaking the mould of easy conformism. This is a book that every British theologian should ponder, and it is only to be hoped that someone will now go and do likewise for Oxford!*

Revd Canon George Pattison,
Lady Margaret Professor of Divinity,
University of Oxford, UK

*David Thompson draws on his extensive knowledge of the nineteenth century to ask whether it is possible to identify a 'Cambridge tradition' in nineteenth-century theology. The pattern that emerges is one that is increasingly characterised by enquiry and openness to the truth. Anyone who wishes to understand what made Cambridge what it is today will profit from this informative study.*

Morna Hooker,
Lady Margaret's Professor of Divinity Emerita,
University of Cambridge, UK

*This book is dedicated to the Faculty of Divinity of the University of Cambridge*

*in memory of Professor Gordon Rupp: scholar, churchman and friend*

# Contents

# Preface

This book has been many years in the making. My fascination for the tradition of theology in Cambridge dates from the late Professor Gordon Rupp's inaugural lecture in November 1969 on 'Hort and the Cambridge Tradition',[1] but at that time my research interests were firmly focused elsewhere. David Newsome's Birkbeck Lectures of 1972, later published as *Two Classes of Men*, were also fascinating, but left me feeling unconvinced, for reasons that I could not identify precisely at that stage. In 1980 I was invited to preach at the Commemoration of Benefactors at my old college, Queens', in Cambridge, and chose to speak about Herbert Ryle, Hulsean Professor, 1887–1901, and President of Queens' from 1896. I was struck by the contrast between him and his predecessor a century earlier, Isaac Milner. Both came from evangelical homes; but Ryle was committed to biblical criticism. Notwithstanding the work of the Cambridge trio, Ryle clearly felt that there was still a significant job to be done; and Hort agreed. What did that mean for the way I was lecturing on the development of biblical criticism in late nineteenth-century England?

The Faculty of Divinity asked me to give a lecture to mark the centenary of the deaths of Joseph Barber Lightfoot in 1989, and the University of Durham also invited me to give one of the commemorative Lightfoot lectures in that year. When I was president of the Cambridge Theological Society in 1993, I used my presidential address to explore some of the themes of early nineteenth-century Cambridge theology. Finally the Faculty invited me to give further commemorative lectures for the deaths of Fenton Hort and Brooke Foss Westcott in 1994 and 2001 respectively. I am grateful for these various invitations, which provoked me to think about the Cambridge theological tradition. From a completely different perspective my involvement in drafting regulations for the various revisions of the Theological Tripos in the last thirty years has also made me think about why we regard particular combinations of subjects and papers as essential or optional.

Unfortunately this book went to press just before the publication of the book by John R. Gibbins, *John Grote: Cambridge University and the Development of Victorian Thought* (Exeter, 2007), which fills in many of the links between Julius Hare and the Cambridge trio, as well as developing an interesting argument about Cambridge Idealism, which also links to James Ward.

I am indebted to many of my colleagues over the years for the ways in which, usually unknowingly, they have prompted my thoughts and questions. Needless to say they are not responsible for anything I have written. In this process of reflection I have become convinced that Hort's formulation of enquiry and

---

1    G. Rupp, 'Hort and the Cambridge Tradition' in *Just Men* (London, 1977), pp. 151–66.

controversy, as a process leading to the formulation of truth is the true mark of the Cambridge tradition.

I am grateful to my wife, Margaret, and my youngest son, Stephen, for editorial work on the manuscript and for their critical comments to make the book more readable. I am also indebted to the staff at Ashgate for their hard work in bringing this book to publication.

May 2007

# Acknowledgements

I am grateful for permission to quote extracts from the *Collected Works of Samuel Taylor Coleridge*, published by Routledge and Princeton University Press as Bollingen Series LXXV.

# Abbreviations

CUL refers to Cambridge University Library.
*CYB* refers to the *Congregational Year Book*.
*DNB* refers to the original edition of the *Dictionary of National Biography*.
*ODNB* refers to the *Oxford Dictionary of National Biography* (Oxford 2004).

Basic biographical information for persons mentioned in the text is taken from the new *Oxford Dictionary of National Biography* unless otherwise stated.

# Introduction

The similarities and differences between Oxford and Cambridge have always been a source of fascination, not least to those who belong to either place (or both). This book explores the question of whether a 'Cambridge tradition' can be identified in theology for the 'long nineteenth century', stretching roughly from the time of the French Revolution to the First World War. Whereas the Oxford Movement is well-known and much written about, is it possible to talk about a Cambridge Movement in the same way?[1] The suggestion of a difference goes back to the nineteenth century itself. Sir Leslie Stephen (1832–1904) wrote with characteristic self-assurance:

> An interesting essay might, I fancy, be written upon the nature and origin of the difference between the Oxford and the Cambridge spirit. Whatever the cause, one distinction is marked. Oxford has long been fertile in prophets; in men who cast a spell over a certain number of disciples, and not only propagate ideas, but exercise a personal sway. At Cambridge no such leader, so far as I can remember, presented himself in my time; and, moreover, Cambridge men were generally inclined to regard their apparent barrenness with a certain complacency. Spiritual guides are troublesome personages. A prophet, perhaps we thought, is apt to be a bit of a humbug, and at any rate a cause of humbug in others.[2]

Presumably Stephen was referring to his own time at Cambridge, where he was an undergraduate from 1850 to 1854, and then a Fellow of Trinity Hall (1854–64); and he also probably had John Henry Newman in mind as an example of an Oxford prophet.

This book is not the essay which Stephen had in mind. It is rather the result of reflection over a period of twenty-five years. When I spoke at Queens' College, Cambridge about Herbert Ryle, Hulsean Professor of Divinity, President of Queens', Bishop of Exeter and Winchester and finally Dean of Westminster, I was intrigued by the fact that he stood for the Hulsean Professorship in 1887 specifically to tackle the problems raised by Old Testament criticism. Yet he was the son of the strongly evangelical J.C. Ryle, Bishop of Liverpool. Similarly Bishop Knox of Manchester was an equally prominent evangelical and his sons moved

---

1   James White's book on *The Cambridge Movement*, for all its interest as an exploration of the Cambridge Ecclesiological Society, is hardly about theology: J.F. White, *The Cambridge Movement: The Ecclesiologists and the Gothic Revival* (Cambridge, 1962).

2   L. Stephen, 'Jowett's Life', in Jowett, B. *The Interpretation of Scripture and other Essays* (London n.d.), p. x; originally published in *The National Review*, May 1897. Noel Annan explored something of the background to Stephen's hostility to Jowett in N. Annan, *Leslie Stephen* (London 1951), pp. 130–41.

in different directions too. But Knox's Oxford-educated sons moved differently from Ryle. Was that a coincidence or was it significant?

This led to various other questions. For example, was it really the case that Cambridge theology was dead in the nineteenth century and the only interesting things were happening in Oxford? Why should English theology be judged by German norms? How do we determine what the most important theological questions in a given period are? Finally, how convincing is it to regard the Cambridge trio of Westcott, Lightfoot and Hort as providing the English 'answer' to biblical criticism? Is that formulation a fair representation of their aims, quite apart from their achievements?

The theme has been tackled in some ways before. David Newsome's Birkbeck Lectures amplified the alleged distinction between Platonists and Aristotelians.[3] They were based on two remarks: Coleridge's comment in his *Table Talk* that 'Every man is born an Aristotelian, or a Platonist' and Edward Strachey's statement in a letter to his aunt that 'Maurice says it is the great evil of everything at Oxford that there is nothing but Aristotelianism. And I find it was the superiority of Cambridge in this respect that made him think it so much better for me to go to the latter university.'[4] Newsome's argument is presented in a characteristically fascinating way, but the situation was more complex. Jowett was a keen editor of Plato, without fitting obviously into Newsome's Platonist characterisation. F.D. Maurice commented in his memoir of Archdeacon Julius Hare that Hare owed little or nothing to Whately: the world of philology and poetry was very different from that of logic and political economy. Maurice also referred to the chasm between the Platonical and the Aristotelian intellects, whilst at the same time noting that this proved the impossibility or lack of necessity of a Broad Church party embracing both.[5] Peter Hinchliff suggested that the Broad Church stream divided into two – one from Coleridge to Maurice and Colenso, the other from Arnold to Stanley, Jowett and Frederick Temple. 'It would be over-simplification,' he added, 'to say one was Cambridge and the other Oxford, but perhaps that had something to do with it.'[6] But the term 'Broad Church' could be abandoned altogether, particularly as the Cambridge 'members' disowned the label.

In any case it is necessary to be careful in generalising about places. Oxford produced Arnold and Jowett as well as Newman and Pusey, and it is not self-evident that one pair was more characteristic of the place than the other. Contemporaries tended to say rather that Cambridge was not subject to the same

---

3   D. Newsome, *Two Classes of Men: Platonism and English Romantic Thought* (London, 1974).

4   2 July 1830: *The Collected Works of Samuel Taylor Coleridge*, xiv, 1: *Table Talk*, ed. C. Woodring (London, 1990), p. 172; F. Maurice, *The Life of Frederick Denison Maurice* (London, 1884), i, pp. 206–7.

5   J.C. Hare, *The Victory of Faith*, ed. E.H. Plumptre (3rd edn, London, 1874), pp. xviii–xix.

6   P. Hinchliff, *God and History: Aspects of British Theology, 1875–1914* (Oxford, 1992), p. 50.

party tensions, and indeed theologically prided itself on a non-party approach. Is this judgement accurate? If so, in what did this non-party approach consist?

The contrast is certainly not between religious commitment and religious indifference. Sometimes theological vigour has been equated with theological partisanship. Oxford therefore seems lively; whereas Cambridge is more readily summarised in Leslie Stephen's words 'You cannot appeal to men's "souls" in the name of the differential calculus' – a reference to the dominance of mathematics in the Cambridge Tripos until at least the mid-nineteenth century.[7] That way of putting the point diminishes the significance of the evangelical tradition: and although Stephen wished to do that, Cambridge theology in the early nineteenth century was dominated by what might be called moderate evangelicals. There was even an intriguing alliance between traditional eighteenth-century theology, which was confident that it was possible to meet scepticism by the application of reason to the understanding of scripture, and the newer evangelical inheritance. The mutual interaction between these rather different approaches gave Cambridge its distinctive character, but involved a reinterpretation of each.

Sir Leslie Stephen has cast a long shadow over the understanding of this period. For many years his rather mournful portrait hung in a room in the old Divinity School in St John's Street. His *History of English Thought in the Eighteenth Century*, first published in 1876, has had an enduring influence. Time and time again Stephen set the tone for the interpretation of particular eighteenth-century thinkers. His charges of covert deism or Unitarianism levelled at a series of Anglican and Dissenting divines have passed into the common understanding, such that it comes as a surprise sometimes to realise how little substance there is to them. No one who regularly sings Isaac Watts's hymns can credibly accept Stephen's insinuation that his views about the trinity '*seem* to have shown traces of the Unitarian tendencies which affected the old dissenters'.[8] What Stephen failed to appreciate were the problems inherently involved in exploring classical trinitarian theology with a Lockean epistemology; but that does not mean that the eighteenth-century divines who failed to appreciate those problems were covert deists, socinians or Unitarians.

Stephen's *History* was the starting point for Jonathan Clark's argument about the ideological origins of English radicalism, but whilst his reintegration of theology into a secularised intellectual history was welcome, the weakness lay in the focus on the political use of theology to support the established order, rather than on theology in its own right. Moreover, although contemporary Anglicans often did castigate Arianism, socinianism and Unitarianism as the sources of political radicalism during the 1790s and 1800s, they conveniently ignored the significance of the fact that several of the proponents were Anglicans who had left the established church in the second half of the eighteenth century, rather than the

---

7    Stephen, 'Jowett's Life', p. x.

8    L. Stephen, *History of English Thought in the Eighteenth Century*, ed. Crane Brinton (London, 1962), ii, p. 328.

dissenters who had been driven out by the Act of Uniformity in 1662.[9] (Stephen might also be claimed as the originator of the Halévy thesis on Methodism and the lack of an English revolution.[10])

Yet Stephen was the son of a prominent evangelical, who had lost his faith, and readily confessed that it caused him no agony at all: 'I was not discovering that my creed was false, but that I had never really believed it.'[11] He originally conceived his *History* in 1870–71 as a history of the Deistic movement, and he finished it just as his first wife died. What he had begun with enthusiasm, he wearied of by the end. In 1895 he said that he 'wrote it with a certain audacity which I do not now possess. I took some things very easily, as it seems to me, and subsequent work, requiring more thorough research, has led me to guess that it is very superficial'. Maitland, his biographer, defended him against his own self-criticism, suggesting that in his desire to be fair 'he had too often repeated of the more unorthodox people what had been said of them by the more orthodox.' He also pointed out that Stephen began his work without any of the bibliographical resources now taken for granted, that he bought the books he used, and did his work at home, rather than in the British Museum.[12] Nevertheless, as his letters reveal, he believed in plain speaking and did not suffer gladly those whom he regarded as fools. Noel Annan commented that the value of Stephen's work was that 'as a good positivist, he does not disguise his method nor his personal interpretations'; the way in which he has often been cited, however, does not always make his personal interpretation clear.[13] Annan's later volume contained a more thorough discussion of Stephen's *History*; and he paid particular attention to Stephen's failure to discuss eighteenth-century thought in a way which did justice to his conviction (expressed in the Introduction) that 'the immediate causes of change [in ideas] are to be sought rather in social development than in the activity of a few speculative minds'.[14]

Generalisations about a whole period are always problematic. Nevertheless it can be claimed that Cambridge theology was more open to the consideration of biblical criticism for most of the nineteenth century. By the time Ryle was elected as Hulsean Professor in 1887, Oxford was moving too: the death of Dr Pusey in 1883 was quite as significant as the publication of *Lux Mundi* in 1889.[15] This is usually attributed to the work of Lightfoot, Westcott and Hort from 1861 to 1892. However, the Cambridge trio did not appear from nowhere: they had been formed in the Cambridge of the 1840s, and that is the first step for some explanation of the road they followed.

---

9   J. Clark, *English Society 1688–1832* (Cambridge, 1985), *passim*, but especially pp. 279ff.
   10  Stephen, *History of English Thought*, ii, p. 367.
   11  F.W. Maitland, *The Life and Letters of Leslie Stephen* (London, 1906), p. 145.
   12  Ibid., pp. 282–3.
   13  Annan, *Stephen*, p. 280.
   14  Stephen, *History of English Thought*, i, p. 11; N. Annan, *Leslie Stephen: The Godless Victorian* (London, 1984), pp. 221–33.
   15  C. Gore (ed.), *Lux Mundi* (15th edn, London, 1904).

The thread that links the various people to be considered in this book is an apologetic one. In the late eighteenth century the threat to Christianity was felt to come from Edward Gibbon and David Hume. Much effort was therefore devoted to showing that miracles were not completely improbable and that Gibbon's implication that the early church Fathers were incredulous forgers could be repudiated. Paley's defence, whether in the *Evidences of Christianity* and *Natural Theology*, or the less well-known *Horae Paulinae* on New Testament interpretation, was based essentially on the improbability of the truth of the accusations levelled at Christianity, and also applied probability to the New Testament by drawing attention to 'undesigned coincidences'. Richard Watson published rational defences of Christianity against both Gibbon and Tom Paine. Herbert Marsh, in his Introduction to Michaelis's work on the New Testament, produced a hypothesis to account for the documentary development of the synoptic gospels with an almost mathematical character.

Evangelicals were less concerned with Christian apologetic than preaching the Gospel, and the influence of evangelicalism on undergraduate religion at the beginning of the nineteenth century was undoubtedly profound. Here for a short period there existed the possibility of a party controversy at Cambridge to parallel what later happened at Oxford. But in the event the formation of a branch of the British and Foreign Bible Society in 1810 did not develop into anything more than a local storm, because in the end the University authorities went along with the scheme, and Marsh, who was its principal opponent, was left high and dry.

Meanwhile a reaction was beginning against Paley's complacency, particularly as expressed in the *Principles of Moral and Political Philosophy*, which were regarded as the epitome of Cambridge utilitarianism. It was associated with Samuel Taylor Coleridge, but the influence of the 'sage of Highgate Hill' was manifested at Cambridge particularly through Julius Hare. Robertson Nicoll wrote that there was a 'characteristic theology of Cambridge' as there was of Oxford, and 'Julius Hare is, in measure, to the one what J.H. Newman is to the other, whether acknowledged or not'.[16] The defence of freedom of enquiry and German theology by Hare and Connop Thirlwall antagonised Hugh James Rose, but impressed the young. From the 1830s the concern of the thinking Cambridge undergraduates was being turned towards what was later called 'the condition of England question'. Men like John Sterling, F.D. Maurice and Charles Kingsley were fearful of the possibility of practical atheism among the working men in the growing cities. For them the concerns of the Tractarians seemed academic, in the worst sense of that word – an Oxford high table spat that provoked much comment in the papers (and in subsequent history) but totally misread the fundamental issues facing the church.

For men of this stamp neither Tractarians nor evangelicals were on the right lines. Tractarians resorted to a doctrine of authority and obedience that was implausible in the changing political world, and did not give working men the credit of being able to think for themselves. Arguments for Christianity were needed, not an appeal to authority. The inspiration of scripture could not be

16  W. Robertson Nicoll, *Princes of the Church* (3rd edn, London, [1922]), p. 22.

taken as read; it had to be justified. This stimulated the further development of New Testament criticism, with a judicious use of German writers, by Westcott, Lightfoot and Hort. Similarly the evangelical tendencies to use the Bible as a 'book to keep the poor in order' (Kingsley's words in *Politics for the People*[17]) and to think the worst of human nature rather than the best were resisted by thinkers such as Maurice, Hort or Westcott. The evangelical way of thinking was usually identified with the Calvinist doctrine of total depravity, emphasis upon which had been strengthened by the evangelical revival, but in many ways it was more Augustinian than exclusively Calvinist.

Cambridge men, perhaps even more than Oxford men, were horrified by the fact that Newman went over to Rome. For them it confirmed their worst fears about the Tractarian tendency, but also about the consequences of party strife. Westcott wrote to his future wife in October 1845 about Newman's move that 'when a man of his learning and practical piety and long experience does such a thing, may not one young, ignorant, and inexperienced doubt?' Next day, he wrote, 'it is said that several more Oxford men intend to follow their example. Let Oxford boast of its divinity – we are not quite so bad as this at Cambridge'.[18] A year later he wrote that he could not 'reconcile the spirit of controversy and that of Christian faith'.[19] Westcott and Hort in different ways sought to construct an alternative theology to the traditional evangelical one, which resulted in Westcott's emphasis on the incarnation and Hort's revaluation of atonement in the context of the church. Both were lovers of St John rather than St Paul.

By the later nineteenth century confidence in this alternative formulation of Christian theology had grown. The acceptance of dissenters into the University was managed without great controversy, though Selwyn College was founded in 1882 to provide a 'safe house' for the Church of England. The Wesleyan W.F. Moulton assisted Westcott and Hort in their work on the Greek text of the New Testament. Other scholars, such as J. Rendel Harris, were welcomed. W. Robertson Smith found refuge at Cambridge from Aberdeen in the 1880s. The Presbyterian Church of England moved its theological college to Cambridge in 1899, thanks to a campaign by the 'Ladies of Castle Brae', Dr Lewis and Dr Gibson, two formidable, and wealthy, Presbyterian women. At Emmanuel Congregational Church in the 1890s, P.T. Forsyth, probably the most impressive Congregational theologian in Britain around the turn of the twentieth century, was minister; and the Baptist T.R. Glover was a member of the congregation and Fellow of St John's College, later to become the author of the best-selling *The Jesus of History*, which made the fortune of the SCM Press in 1917.

These men (and with the exception of Drs Lewis and Gibson they were men) cannot be treated as though they represented a Cambridge party in theology, which could be differentiated from evangelicals and Tractarians. That would be the last thing that any of them would have wished. But there was a distinctive voice and,

17  *Politics for the People*, no. 3 (20 May 1848; repr. New York, 1971), p. 58.
18  Westcott to Mary Whittard, 19 and 20 May 1845: A. Westcott, *Life and Letters of Brooke Foss Westcott* (London, 1903), i, p. 57.
19  Westcott to Mary Whittard, 8 November 1846: ibid., i, p. 77.

for whatever reasons, it has hitherto been presented only as a supplement to a dominant narrative which is based elsewhere.

What then counts as 'the Cambridge tradition'? Most writers on the subject have considered the thought of those educated at Cambridge, usually without reference to their involvement in teaching at the time of their writing. Indeed, since there was no systematic undergraduate education in Theology until the 1870s, it is not easy to make active teaching involvement a qualification for being part of the 'Cambridge tradition'. How significant, therefore, would we consider the work of William Paley, most of whose published works were written after he had ceased to be an active teacher in the University and had moved to his various benefices in Carlisle, Sunderland and Lincoln? Julius Hare was as influential after he left Cambridge as he was while he was present. Much of Westcott's work was done before his return to Cambridge as Regius Professor in 1870, and much of Hort's significant work, including his Hulsean Lectures, was done while he was vicar of St Ippolyts near Hitchin, in Hertfordshire. F.D. Maurice spent only a brief time in Cambridge as Knightbridge Professor of Philosophy, but he cannot be omitted on those grounds alone. These considerations require a discussion that is more sensitive to changes over time as various people come and go. It also must acknowledge the significance of the institutional structure of the University and the Colleges. Thus, for example, the abolition of the prohibition on the marriage of Fellows was quite as important as the abolition of religious tests for the career patterns of Cambridge dons in enabling them to remain an active part of the University for longer periods.

The most important change in the nineteenth century – which cannot be dated precisely – was that it ceased to be possible to view the University as part of the Church of England. Instead it gradually became an institution in its own right, certainly not secular in the modern sense, but at least institutionally detached from the church. Any listing of the offices held by senior members of the University before the church reforms of the 1830s illustrates the intimate and intricate interrelationship of University and church. This pluralism survived the reforms of the 1830s. In the 1820s Herbert Marsh, Lady Margaret's Professor, was Bishop of Peterborough and John Kaye, Regius Professor of Divinity, was Bishop of Bristol. Only when Kaye was translated to Lincoln in 1827 did he resign his chair. His successor, Thomas Turton, was Dean of Peterborough from 1830 to 1842 and then Dean of Westminster: he resigned his chair when he became Bishop of Ely in 1845. William Selwyn, Lady Margaret's Professor 1855–75, had been a residentiary Canon of Ely since 1830 and remained so. J.A. Jeremie, Regius Professor 1850–70, was Subdean and then Dean of Lincoln, provoking hostile comment from Benson for hanging on to the chair after he became Dean. Lightfoot was a Canon of St Paul's and Westcott was first a Canon of Peterborough and then of Westminster. Those who did not have cathedral preferment might expect a parish. G.E. Corrie, Norrisian Professor 1838–54, became Rector of Newton, the most prosperous living in the gift of the Bishop of Ely in 1851, and was an active parish priest and rural dean, as well as being Master of Jesus. John Blunt, Lady Margaret's Professor 1839–55, was actually unusual in resigning his parish when he became a professor and in residing continuously in Cambridge. Hort never held any canonry and died as a Professor.[20]

There were vital links of patronage here. Apart from the Lady Margaret's chair, the professorships were not well endowed. Those who held them rarely came from families with means. The sheer necessity of pluralism to maintain the style of life expected was an unavoidable fact of university life. Two rather different examples illustrate the point. George Corrie's career depended almost entirely on the patronage of Turton. It was Turton as Tutor of St Catharine's College, who offered him the post of Assistant Tutor in 1817, which led him to stay in Cambridge. When Turton became Lucasian Professor of Mathematics in 1822, Corrie succeeded to the Tutorship. Turton had no direct hand in Corrie's election as Norrisian Professor in 1838, but when he became Bishop of Ely in 1845, Turton made Corrie his examining chaplain, appointed him Master of Jesus in 1849 and gave him the Rectory of Newton in 1851. William Selwyn's election as Lady Margaret's Professor in 1853 was rather different. The electors then were DDs and BDs of the University, a majority of whom were Johnians because of the St John's statute which required those eligible to proceed to the BD and DD degrees. In 1855 the Vice-Chancellor changed his mind about the voting procedure in the middle of the election: Selwyn and Harold Browne got 43 votes each and the Vice-Chancellor gave a casting vote to Selwyn. William Whewell, Master of Trinity, who had left the Senate House because he thought the voting would take most of the day, returned to discover the vote he intended to cast for Browne was too late. But Selwyn, who was well off and did not need the Lady Margaret's stipend of *c.* £1,500 per annum, secured a grace of the Senate to enable him to pay £700 per annum to the Norrisian Professor so long as it was held by Browne.[21]

The significance of the University within the Church of England also explains the controversy over the place of theology in the curriculum. In 1834 Connop Thirwall was dismissed from his Tutorship at Trinity by the Master, Christopher Wordsworth, for publishing a pamphlet advocating the admission of dissenters to Cambridge. He argued that, since theology did not figure in the curriculum and since compulsory college chapel attendance did more harm than good, there was no solid reason for denying admission to dissenters. The movement of 1834 was unsuccessful, but the result was a heightened fear of change imposed from outside and a greater impetus to make something more of theology as a subject of study in the University. A Voluntary Theological Examination was introduced in 1841, as the result of the report of a Theology Syndicate. The Theological Tripos was introduced in 1871.

--------

20  For the significance of Hort within the Faculty of Divinity, see G. Rupp, 'Hort and the Cambridge Tradition' in *Just Men* (London, 1977), pp. 151–66; C.N.L. Brooke, *A History of the University of Cambridge* (Cambridge, 1993), iv, pp. 9–14, 137–8.

21  D.A. Winstanley, *Early Victorian Cambridge* (Cambridge, 1940), pp. 327–8; Romilly's Diary, 29 Jun 1855: M.E. Bury and J.D. Pickles, *Romilly's Cambridge Diary 1848–1864* (Cambridge, 2000), p. 212.

Whewell's letters to Archdeacon Hare and others in 1841–42 show that the reluctance to introduce examinations in theology was not simply reactionary. Whewell (1794–1866) had been Knightbridge Professor of Moral Philosophy since 1838 and became Master of Trinity in 1841. Winstanley thought he had effected a decisive shift in the teaching of philosophy in the University. But he was not enthusiastic about including theology more formally in the University's curriculum because he thought that it would depend too much on examinations; and there was no money for the endowment of new chairs. In another letter to Hare he wrote:

> though most of the old lectures have lost their power in men's eyes, Blunt's on Pastoral Theology have been crowded. Corrie's [Norrisian] have had of course a good attendance, and he says great attention paid; mine have been well filled hitherto, nor have Sedgwick's lost their popularity. It is true neither Blunt, Corrie, Turton, nor Mill [Regius Professor of Hebrew] are men to create a new system, which is what we want, but if the right professor can be put in his place he will not be destitute of hearers and disciples.[22]

Whewell at this time was wondering whether there was a way of getting F.D. Maurice back to Cambridge: that only happened after his own death, when Maurice became Knightbridge Professor in succession to John Grote in 1866. But Whewell is a representative of the transition. He held no ecclesiastical preferment, and his position was essentially that of Master of Trinity (and Vice-Chancellor from time to time). From 1840 it was no longer possible for Deans of Cathedrals to be non-resident, though residentiary canons only had to live in during their residence. By the end of the century, with one or two exceptions in the Faculty of Divinity itself, the separation of church and University was complete.

Finally it is easy to forget that people change their minds, and that this propensity qualifies any simple characterisations of them. In particular, they are often characterised in terms of where they ended up, rather than where they began or at any intermediate point along the way. Thus John Henry Newman is usually described as a Catholic, sometimes with a deliberate ambiguity intended to minimise the significance of his move from the Church of England to the Church of Rome. No one would think of denying that he changed his opinions, but this point is somehow detached from the way in which he is described. In the eighteenth century Edmund Burke changed his political views as a result of the French Revolution; and in the same way Cambridge men changed their theological opinions – and continued to do so in the following century.

No book on the Cambridge tradition can say everything. There is deliberately no detailed discussion of the development of the Natural Sciences in Cambridge and their implications for theology, nor the philosophical tradition developed by Henry Sidgwick. These developments were undoubtedly significant. However, much has already been written about Cambridge science in the 1830s, and the

---

22 M. Stair Douglas, *The Life and Selections from the Correspondence of William Whewell* (London, 1881), p. 249.

significance of Charles Darwin; less has been written about the importance of history.[23] The biblical work of the trio was more indebted to the methods of history than physics, and geology and evolutionary biology are in an important sense historical. An important book on Sidgwick has recently appeared,[24] and Sidgwick's successors tended to move away from the theological. This book concentrates on those aspects of Cambridge on which relatively little has been written, beyond the classic Victorian biographies, which are now over a century old.

One article in the last twenty years, by Alan Waterman, examines Cambridge theology at the end of the eighteenth century.[25] In the 1970s two books were written about William Paley.[26] The most significant general study is undoubtedly that of Gascoigne; others tend to move in the direction of politics or economics.[27] The only work done on Herbert Marsh is R.K. Braine's unpublished Cambridge PhD dissertation.[28] John Brooke wrote a valuable essay on Whewell in 1991, but (apart from John Yule's unpublished dissertation) the main emphasis in that period has come in the history of science.[29] For Julius Hare, Merrill Distad's book of 1979 is valuable, and Julie Lethaby discussed his work on Luther in her unpublished Cambridge PhD dissertation.[30] Maurice is always being written about, but not usually in a Cambridge context: Jeremy Morris's book is the most recent study.[31] There is still no adequate biography of Lightfoot, but Geoffrey Treloar's work is invaluable.[32] Graham Patrick has published a useful little study of Hort and a longer biography of Westcott.[33] There is a brief reference to the trio in Robert Morgan's essay on Anglican reactions to German gospel criticism, and a rather

23  An obvious exception was Duncan Forbes, *The Liberal Anglican Idea of History* (Cambridge, 1952), although even there Arnold and Stanley counted for as much as some of the Cambridge figures.

24  B. Schultz, *Henry Sidgwick: Eye of the Universe* (Cambridge, 2004).

25  A.M.C. Waterman, 'A Cambridge "Via Media" in Late Georgian Anglicanism', *Journal of Ecclesiastical History*, xlii, 3 (July 1991).

26  M.L. Clarke, *Paley: Evidences for the Man* (London, 1974); D.L. LeMahieu, The Mind of William Paley (Lincoln, Nebraska, 1976). See also the important sections on Paley in P. Addinall, *Philosophy and Biblical Interpretation* (Cambridge 1991), pp. 35–55, 86–106.

27  J. Gascoigne, *Cambridge in the Age of the Enlightenment* (Cambridge, 1989).

28  R.K. Braine, 'The Life and Writings of Herbert Marsh' (unpublished Cambridge PhD dissertation, 1989).

29  J.H. Brooke, 'Indications of a Creator: Whewell as Apologist and Priest' in M. Fisch and S. Schaffer (eds), *William Whewell: A Composite Portrait* (Oxford, 1991); J.D. Yule, 'The impact of science on British religious thought in the second quarter of the nineteenth cenutry' (unpublished Cambridge PhD dissertation, 1976).

30  M.N. Distad, *Guessing at Truth* (Shepherdstown, West Virginia, 1979); J.I. Lethaby, '"A Less Perfect Reflection": Perceptions of Luther in the Nineteenth-century Church of England' (unpublished Cambridge PhD dissertation, 2001).

31  J.N. Morris, *F.D. Maurice and the Crisis of Christian Authority* (London, 2005).

32  G.R. Treloar, *Lightfoot the Historian* (Tübingen, 1998).

33  G.A. Patrick, *F.J.A. Hort: Eminent Victorian* (Sheffield, 1988); G.A. Patrick, *The Miners' Bishop* (2nd edn, Peterborough, 2004).

longer discussion in Peter Hinchliff's stimulating book on *God and History*.[34] There was a conference at Aberdeen in 1995 to mark the centenary of the award of Forsyth's DD, the proceedings of which were published, but obviously the main theological emphasis fell on the post-Cambridge period; little has been written on T.R. Glover's theology.[35] But no one has examined the whole story. A new look is timely.

---

34 R.C. Morgan, '"Non Angli sed Angeli": Some Anglican Reactions to German Gospel Criticism' in S. Sykes and D. Holmes (eds), *New Studies in Theology 1* (London, 1980); Hinchliff, *God and History: Aspects of British Theology, 1875–1914*.

35 T. Hart (ed.), *Justice the True and Only Mercy: Essays on the Life and Theology of Peter Taylor Forsyth* (Edinburgh, 1995).

# Chapter 1

# The End of the Eighteenth Century

It is a very wonderful thing, that a being such as man, placed on a little globe of earth, in a little corner of the universe, cut off from communication with the other systems which are dispersed through the immensity of space, imprisoned as it were on the spot where he happens to be born, almost utterly ignorant of the variety of spiritual existences, and circumscribed in his knowledge of material things, by their remoteness, magnitude, or minuteness, a stranger to the nature of the very pebbles on which he treads, unacquainted, or but very obscurely informed by his natural faculties of his condition after death; it is wonderful, that a being such as this should reluctantly receive, or fastidiously reject, the instruction of the Eternal God! or, if this is saying too much, that he should hastily, and negligently, and triumphantly conclude, that the Supreme Being never had condescended to instruct the race of man.[1]

This arrestingly rhetorical passage could only come from an eighteenth-century writer, aware of the Copernican and Newtonian revolutions in thought, yet convinced that Christianity was true. It is, as it were, poised between the worlds of the Reformation and the later challenges of nineteenth-century science. The author was Richard Watson (1737–1816), Regius Professor of Divinity at Cambridge from 1771, and it comes almost midway through the Preface to his six-volume collection of Theological Tracts, published in 1785.

The work was dedicated to Queen Charlotte. As a wife and mother she was an example of the sex, which was expected to provide the first principles of religious education; and since its purpose was to preserve youth from infidelity, Watson felt his dedication was appropriate. His specified intention was to give 'young persons of every denomination, and especially to afford the Students in the Universities, and the younger Clergy, an easy opportunity of becoming better acquainted with the grounds and principles of the Christian Religion than, there is reason to apprehend, many of them at present are'.[2] Watson did not contribute anything himself to the collection. The works included came from the late seventeenth and eighteenth centuries and were primarily concerned with the authenticity of scripture and the reasonableness of Christianity. Locke's essay with the latter title was included, as was Nathaniel Lardner's *History of the Apostles and Evangelists* (1760) and his *Argument for the Truth of Christianity* (1764). Samuel Clarke's *Discourse concerning the unchangeable Obligations of Natural Religion and the Truth and Certainty of the Christian Revelation* (1705), David Hartley's *Truth of*

---

1    R. Watson, *A Collection of Theological Tracts* (2nd edn, London, 1791), i, p. ix.

2    Ibid.

*the Christian Religion* (1749), and Joseph Addison's posthumous treatise of the same title were there; as were Thomas Secker's *Charges* (1769) as a guide to the pastoral duties of the clergy. By his own account nearly a thousand copies were sold in less than three months; a second edition was published in 1791.

Watson has not had a good press as Regius Professor.[3] Norman Sykes described him as having 'an individual creed, strikingly different from the official articles of subscription of the Established Church'.[4] On the other hand, he might have articulated what many others believed, but did not dare to say, since one of his striking characteristics was a readiness to say what he thought, regardless of the consequences. The key to Watson's theology was John Locke, and it is no coincidence that *The Reasonableness of Christianity* was reprinted in Watson's collection.[5] In 1775 Watson advised his former pupil Lord Granby, who had just become MP for the University, to read Bacon and Locke, together with Shakespeare; and of Locke he said that all of his writings 'may be read over and over again with infinite advantage'.[6] Moreover Edmund Law, who in many ways was a critic of Watson, also edited an edition of Locke's *Works*. He noted the way in which Newtonian mathematics 'together with Mr Locke's *Essay* [and] Dr Clarke's works went hand in hand through our public schools and lectures'. By contrast the Heads of Houses at Oxford had attempted to ban the study of Locke's *Essay on Human Understanding* in 1703, though with only limited success.[7] Watson affirmed that 'the truth of the Christian religion depends upon testimony … and I consider the testimony concerning the resurrection of Jesus (and that fact is the corner-stone of the Christian church) to be worthy of entire credit'.[8] This captures in a single sentence the significance attached to evidences of Christianity in general, and the authenticity of the New Testament in particular, which was to determine the pattern of theological study in eighteenth-century Cambridge, and ultimately to lead to the development of biblical criticism.

Locke's influence was significant in Cambridge, not only for the thought of dons, but also for undergraduates. In the disputations in the Senate House in the Lent Term of the third year students were expected to argue propositions with one another. Usually two of these were mathematical and one philosophical. The written examination in the Senate House, which followed later, also contained a predominance of mathematical questions, but there were questions on

---

3     See, for example, D.A. Winstanley, *Unreformed Cambridge* (Cambridge, 1935), pp. 106–7.

4     N. Sykes, *Church and State in England in the Eighteenth Century* (Cambridge, 1934), p. 351.

5     Watson, *Theological Tracts*, iv, pp. 1–108.

6     Letter of 15 August 1775, R. Watson, *Anecdotes of the Life of Richard Watson* (2nd edn, London, 1818), i, p. 82.

7     J. Gascoigne, *Cambridge in the age of the Enlightenment* (Cambridge, 1989), p. 174, quoting T. Fuller, *The history of the University of Cambridge*, ed. J. Nichols (Cambridge, 1840), p. 214; L.S. Sutherland and L.G. Mitchell, *The History of the University of Oxford: v The Eighteenth Century* (Oxford, 1986), pp. 570–90.

8     Watson, *Anecdotes*, i, p. 24, quoted Sykes, *Church and State*, p. 351.

philosophy.[9] In all questions students were expected to argue using major and minor premises, and drawing conclusions from them. This is one explanation of the surviving importance of geometry. Watson provided a list of the propositions to be debated in 1762: twenty-eight were mathematical or scientific; forty-eight were philosophical or theological.[10] It is true, as is usually said, that mathematical questions increasingly dominated, under the influence of Newton, but philosophical questions also had to be discussed, and here the influence was Locke.

Nor was this development simply a matter of intellectual fashion, though it was that. Eighteenth-century England still lived in the shadow of the religious wars of the previous century, not least the English Civil War. Although Bonnie Prince Charlie's invasion in 1745 is nowadays regarded as a romantic episode doomed to fail, he did get as far as Derby; and the threat of Popery assumed a new reality. Politically, the fear was of foreign domination – now by France rather than Spain – but theologically, the worry was that the differences between Protestantism and Roman Catholicism were perceived in issues of speculative theology, which were not amenable to resolution by reason, but only by appeal to religious authority, an argument which rapidly became circular. When the Hanoverians secured the throne in 1714, they also needed to secure a base in the Universities: in May 1724, at the instigation of Edmund Gibson, Bishop of London, George I informed the Vice-Chancellors of Oxford and Cambridge of his intention to found Professorships of Modern History at both universities and royal letters patent to establish the Cambridge chair were issued in September 1724.[11] Generally speaking, the Whig political success was more complete (though not entirely so) in Cambridge than Oxford. Hence the significance of Locke's influence was both political – the doctrine of consent – as well as theological – toleration, or faith and reason.[12] Locke's understanding of toleration did not extend to Roman Catholics, but his conviction that all significant theological questions could be settled by using human reason to interpret the Bible, was felt to be consonant with the traditional Protestant emphasis on 'sola scriptura'. It is widely agreed now that Locke did not go along the Deist road, which concentrated on natural religion and made the appeal to revealed religion irrelevant, and this is why eighteenth-century Anglican, Dissenting and Scottish divines could appeal to him with such confidence.

Watson became a Fellow of Trinity in 1760 and was elected Professor of Chemistry in 1764; he immediately set about learning Chemistry and within

---

9    P. Searby, *A History of the University of Cambridge, iii 1750–1870* (Cambridge, 1997), pp. 154–63; M.L. Clarke, *Paley: Evidences for the Man* (London, 1974), pp. 6–8.

10    Watson, *Anecdotes*, i, pp. 37–43.

11    Winstanley, *Unreformed Cambridge*, pp. 154–5.

12    Questions, illustrating these themes, referred to by Watson were: 'Recte statuit Lockius de humana libertate?', 'Homines a muneribus publicis non recte excluduntur ob religiosas opiniones?', 'Supremo magistratui resistere licet, si respublica aliter servari nequit?', and 'Rectestatuit Lockius de distinctis fidei et rationis provinciis?: Watson, *Anecdotes*, i, pp. 41–2.

fourteen months read a course of lectures to 'a very full audience, consisting of persons of all ages and degrees, in the University'. This was the more significant since students were under no obligation to attend lectures in Chemistry at all. His collection of *Chemical Essays*, published in 1781, was commended by Sir Humphrey Davy, and in 1787 he was advising the Government on how to strengthen gunpowder![13] However, when the Regius Chair of Divinity became vacant in 1771 as a result of the early death of Dr Rushforth, Watson set about securing the support of the electors, and also the King's mandate to be created a Doctor of Divinity without fulfilling the usual Act in order to be eligible for election. He had to write on two subjects: the reconciliation of the genealogies in Matthew and Luke, and the interpretation of 1 Cor 25:29 on baptism for the dead. Upon submitting these two pieces to the electors, he was asked to write a Latin dissertation of an hour's length on Genesis 10:32 (the division of the nations according to the families of the sons of Noah after the flood); this was read in the Divinity Schools a fortnight later, and he was elected unanimously the next day.[14] The distance between these exercises and the preoccupations of later eighteenth-century theology is striking. Watson was clearly popular. In his *Reminiscences* Henry Gunning remarked that the first time he presided in the Divinity School at a disputation, it was crowded to excess. On the first occasion, because the Opponents were 'alarmed at the thought of exhibiting before such a crowded audience as the high reputation of the Regius Professor of Divinity could not fail to draw together', they did not appear; but Watson dashed the Respondent's hopes of not having to defend his thesis by questioning him himself. Disputations did not always proceed so smoothly. Gunning described the Act kept by Isaac Milner for his BD, where both Milner and his opponent, Henry Coulthurst, repeatedly talked across one another and failed to respond to the arguments presented. Watson two or three times made ineffectual attempts to enforce the rules of disputation but neither took any notice, and he resumed his seat in despair leaving them to finish in their own way. Apparently the Divinity School was crowded for most of Watson's time, but latterly the numbers began to decline because some of the Colleges changed the hour of dinner from 1.00 to 3.00, provoking Watson to make an adverse comment on this in one of his Commencement speeches.[15]

Watson did not hesitate to join the agitation against the requirement for clergy to subscribe to the Thirty-Nine Articles which culminated in the Feathers' Tavern Petition to the House of Commons of 1772. He published two letters under the pseudonyms of 'A Christian Whig' and 'A Consistent Protestant', and circulated them to all MPs on the day before they considered the Petition. He argued that it was inappropriate for the church to require subscription to any human confession

---

13   Watson, *Anecdotes*, i, pp. 33, 45–6, 141, 236–7, 240–41; Winstanley, *Unreformed Cambridge*, p. 145. Three other volumes of *Chemical Essays* followed in 1781, 1782 and 1785.

14   Watson, *Anecdotes*, i, p. 56–61.

15   H. Gunning, *Reminiscences of the University, Town and County of Cambridge* (London, 1854), i, pp. 46–8.

of faith other than a declaration that the scriptures contained the will of God; and he gloried in the fact that both his political and theological ideas were so close to those of Bishop Hoadly, even though he claimed that he only discovered this later.[16] The Petition was overwhelmingly defeated in the House of Commons, and this forced those of unitarian views to declare themselves: the Essex Street congregation was established in London in 1774.[17] Watson's friend, John Jebb, who was two years his senior and with whom he had been Moderator in 1763, when Paley was Senior Wrangler, identified himself with the new congregation; but Watson did not and there is no reason to suppose that Watson was tempted to adopt unitarian views.

Watson always thought that the American war was unjust, and that its consequences would be bad for Britain. In 1776 he preached the Restoration Sermon before the University, when the war with the American Colonists was already going badly, and published it under the title 'The Principles of the Revolution Vindicated'.[18] The poignancy of its being a Restoration Day Sermon may have accentuated its significance and it gave great offence to the Court: he always regarded it as the obstacle to his subsequent promotion. In 1782 during Lord Shelburne's ministry he became Bishop of Llandaff at the instigation of Grafton, but he got no further, despite several appeals to William Pitt.[19] In 1787, when he was 50, his doctors advised him to discontinue his University duties, and he secured the approval by the Senate of a grace appointing Dr Thomas Kipling as his deputy and giving him a stipend.[20] The previous year Watson had been left an estate in Sussex by an old friend and he presumably used the proceeds of its sale (£23,500) to purchase Calgarth Park on the shores of Lake Windermere in his native Westmorland. He retired there and devoted the rest of his life to the improvement of land and the planting of trees.[21] When he left Cambridge he had been a Fellow of Trinity since 1760, and had regularly acted as Moderator in the Divinity Schools. Clearly the medical advice was effective since he lived nearly another thirty years!

The Preface to Watson's *Theological Tracts* gave a clear account of his objectives and his own views. 'There is a fashion in study as in other pursuits,' he wrote, 'and the taste of the present age is not calculated for making great exertions in Theological Criticism and Philology.'[22] Rather his aim was to provide young

---

16  Ibid., i, pp. 65–70.

17  Gascoigne, *Cambridge in the Age of the Enlightenment*, pp. 194–6; Sykes, *Church and State*, pp. 352–3; A.M.C. Waterman, 'A Cambridge "Via Media" in Late Georgian Anglicanism', *Journal of Ecclesiastical History*, xlii, 3 (July 1991): 425–7. Although Waterman is right about the *content* of Watson's belief, his position on subscription does justify Sykes's remark about his 'individual creed'.

18  Watson, *Anecdotes*, i, pp. 71, 88–95.

19  Gascoigne, *Cambridge in the Age of the Enlightenment*, p. 194.

20  Kipling was Senior Wrangler in 1768, and edited the *Codex Bezae* in 1798: J.R. Tanner (ed.), *Historical Register of the University of Cambridge* (Cambridge, 1917), p. 453.

21  Watson, *Anecdotes*, i, pp. 94–5, 155, 233–4, 296–7, 304, 308.

22  Watson, *Theological Tracts*, i, p. v.

clergy with 'a well grounded persuasion that Christianity is not a *cunningly devised fable, but the power of God unto salvation to every one that believeth*'. This was to be achieved by enabling them to come to a rational conviction of the truth of Christianity, 'resulting from a comprehensive view of the proofs by which it is established'.[23] The nature of the clerical life meant that they had to learn how to think for themselves, and for this they needed not so much new books as an inclination 'to explore the treasures of the old ones'.[24] Watson believed that 'great ends of all our studies, and all our pursuits' should be 'a steady faith, a rational piety, [and] a true Christian charity of mind' – a significant trio – and the best way to ensure this was by the frequent reading of the scriptures.[25] He drew particular attention to the convincing proofs of the Christian Religion contained in volumes 1, 4 and 5.[26] So while acknowledging that 'unbelievers attempt to make proselytes to infidelity' by pressing upon them the authority of writers like Bolingbroke, Voltaire, Helvetius, Hume and other Deistical writers, he listed fifteen others (including Newton and Locke) who were professed believers in Christianity. However, neither the truth nor the falsehood of Christianity could be established by authorities.[27]

The foundation of all Christian truth, therefore, was the Bible: 'there is no certainty of truth but in the word of God.' 'All other foundations, whether they be the decisions of councils, the confessions of churches, the prescripts of popes, or the exposition of private men' had to be regarded as 'sandy and unsafe'.[28] But it was necessary to take advantage of 'the united labours of learned men in every country'; thus 'the freedom of inquiry ... which has subsisted in this country during the present century' had been of great assistance to Christianity. The Christian Religion had nothing to fear from 'the strictest investigation of the most learned of its adversaries', and 'it is no small part of the province of a teacher of Christianity, to distinguish between the word of God, and the additions which

---

23    Ibid., p. vi (emphasis original).
24    Ibid., p. vii.
25    Ibid., p. ix.
26    These were J. Taylor, *A Scheme of Scripture-Divinity* (1762); P. Allix, *Reflexions upon the Books of the Holy Scripture, to establish the Truth of the Christian Religion* (1688); J. Locke, *The Reasonableness of Christianity* (1727); S. Clarke, *A Discourse concerning the unchangeable Obligations of Natural Religion, and the Truth and Certainty of the Christian Revelation* (1705); J. Smith, *A Discourse on Prophecy* (1656); J. Shute Barrington, *An Essay on the Teaching and Witness of the Holy Spirit* (1725), G. Benson, 'An Essay concerning Inspiration', 'An Essay concerning the Unity of Sense: to shew that no Text of Scripture has more than one single Sense' and 'An Essay on the Man of Sin', from *Paraphrase and Notes on St Paul's Epistles* (1752); D. Hartley, *On the Truth of the Christian Religion* (1749); J. Addison, *On the Truth of the Christian Religion* (?1730), N. Lardner, *Of the Argument for the Truth of Christianity* (1764); J. Macknight, 'All the Actions recorded in the Gospels are probable' and 'Of the Argument for the Truth of the Christian Religion arising from the conversion of the world to Christianity', from *The Truth of the Gospel History* (1763); and G. West, *Observations on the History and Evidence of the Resurrection of Christ* (1767).
27    Watson, *Theological Tracts*, i, p. xi.
28    Ibid., p. xii.

men have made to it'.[29] The objections of unbelievers were frequently directed at 'mere human system' rather than Christianity: 'The effect of established systems in obstructing truth, is to the last degree deplorable: every one sees it in other churches, but scarcely any one suspects it in his own.'[30]

Here he came to the heart of his argument. The lesson every one needed to learn from church history was Moderation: 'Want of genuine moderation towards those who differ from us in religious opinion, seems to be the most unaccountable thing in the world'.[31] It was not surprising that Roman Catholics should light up the fires of the inquisition, since they believed in the infallibility of their church; but Protestants could never justify that on the basis of their principles:

> A suspicion of fallibility would have been a useful principle to the professors of Christianity in every age; it would have choked the spirit of persecution in its birth, and have rendered not only the church of Rome, but every church in Christendom, more shy of assuming to itself the proud title of Orthodox, and of branding every other with the opprobrious one of Heteredox, than any of them have hitherto been. There are, you will say, doubtless, some fundamental doctrines in Christianity. – *Paul*, the Apostle, has laid down one foundation; and he tells us, that *other foundation can no man lay, than that is laid, which is Jesus – The Christ.* – But this proposition – Jesus is the Messiah – includes, you will reply, several others, which are equally true. I acknowledge that it does so; and it is every man's duty to search the Scriptures, that he may know what those truths are; but I do not conceive it to be any man's duty, to anathematize those who cannot subscribe to *his* catalogue of fundamental Christian verities.[32]

Watson had no regard for latitudinarian principles, nor for any principles, but the principles of Truth; so it was necessary for everyone to examine each side of controverted questions. Thus the clergy ought to satisfy themselves of the external and internal evidences for the truth of the Gospel, but having done that, their time would be more usefully employed discharging their pastoral office with fidelity than in weighing the importance of 'all the discordant systems of faith'. He looked forward to the day 'when Theological Acrimony shall be swallowed up in Evangelical Charity, and a liberal toleration become the distinguishing feature of every church in Christendom'.[33] Similarly he hoped that people would come to see that diversity in religious opinions could exist 'without endangering the common weal', and that no one should be hindered in the exercise of their natural rights on the grounds of religion:

> These enlarged sentiments proceed not, I would willingly hope, from what the Germans have called *Indifferentism* in Religion; but partly from a perfect knowledge of its true end, which is Charity; and partly from that consciousness of intellectual weakness,

---

29    Ibid., p. xiii.
30    Ibid., p. xiv.
31    Ibid.
32    Ibid., p. xv.
33    Ibid., p. xviii.

which is ever most conspicuous in minds the most enlightened; and which, wherever it subsists, puts a stop to dogmatism and intolerance of every kind.[34]

Finally he apologised to those Anglicans who 'never read dissenting Divinity' for having made so much use of the works of Dissenters in this Collection; but that was because he considered whether the works suited his purpose, not where they came from. He also added a list of the questions for disputations for the degrees of BD or DD in the last 25 to 30 years. Watson rightly anticipated the antipathy of certain Anglicans, because the collection was ill received by the bishops precisely on the grounds it included tracts written by Dissenters; the Archbishop of Canterbury did not acknowledge receipt of his set, and the Archbishop of York objected to it being given to a young man who was going out to Canada as chaplain to a nobleman.[35]

What stands out is the essentially apologetic nature of most of the works included. Those concerned with the teaching of theology realised that they no longer lived in a world in which the truth of Christianity could be taken for granted. Ironically, an archetype of Victorian agnosticism such as Leslie Stephen painted a picture of eighteenth-century theology in such a way as to suggest that it was remote from any crisis of faith and that it exuded an air of complacency. Perhaps Stephen confused the positive nature of their conclusions with the significance of the questions they asked.

Two of Watson's own works were essentially apologetic. In 1776 he published *An Apology for Christianity* as a refutation of chapters 15 and 16 of Gibbon's *Decline and Fall of the Roman Empire*. He began by affirming his support for free inquiry in religious matters and his regard for 'the right of private judgment, in every concern respecting God and ourselves, as superior to the control of human authority'.[36] He then proceeded in the following chapters to discuss the five secondary causes alleged by Gibbon as the reason for the success of Christianity, in addition to the primary cause – 'the evidence of the doctrine itself and the ruling providence of its great Author'.[37] Thus, he doubted whether the inflexibility and intolerance of Christian zeal would be judged to be the most effective missionary strategy (Letter 1); he doubted whether the Christian doctrine of a future life corresponded to contemporary Roman expectations and pointed out that the doctrine of the Millennium took several centuries to establish itself among Christian thinkers (Letter 2). In Letter 3, where he dealt with miracles, he noted that, according to Locke's definition of knowledge, miracles could 'neither be the object of sense nor of intuition, nor consequently of demonstration'. Thus we could not, 'philosophically speaking, be said to know, that a miracle has ever been performed'. 'But in all the great concerns of life, we are influenced by probability

34   Ibid., pp. xviii–xix.
35   Watson, *Anecdotes*, i, pp. 222–3.
36   R. Watson, *An Apology for Christianity* (Cambridge, 1776), pp. 1–2.
37   E. Gibbon, *The History of the Decline and Fall of the Roman Empire*, ed. Milman, Guizot and Smith (London, 1908), ii, p. 152; Watson *Apology for Christianity*, p. 5: Watson omits 'great'.

rather than knowledge; and of probability the same great author established two foundations – a conformity to our own experience and the testimony of others.'[38] Thus on historical grounds, Watson held that Gibbon had no reason to suppose that miracles were unusual.

In Letter 4 he argued against the view that early Christian virtues were due either to their being previously notorious sinners or to a wish to move up in society, and interestingly commented that 'Christianity troubles not itself with ordering the constitutions of civil societies, but levels the weight of all its influence at the hearts of the individuals which compose them' – a sentiment with an almost evangelical ring to it.[39] In Letter 5 he tackled Gibbon's criticism of the origin and progress of episcopal jurisdiction and the pre-eminence of the metropolitan churches, particularly the Church of Rome: again he conceded the truth of some of the criticisms, but suggested that they did not discredit the whole enterprise. Watson's final letter concerned Gibbon's sixteenth chapter in which he had criticised the persecuting zeal of the early Christians: he did not so much defend the church as suggest that the image of the benevolent tolerance of the Roman Empire was mistaken. In conclusion he attacked the naivety of Gibbon's belief that the religion of Nature would rid society of superstition and a priesthood. Pointing out that the truths of mathematics or science were equally incomprehensible to convinced sceptics, he acknowledged the various contradictions in the biblical record but concluded:

> if your mind is so disposed, you may find food for your scepticism in every page of the Bible, as well as in every appearance of nature; and it is not in the power of any person, but yourselves, to clear up your doubts; you must read, and you must think for yourselves, and you must do both with temper, with candour, and with care.[40]

So he ended again with Locke's advice to a young man: 'Study the Holy Scriptures, especially the New Testament: therein are contained the words of eternal life. It had God for its author, salvation for its end, and truth without any mixture of error for its matter.'[41]

It is not surprising that he annoyed some critics by what he was prepared to concede. Many of the problems about scripture which were still to be vexing Christians a century later were cheerfully acknowledged by Watson with the argument that scepticism was even less plausible than Christianity. John Jebb wrote to him appreciatively and said that he hoped that it would 'remove the

---

38    Watson, *Apology for Christianity*, pp. 88–9.
39    Ibid., p. 111.
40    Ibid., p. 265.
41    Ibid., p. 268. Watson's footnote says the quotation comes from Locke's *Posthumous Works*. It does not come from the work of that title but from 'A Letter to the Revd Mr Richard King' (25 August 1703), in *A Collection of Several Pieces of Mr John Locke never before printed or not extant in his Works* (London, 1720), pp. 345; also in *The Works of John Locke* (7th edn, London, 1768), iv, p. 638. Locke's original says 'Let him study the Holy Scripture …'.

prejudices of many well disposed Deists, and be the happy means of converting them to the truth'.[42]

Twenty years later Watson responded to Part II of Tom Paine's *Age of Reason* in *An Apology for the Bible*. He did not think that Paine had produced any novel objections to revealed religion, and he acknowledged his sincerity; but he lamented that his talents had not been better used. Indeed with characteristic sharpness he observed that 'it would have been fortunate for the Christian world, had your life been terminated before you had fulfilled your intention [of publishing his thoughts on religion]'.[43] Significantly he invoked Locke's definition of conscience as 'merely our own judgment of the moral rectitude or turpitude of our own actions',[44] and as such conscience could be 'no criterion of moral rectitude, even when it is certain, because the certainty of an opinion is no proof of its being a right opinion'. Hence Paine needed to take account of the fact that thousands of learned and impartial men in all ages had embraced revealed religion as true. Watson suggested that Paine's argument that there was no evidence for believing the Bible to be the Word of God on moral grounds would not hold, since natural disasters such as earthquakes could as justly be regarded as being as evil as God's command to the Israelites to destroy the Canaanites; the same argument worked against natural religion as revealed religion.[45] It was no stranger that God should have revealed himself to men and women in the first ages of the world than that there was 'water, and earth, and air, and fire; that there is a sun, and moon, and stars'.[46] Watson then addressed Paine's criticism of the authenticity of the Bible, by distinguishing between genuineness and authenticity; a genuine book was written by the person named as the author; an authentic book 'is that which relates matters of fact, as they really happened'.[47]

Thus, whilst Watson made it clear that he did not think that Paine's objections to the Mosaic authorship of the Pentateuch stood up, he also argued that they proved nothing about the truth of what was said; and he developed the same arguments in relation to the authorship of Joshua, Samuel, and the Psalms. He became more heated in his discussion of Isaiah 44–45 and Paine's claim that these were written at least 150 years after Isaiah was dead, affirming strongly that these were prophecies written before Cyrus was born and referring to the similar arguments of Porphyry and Voltaire: 'We will not, Sir, give up Daniel and St Matthew to the impudent assertions of Porphyry and Voltaire, nor will we give up Isaiah to your assertion. Proof, proof is what we require, and not assertion.'[48]

Turning to the New Testament, he criticised Paine's argument that, whereas the agreement of all the parts of a story does not prove the story to be true, the

42   Watson, *Anecdotes*, i, pp. 98, 102.
43   R. Watson, *An Apology for the Bible* (7th edn, London, 1797), p. 5.
44   Ibid., p. 7.
45   Ibid., pp. 16–19.
46   Ibid., p. 28.
47   Ibid., p. 34. Note the anticipation of Ranke's famous remark about history 'wie es eigentlich gewesen'.
48   Ibid., p. 158.

disagreement of the parts proves that the whole cannot be true.[49] Watson, however, considered it entirely natural that there should be differences in such accounts. One of the first examples he discussed was the question of the genealogies of Christ in Matthew and Luke – perhaps drawing on what he had written on this when elected Regius Professor.[50] Thus he concluded his discussion of the resurrection by saying:

> Great and laudable pains have been taken by many learned men, to harmonize the several accounts given us by the evangelists of the resurrection. It does not seem to me to be a matter of any great consequence to Christianity, whether the accounts can, in every minute particular, be harmonized or not; since there is no such discordance in them, as to render the fact of the resurrection doubtful to any impartial mind.[51]

In his Conclusion he argued against Paine's assertion that 'It has been the scheme of the Christian Church, to hold man in ignorance of the Creator, as it is of government to hold him in ignorance of his rights'. He refuted both claims, suggesting that

> the most unlearned congregation of Christians in Great Britain have more just and sublime conceptions of the Creator, a more perfect knowledge of their duty towards him, and a stronger inducement to the practice of virtue, holiness, and temperance, than all the philosophers of all the heathen countries in the world ever had, or now have.[52]

Likewise 'all wise statesmen are persuaded, that the more men know of their rights, the better subjects they will become'.[53] For his own part Watson would not ridicule the rights of man.

> I have long ago understood, that the poor as well as the rich, and the rich as well as the poor, have by nature some rights, which no human government can justly take from them, without their tacit or express consent; and some also, which they have no power to surrender to any government.[54]

But he was firmly against 'that democratic insanity, which would equalize all property, and level all distinctions in civil society'.[55] It is significant that between 1776 and 1796 Watson had himself joined the ranks of the landed gentry. Interestingly, he outlined the differences between deists and Christians in terms of their understanding of the Maker of heaven and earth, and the prospect of a future state. And his final words were that the root of infidelity was principally

---

49  Ibid., p. 223.
50  See note 14 above.
51  Watson, *Apology for the Bible*, pp. 291–2.
52  Ibid., pp. 351–2.
53  Ibid., p. 353.
54  Ibid., p. 355.
55  Ibid., p. 356.

fixed among the great and opulent, but Paine was endeavouring to spread the malignity of its poison through all classes of the community. Watson was most anxious to preserve the merchants, manufacturers and tradesmen of the kingdom from this; and he was equally concerned about the rising generation of both sexes.[56]

In his *Anecdotes* Watson described his own theological position in this way:

> I determined to study nothing but my Bible, being much unconcerned about the opinions of councils, fathers, churches, bishops, and other men, as little inspired as myself ... The Professor of Divinity had been nick-named *Malleus Haereticorum*; it was thought to be his duty to demolish every opinion which militated against what is called the orthodoxy of the Church of England. Now my mind was wholly unbiassed; I had no prejudice against, no predilection for the Church of England; but a sincere regard for the *Church of Christ*, and an insuperable objection to every degree of dogmatical intolerance. I never troubled myself with answering any arguments which the opponents in the divinity-schools brought against the articles of the church, nor ever admitted their authority as decisive of a difficulty; but I used on such occasions to say to them, holding the New Testament in my hand, *En sacrum codicem!*[57]

It is not therefore surprising that he encountered opposition from those of more traditional views. He has been criticised for his charitable view of the Duke of Grafton, Chancellor of the University (1768–1811), who attended Theophilus Lindsay's congregation in Essex Street, London, from 1774. Watson said that he 'never attempted either to encourage or to discourage his profession of *Unitarian* principles; for I was happy to see a person of his rank, professing with intelligence and with sincerity Christian principles'.[58] Charles Smyth was clearly disconcerted by the fact that Watson regarded Unitarians as Christian; but Smyth believed that 'a Regius Professor of Divinity who is distinguished chiefly, in his academic character, by the liberality of his opinions, is never an unmixed blessing to the University'.[59] Alan Waterman thought that Sykes was deceived by Watson's 'boastful, octogenarian ramblings', and considered that the Preface to his *Theological Tracts* suggested a rather different picture.[60] Waterman implied that Watson became more conservative as a result of the French Revolution. Whilst it is certainly true that he did not indicate his hostility to levelling democratic ideas in 1776 in the same way as he did in 1796, there is no reason to suppose that a loyalty to Lockean natural rights and contractual principles entailed the democratic ideas of the French Revolution. Nor is there any significant difference between the affirmations in the *Anecdotes* and the corresponding points in the Preface to the *Theological Tracts*. There is the same commitment to scripture, the same objection to 'dogmatical intolerance', in each, and the same reluctance to accept

56    Ibid., pp. 381–3.
57    Watson, *Anecdotes*, pp. 62–3.
58    Ibid., i, p. 75.
59    C. Smyth, *Simeon and Church Order* (Cambridge, 1940), pp. 103, 107.
60    A.M.C. Waterman, 'A Cambridge "Via Media" in Late Georgian Anglianism', *Journal of Ecclesiastical History*, xlii, 3 (July 1991): 425.

the Articles as authoritative in themselves. Perhaps one of the lasting legacies of the Victorian view is to suppose that an openness to theological questioning is incompatible with a personal conviction of the truth of Christianity. Yet if there is a Cambridge tradition in theology, it is that the two are not incompatible.

What was true of Watson is even more true of his better remembered near-contemporary, William Paley (1743–1805). Watson was one of the two Moderators when Paley was Senior Wrangler in 1763. Both were from the north. Paley was born in Peterborough, but his father was from Giggleswick in Yorkshire, and became Master of Giggleswick School; Watson was born in Heversham, Westmorland, barely thirty miles away, and went to Heversham Grammar School. It is often noted that when Paley proposed for his oral disputation the question 'Aeternitas poenorum contradicit divinis attributis', Watson accepted it without question. When, however, the Master of Christ's, Dr Thomas, who was also Dean of Ely, insisted that he should not propose such a question, Watson suggested the insertion of 'non', and in that form both it and Paley passed.[61] After three years teaching at a school in Greenwich until he was of age for ordination, he was ordained to a curacy at Greenwich Parish Church, and then elected to a Fellowship at Christ's, where he remained until 1776. He was a conscientious teacher, and in 1775 and 1776 he gave a course of Divinity lectures for BAs who were intending to be ordained, itself something of an innovation.[62] Paley showed the same regard for Locke as Watson. An old pupil of his – probably William Frend – described Paley teaching with 'a ragged Locke upon his left knee', the pages of which he would turn over with the utmost rapidity; and in the Greek Testament class

> We had not, you may be sure, any rigmarole stories about the Trinity, or such stuff; the five points [between Calvinists and Arminians] were left to repose in antiquated folios; the Thirty-nine Articles were never hinted at; the creed of Calvin ... was never thought of; and Paley seems to have taken throughout for his model Locke on the Reasonableness of Christianity and his comments on the Epistles.[63]

Paley was a supporter of the movement to abolish subscription to the Thirty-Nine Articles, both for clergy generally and for Cambridge graduates in particular; though he never signed the Feathers Tavern Petition, alleging, presumably in jest, that 'he could not afford to keep a conscience'.[64] The parliamentary petition failed to gain support because of opposition in the House of Lords, but a limited success was secured in Cambridge in June 1772, when the Senate unanimously supported a grace to substitute for subscription to the Articles a declaration,

---

61   Clarke, *Paley*, pp. 7–8.

62   Ibid., pp. 13–15; cf. D. Reynolds (ed.), *Christ's: A Cambridge College over Five Centuries* (London, 2004), pp. 91–101.

63   *Universal Magazine*, iv (1805): 414–17, cited in Clarke, *Paley*, pp. 15–16, and F. Knight, *University Rebel: The Life of William Frend (1757–1841)* (London, 1971), pp. 25–7.

64   G.W. Meadley, *Memoirs of William Paley, DD* (2nd edn, Edinburgh, 1810), p. 89.

by those being admitted to the BA degree, that they were *bona fide* members
of the Church of England as by law established. In 1779 this was extended to
Bachelors of Law, Physic and Music, and to Doctors of Music, but the MA
and the Divinity Degrees remained protected.[65] When Edmund Law, Master of
Peterhouse and the father of Paley's great friend and colleague at Christ's, John
Law, published a pamphlet in defence of not requiring subscription in 1774, it
was answered by Thomas Randolph, President of Corpus Christi College, Oxford.
Paley published a defence of Law's pamphlet under the pseudonym, 'A Friend
of Religious Liberty', in which he suggested that the church might dismiss many
of the Articles 'and convert those which she retains into terms of peace'. In so
doing 'a greater consent may grow out of inquiry than many are at present aware
of'.[66] Edmund Law had become Bishop of Carlisle in 1769, though he continued
to spend most of the year in Cambridge. Paley served as Law's Chaplain on his
annual visits to Carlisle, and in 1775 was presented to the rectory of Musgrave
in the diocese. In the following year he resigned his Fellowship, married, and
was presented to the vicarages of St Laurence, Appleby and Dalston, the latter
being the parish in which the Bishop's Palace was situated. In 1782, when John
Law became Bishop of Clonfert, Paley became Archdeacon of Carlisle in his
place. Paley never returned to Cambridge, despite being offered the Mastership
of Jesus College in 1789.[67]

Paley's *Principles of Moral and Political Philosophy* (1785) contained much of
the material he had used in his Cambridge lectures. Although in many respects he
followed Locke in making the pursuit of happiness the motive of human virtue, he
linked this with the will of God, not least by making 'everlasting happiness' – that
is, heaven, the ultimate end. Thus LeMahieu saw this as the point at which Paley's
three major works, the *Principles* (1785), the *Evidences of Christianity* (1794)
and *Natural Theology* (1802), become a 'coherent system of thought'.[68] In fact,
Paley went beyond Locke, particularly in his discussion of political philosophy
by denying the notion of an original compact as historically unfounded, and
in its place substituting 'the will of God as collected from expediency'.[69] The
advantage of this was to link an essential political pragmatism to the notion of
God's will, again coming very close to the view that 'whatever is, is right'. But
it meant that in the age of the French Revolution, Paley's political philosophy
was definitely on the conservative side, notwithstanding his famous analogy of
the pigeons as an explanation of the injustices of private property which gave

---

65   Winstanley, *Unreformed Cambridge*, pp. 303–16; Searby, *History of the University*,
iii, pp. 406–10.

66   W. Paley, *Defence of the Considerations on the Propriety of requiring a Subscription
to Articles of Faith*, in R. Lynam, *Works of William Paley* (London, 1825), iv, p. 385;
Meadley, *Memoirs*, p. 92.

67   Meadley, *Memoirs*, p. 152.

68   D.L. LeMahieu, *The Mind of Willliam Paley* (Lincoln, Nebraska, 1976),
p. 121.

69   W. Paley, *The Principles of Moral and Political Philosophy* (London, 1824),
pp. 287, 294; cf. Meadley, *Memoirs*, p. 133.

him the nickname 'Pigeon Paley', and allegedly ruined for ever his chances of a bishopric under George III.[70]

Paley retained the classic Cambridge defence of free enquiry, and, while defending the principle of the establishment of religion, also argued for 'complete toleration' for dissenters, rather than the 'partial toleration' which then existed. He even distinguished between the religious opinions of Roman Catholics and their political views, thinking that it was not helpful to link exclusion to religious views when political views were at stake. Repeating the terminology of 'articles of peace' used in his defence of Law's pamphlet, Paley saw

> no reason why men of different religious persuasions may not sit upon the same bench, deliberate in the same council, or fight in the same ranks, as well as men of various or opposite opinions upon any controverted topic of natural philosophy, history or ethics.[71]

Thus 'a comprehensive national religion, guarded by a few articles of peace and conformity, together with a legal provision for the clergy', coupled with 'a *complete* toleration of all dissenters' would be not only just and liberal, but 'the wisest and safest system', because it united all the perfections of a religious constitution – 'liberty of conscience, with means of instruction; the progress of truth, with the peace of society; the right of private judgment, with the care of the public safety'.[72]

Paley's *Moral and Political Philosophy* was introduced into the Cambridge examinations by Thomas Jones of Trinity in 1786, only a year after its publication. Henry Gunning was one of the earliest to be examined on Paley, and described waiting on Jones in 1787 with his questions, 'which were on the second and third sections of Newton, and Paley on Utility'. By the beginning of the nineteenth century a knowledge of Paley was sufficient.[73] Charles Darwin, writing of his own time at Christ's from 1828, noted that 'The logic of [Paley's] book, and as I may add of his Natural Theology, gave me as much delight as did Euclid'.[74] The *Natural Theology* was his last book, completed in 1802 and written at the suggestion of Shute Barrington, the Bishop of Durham. He wrote it when he was suffering considerable pain, which gives an added poignancy to his remark that 'a man resting from a fit of the stone or gout, is, for the time, in possession of feelings

---

70    Paley, *Principles*, p. 62; LeMahieu, *Mind of Paley*, p. 24. Paley compared the unequal distribution of property to the fortunes of a flock of pigeons with one, 'the weakest, perhaps worst, pigeon of the flock', guarding and wasting a heap of what all the others had gathered.

71    Paley, *Principles*, pp. 403, 414.

72    Ibid., p. 417.

73    Clarke, *Paley*, p. 127; Gunning, *Reminiscences*, i, p. 81; D.A. Winstanley, *Early Victorian Cambridge* (Cambridge, 1940), p. 151.

74    N. Barlow (ed.), *Autobiography of Charles Darwin* (London, 1958), p. 59, cited in Reynolds, *Christ's*, p. 100.

which undisturbed health cannot impart'.[75] This observation comes towards the end of the book, where he is arguing against the view that natural evil is an argument against the existence of God; on the contrary he suggests that pain and other misfortunes, when understood in the context of divine providence and earthly life as the preparation for a future state, made perfect sense. The coupling of these arguments was to be important when they were attacked later in the century.

The *Natural Theology* was probably the most comprehensive summary of the design argument for the existence of God written up to that point, although it was to be sustained well into the new century by a series of Cambridge scientists. It completed the critique of Hume's *Dialogues on Natural Religion*, which Paley had begun in his *Evidences of Christianity*. Its well-known opening, arguing that the difference between a stone and a watch was that in the latter 'its several parts are framed and put together for a purpose', and the 'inevitable inference' 'that the watch must have had a maker' was developed over several hundred pages in relation to all kinds of plants and animals.[76] The problem, however, is whether the analogy between the watch and complex natural plants and animals really does hold good, such that both can be regarded as the product of a designer.[77]Nevertheless the argument fascinated Darwin and at first he found it completely convincing; one might almost suggest that it set the programme for Darwin's own work. Interestingly, he did not abandon Christianity because he came to doubt design: by his own account it was a rejection of the morality of God as depicted in the Old Testament that initiated the process, and it was confirmed by his rejection of the doctrine of everlasting punishment. The replacement of Paley's design argument by 'the law of natural selection' came later.[78]

Paley's two books from the 1790s, the *Horae Paulinae* (1790) and *The Evidences of Christianity* (1794), were concerned, in rather different ways, to defend the credibility of revealed religion. Both were translated into German and published in 1797, one in Helmstädt, the other in Leipzig – a relatively rare honour for Cambridge writers at this time.[79] The *Evidences* are well-known, and tackled Hume's criticism of miracles. The *Horae Paulinae* is less well-known now, and is less easy to read, precisely because so much of it is a detailed examination of particular texts selected to illustrate Paley's basic argument. It was an examination of Paul's epistles and a comparison of them with the Acts of the Apostles. 'By assuming the genuineness of the letters, we may prove the substantial truth of the history,' he began, 'or, by assuming the truth of the history, we may argue strongly in support of the genuineness of the letters.' But Paley assumed neither;

---

75    W. Paley, *Natural Theology* (15th edn, London, 1815), p. 497; cited in Meadley, *Memoirs*, p. 205, though Meadley writes 'severe pain' rather than 'a fit of the stone or gout'.

76    Paley, *Natural Theology*, pp. 1–3. Leslie Stephen pointed out that this analogy was not original to Paley: L. Stephen, *History of English Thought in the Eighteenth Century*, ed. Crane Brinton (London, 1962), i, p. 347; cf. LeMahieu, *Mind of Paley*, pp. 60–61.

77    P. Addinall, *Philosophy and Biblical Interpretation* (Cambridge 1991), pp. 46–9.

78    Barlow, *Autobiography of Charles Darwin*, pp. 85–7. The Cambridge University Library's set of Paley's *Complete Works* was presented by the executors of Mrs Darwin in 1899.

79    Meadley, *Memoirs*, pp. 156, 169.

instead his argument was intended to show that even in the absence of 'any extrinsic or collateral evidence' a comparison of the different writings would 'afford good reason to believe the persons and transactions to have been real, the letters authentic, and the narration in the main to be true'.[80] His argument was an interesting reversal of the design argument. If either the history were derived from the letters, or vice versa, or if both were founded on a common source, the conformity would be the effect of design: 'in examining, therefore, the agreement between ancient writings, the character of truth and originality is undesignedness.'[81] He readily acknowledged that his aim was to prove the 'substantial truth' of the narrative, affirming that nothing more than this could ever be established by historical enquiry; he also declared that he had advanced nothing which he did not think probable; 'but the degree of probability, by which different instances are supported, is undoubtedly very different'.[82] On the other hand, each instance was independent of all the rest, yet whatever established the authenticity of one epistle to some extent established the authority of the rest. Although several writers had attempted to give a continuous account of St Paul from his letters and Acts taken together – and Paley depended very much on Lardner's work in this respect – no one had attempted the same kind of argument before; and he hoped that the book might 'add one thread to that complication of probabilities by which the Christian history is attested'.[83] His conclusion, however, was an interesting anticipation (though very differently grounded) of J.B. Lightfoot's response to German New Testament criticism some seventy years later. The collective force of the evidence for the authenticity of the Pauline epistles gave grounds for entertaining the basic credibility of the gospels, not least in terms of the contested question of miracles.

The argument from probability was much more prominent in the *Evidences*. That confidently began with the affirmation that he considered it 'unnecessary to prove that mankind stood in need of a revelation'.[84] Nor could a revelation be made in any way but by miracles: 'consequently, in whatever degree it is probably, or not very improbable, that a revelation should be communicated to mankind at all; in the same degree is it probable, or not very improbable, that miracles should be wrought'. But he hastened to assure his readers that he was not assuming the attributes of the Deity or the existence of a future state in order to prove the reality of miracles. 'That reality always must be proved by evidence. We assert only, that in miracles adduced in support of revelation, there is not any such antecedent improbability as no testimony can surmount.'[85] In Paley's view Hume had stated 'the case of miracles to be a contest of opposite improbabilities ...

---

80    W. Paley, *Horae Paulinae, or The Truth of the Scripture History of St Paul Evinced*, ed. T.R. Birks (London, 1850), p. 1.

81    Ibid., p. 3.

82    Ibid., p. 7.

83    Ibid., p. 8.

84    W. Paley, *Evidences of Christianity*, ed. T.R. Birks (new edn, London, n.d.), p. 31.

85    Ibid., p. 32.

whether it be more improbable that the miracle be true, or the testimony false'.[86] Paley rejected the view that the improbability of the truth of miracles was the same for believers as unbelievers; and he suggested that the question of how the historical testimony to miracles had arisen, which Hume regarded as irrelevant, could not be so easily dismissed. The substance of the book which followed consisted of a detailed examination of the testimony for Christianity, based on both ancient and modern sources. Paley's conclusion also reflected a characteristic emphasis of the Cambridge theology of his time, that the habit of presenting the doctrines of Christianity before any consideration of its proofs was likely to put people off. However, 'the truth of Christianity depends upon its leading facts, and upon them alone'.[87]

The common strands between Watson and Paley are now apparent. Both laid emphasis on probability, following Berkeley. Both made a sharp distinction between the facts of Christianity, which could be demonstrated, and the doctrines, which were more open to discussion. Both laid great emphasis on free enquiry and the use of reason, drawing on the inheritance of Locke. Paley's works were more substantial and had a wider circulation; the lucidity of his argument was extremely attractive, giving some sense of what he must have been like as a teacher. For both the agenda they sought to combat was set by the seventeenth- and eighteenth-century sceptics, of whom Gibbon was simply the latest example. Their principal argument was that the biblical documents were either forged or the result of some kind of ecclesiastical conspiracy. Although Paley's time as a teacher at Cambridge was quite short, this was the period in which the ideas set out in his later books took shape, and the books themselves rapidly became required reading. Nevertheless in Germany a rather different direction had been followed, and at the turn of the century Cambridge had one teacher who was in touch with this – Herbert Marsh.

---

86    Ibid., p. 35.
87    Ibid., p. 364.

# Chapter 2

# Herbert Marsh and the Beginning of Biblical Criticism

> The author had been frequently asked during his residence in Germany, 'What is the plan of study adopted in your Universities for those, who are designed to take Orders, to what branches of Divinity do they particularly attend, and how many years must a student have heard the different courses of theological lectures before he is admitted to an office in the church?' He was unable at that time to give a satisfactory answer, because theological learning forms no necessary part of our academical education; but he hopes that due attention will in future be given to a study that is at present more neglected than it deserves.[1]

The author in question was Herbert Marsh (1757–1839); the book was *An Essay on the Usefulness and Necessity of Theological Learning to those who are designed for Holy Orders*, published in 1792 and based on a 'Discourse lately held before the University of Cambridge'.

In many ways Marsh was a bridge between late eighteenth-century Cambridge and the new world of the nineteenth century; and he was unique in his own day, and for some time to come, in having spent a considerable time in Germany.

In his essay he pointed out that it was much more difficult to study the New Testament than was often supposed, particularly because of over-familiarity with its English translation. It was further complicated by the fact that, instead of impartially examining scripture to discover the truth in whatever form it presented itself, people began with 'a system already adopted'.[2] Although there were rules for the interpretation of scripture, writers were unwilling or unable to adopt them. Thus first, 'we must commence the study of the New Testament with a mind free and unprejudiced by party, we must lay aside all system, and forget, if possible, for a time, even the church, of which we are members'.[3] Here are echoes of Watson's suspicion of 'system'. It was also necessary to study the original languages and the contemporary modes of thought and expression. Secondly,

---

1    H. Marsh, *An Essay on the Usefulness and Necessity of Theological Learning to those who are designed for Holy Orders* (Cambridge, 1792), flyleaf. The Library of the Faculty of Divinity in Cambridge has a bound set of Marsh's Works, and this is in volume viii. The set was given by Dr J.E.B. Mayor of St John's College (University Librarian and later Professor of Latin, who was just below Westcott in the Classical Tripos List for 1848) to Professor Westcott in 1884 for the Library, but they were probably bound up in the 1840s or 1850s: no uniform edition of Marsh's Works was published.

2    Ibid., p. 8.

3    Ibid., p. 9.

theological learning was a means of promoting love and charity, and whilst pride and arrogance tended to be the marks of those whose knowledge was limited, 'we almost invariably find that humility and moderation are the distinguishing virtues of those, whose views are enlarged, and whose notions are enlightened'.[4] Marsh's own fiercely controversial nature makes this comment sound slightly ironical. Finally, Marsh rejected the view that theological learning was useless to the preacher: 'Zeal without learning produces only wild enthusiasm, but if it be tempered by a general and liberal erudition, it will be attended with meekness and charity, the greatest ornaments of the Christian name.'[5]

Marsh's work reflected the way in which the question of the authenticity of scripture was moving on from the world of Paley. However, his translation into English of J.D. Michaelis's *Introduction to the New Testament*, which was advertised as being in the press in a concluding end-note to the *Essay*, has led historians of New Testament scholarship to see him as a pioneer of biblical criticism in England, particularly because of his theory about the origins of the synoptic gospels. The danger of this approach is its teleological nature. Marsh's starting point was exactly the same as that of Paley's *Horae Paulinae* and Watson's *Apology for the Bible* or indeed his *Apology for Christianity*. The dominating issue raised by eighteenth-century scepticism was the authenticity of the Bible in general, and the New Testament in particular.

It is no surprise that Marsh, like Watson and Michaelis, based much of his defence of the New Testament on the work of the dissenting minister Dr Nathaniel Lardner. His seventeen octavo volumes on *The Credibility of the Gospel History*, published between 1727 and 1755, had become a classic through their exhaustive examination of the patristic sources. In fact, the subtitle, while characteristically long, was very revealing: 'The Facts occasionally mentioned in the New Testament confirmed by Passages of Ancient Authors, who were contemporary with our Saviour, or his Apostles, or lived near their time; with an appendix concerning the time of Herod's death.' In other words, the central issue was to demonstrate that there was no reason to suppose that the gospels were fables. It is also interesting that, despite the comments about Lardner's Socinianism made by Watson in the Preface to his *Tracts*, when Lardner's *Collected Works* were printed by public subscription in 1788, the List of Subscribers included a significant number of members of both Universities. Out of some 500 subscribers listed, there were nine Fellows of Oxford Colleges and seventeen Fellows of Cambridge Colleges, including the Vice-Chancellor, the Master of Magdalene and the Norrisian Professor; there were fourteen other members of Oxbridge Colleges listed, and ten Bishops including Watson. The Duke of Grafton, Chancellor of Cambridge, was also a subscriber.[6]

---

4    Ibid., p. 11.
5    Ibid. p. 13.
6    N. Lardner, *The Works of Nathaniel Lardner, DD in eleven volumes* (London, 1788), i, pp. vii–xix.

Even more significant for the present purpose is the distinction which Lardner drew between internal and external evidences for the truth of the New Testament:

> The internal evidence depends on the probability of the things related, the consistence of the several parts, and the plainness and simplicity of the narration. The external evidence consists of the concurrence of other ancient writers of good credit, who lived at, or near the time, in which any things are said to have happened; and who bear testimony to the books themselves, and their authors, or the facts contained in them.[7]

Lardner's distinction was followed by Watson, Paley, Michaelis and Marsh. What Michaelis and the other German critics added was a more detailed examination of textual variants – the beginning of what was to become the 'lower criticism' – although originally this was seen as part of the internal evidence. Unless the role of biblical criticism in a wider argument between Christianity and scepticism is remembered, it is impossible to understand why its conclusions were felt to matter so much. This penumbra of wider issues was much closer to the consciousness of later nineteenth-century writers than it became in the twentieth century, when biblical criticism became an established part of University courses.

Born in the year that Watson was Moderator in the Tripos for the first time, Marsh came from a rather different kind of family. Herbert grew up in Faversham, where his father was vicar, and went to Faversham Grammar School, before moving to the King's School, Canterbury. In 1770 he became a king's scholar. His cousin on his mother's side was William Frend, who was a contemporary at Canterbury. Marsh went to St John's College as a foundress scholar in 1775; he was Second Wrangler in 1779 and became a foundress Fellow of St John's in the same year.

In 1785 Marsh was given leave to travel to Egypt and Arabia. On his way he visited Göttingen to discuss learning Arabic with the biblical scholar, J.D. Michaelis (1717–91), who was Professor of Oriental Languages in the University there from 1746 until his death. However, while staying in Leipzig for the winter, his asthma worsened and he was bedridden for most of the next three years. His reading of H.S. Reimarus challenged his understanding of biblical inspiration, but his hopes of translating Gottfried Eichhorn's *Introduction to the Old Testament* were dashed by the advice of Dr Kipling (Watson's deputy) that it would be too radical for the Cambridge University Press to publish. Instead he was invited to translate Michaelis's *Introduction to the Sacred Writings of the New Covenant*, which he did with extensive notes. The first edition of 1750 had already been translated into English, but the fourth edition of 1788, which Marsh translated, was considerably amplified, reflecting the advances in scholarship in the intervening period.

Volumes 1 and 2 (the second in two parts) were published in 1793, and Volumes 3 (in three parts) and 4 followed in 1801. Marsh developed his own theory on

---

7    N. Lardner, *The Credibility of the Gospel History* in *Works*, i, p. 3.

the origin of the first three gospels, which he had completed by 1798, and which appeared in Volume 3, part 2, as well as being published separately. But Marsh did not publish any of his own notes on Volume 4, which was concerned with the Epistles and the Apocalypse, because of his return from Leipzig to Cambridge; and he never returned to the matter. From 1798 to 1800 he had been distracted into politics, by feeling the need to publish a defence of British policy towards France against its critics at home and abroad.[8] A detailed account of Michaelis's *Introduction* itself is unnecessary; instead the focus will be on Marsh's original purpose in translating the work, the significance of the points at which he disagreed with Michaelis and the importance of his own work. The reviews provide a convenient reference point for such a discussion: on the whole the reception of volumes 1 and 2 in 1793–95 was more friendly than that of volumes 3 and 4 in 1803–04. Indeed both the *Critical Review* and the *Monthly Review* concluded their reviews of the first two volumes by saying that Marsh deserved some appropriate reward from the church.[9] This was not repeated in the second round of reviews.

The apologetic significance of Marsh's work was immediately noted by the *Monthly Review*: 'We deem the contents of these volumes not only interesting in the highest degree to believers, for we consider them also as peculiarly demanding the examination of infidels. The basis of Christian faith is here searched to the bottom.'[10] The reviewer's argument became clear later when he observed, 'Prove the sacred books to be a forgery, or to be written by persons who borrowed the names of Evangelists and Apostles, and the superstructure of faith falls to the ground'.[11] Thus Michaelis's conclusion that it was certain 'that the sacred writings have been transmitted from the earliest to the present age without material alteration' was not only a comment about textual certainty but part of a demonstration of the truth of Christianity.[12] Even the *British Critic*, which was more reserved, having criticised Michaelis for indulging in ingenious but ill-founded innovation, praised Marsh for standing forward in general 'as an able defender of the ancient translators and commentators against attacks of this nature'.[13]

---

8     J.D. Michaelis, *Introduction to the New Testament*, trans. H. Marsh (4th edn, London, 1823), iii, Preface, p. iii. This defence was written first in German and published at Leipzig under the title *Historische Übersicht der Politik Englands und Frankreichs* in February 1799. His starting point was that the Franco-British War had been condemned by some writers (in both Britain and Germany) as unnecessary and unjust and defended by others on grounds of expediency and justice: both, however, assumed that the choice of war or peace lay with the British Government. Marsh set out to demonstrate on the basis of an examination of the French official and unofficial records that 'not the British Ministry, but the French rulers alone, were the authors of the war': H. Marsh, *The History of the Politicks of Great Britain and France* (London, 1800), pp. i, iii–iv, xi.

9     *Critical Review*, ix (December 1793): 429; *Monthly Review*, xviii (September 1795): 36.

10    *Monthly Review*, xvii (July 1795): 296.

11    Ibid.: 304.

12    Michaelis, *Introduction to the New Testament*, ii–I, p. 2.

13    *British Critic*, iv (August 1794): 170.

One issue which emerged clearly, even if it was not resolved, was the way in which any judgements about the historical reliability of the New Testament related to the understanding of inspiration. Michaelis had begun his discussion of the authenticity of the New Testament with Paul's epistles, and then moved to the gospels. Michaelis's note recommended Lardner's *Credibility of the Gospel History* and Gottfried Less's *Truth of the Christian Religion* (though Marsh noted that he meant his *History of Religion*, Göttingen, 1786).[14] Michaelis also argued that the testimony of heretics and opponents of Christianity such as Celsus and Porphyry was actually a powerful witness for the antiquity of the New Testament, as Chrysostom had remarked in his Sixth Homily.[15] When, however, Michaelis argued that the question of whether the books of the New Testament were inspired was less important than the question of whether they were genuine, Marsh disagreed, saying that, although the truth of Christianity was independent of the existence of the New Testament, the proof of the truth did in practice depend on it.[16] Michaelis went on to suggest that inspiration was more important for the epistles than it was for the historical books, and that 'it would be no detriment to the Christian cause to consider [the evangelists as human evidence] in matters of historical fact'; Marsh simply commented that this was not a new distinction, going back to Grotius and the dispute between the Dominicans and the Jesuits.[17] Michaelis, recognising that Protestants could not base their authority for the inspiration of scripture in the church, therefore fell back to apostolic authorship as the ground for the inspiration of the New Testament.[18] Thus he hesitated to acknowledge the inspiration of the Gospels of Mark and Luke, and also Acts, and instead took the view, for which there was support in the church Fathers, that theirs was an inspiration derived from Peter and Paul – a view accepted by Marsh, who pointed out that, in effect, this was acknowledged by Eusebius and others of the ancient Fathers.[19] The *British Critic* in 1802, by contrast with 1794, cited Michaelis's doubts about the divine inspiration of Mark and Luke, which were amplified when the gospels were being considered one by one in Volume 3, as an illustration of 'that bold latitude of opinion, in which the German divines, with little benefit to truth or reason, are so prone to indulge themselves'; nor did it acknowledge that Michaelis produced arguments, based on the Fathers, for deciding on balance that they were inspired.[20]

Michaelis's distinction between history and inspired text in the gospels was clearly controversial. He returned to this issue in Volume 3. He noted that the *Wolfenbüttel Fragments* suggested that the resurrection of Christ was a false and idle tale, because the accounts of it differed; but he had repudiated this in

---

14    Michaelis, *Introduction to the New Testament*, i, pp. 12, 353.
15    Ibid., pp. 39–44.
16    Ibid., pp. 72, 378–9.
17    Ibid., pp. 75, 380.
18    Ibid., pp. 76–9.
19    Ibid., pp. 87–92, 387–9.
20    *British Critic*, xx (December 1802): 670.

1783.[21] On the contrary Michaelis believed that the discrepancies showed that 'the Evangelists did not write in concert'; and a few pages later he reminded his readers that he did not think inspiration extends to recounting of historical facts.[22] The *Monthly Review* agreed with this point, but added:

> It *might* be advantageous to Christianity to have it proved that, in the largest sense of the word, the Evangelists *were* divinely inspired; but, should it be fully proved that they were *not* divinely inspired, even in the most limited sense of the word, so that the works of the Evangelists would be intitled to no greater degree of credit than we allow to the histories of Xenophon, Livy, or Froissart, still there would be sufficient ground for our belief in the history of Christ.[23]

In the mind of the reviewer historical truth was more important than inspiration. The *Critical Review*, in reviewing the pamphlet published in response to Marsh entitled *A Caution to Students in Divinity*, was more blunt: 'No true history can be the more true for its being inspired; and if in any inspired history discordances occur which cannot be solved, we must in such cases at least, give up the inspiration.'[24]

This highlights the problems caused by Michaelis's failure to give a complete definition of what he understood by inspiration. Marsh had himself noted the difficulties caused by this and listed six or seven different possibilities, without offering any judgement himself. What he did say was that

> a writer who receives inspiration in recording historical facts which he knew before, cannot be said to have had a revelation; and even the latter may exist without the former, since, if the doctrines which were revealed by Christ, had been recorded by the Apostles, without any intervention of the Deity, during the act of writing, we should have had a revealed religion without inspiration.[25]

A few pages later Marsh noted that the truth of Christianity did not depend on the authenticity of the New Testament, since it was as true within ten years of the death of Christ before the New Testament was written, as it was today; on the other hand, it was impossible for us '*to prove* the divine origin of Christianity' unless the New Testament was authentic.[26]

The emphasis of the reviewers on this point was different in the 1790s from a decade later. The *British Critic* in 1794 approved of what it called Marsh's note on chapter 10 'that there is no medium between adopting in general the doctrines, which the New Testament literally contains, and rejecting the whole as an improper criterion of faith', though the words quoted come from Marsh's

---

21   See *Reimarus: Fragments*, ed. C.H. Talbert (London, 1971), pp. 153–200.

22   Michaelis, *Introduction to the New Testament*, iii-I, pp. 5, 26–7.

23   *Monthly Review*, xxvi (December 1801): 397.

24   *Critical Review*, xxxvi (September 1802): 65.

25   Michaelis, *Introduction to the New Testament*, i, pp. 375–6; the quotation is on p. 376.

26   Ibid., pp. 378–9.

summary of the chapter in his Preface rather than a note.[27] The *Monthly Review* declared that the interest of revelation

> has been highly injured by endeavouring to affix, on every book and passage of Scripture, an equal degree of authenticity; when in fact the evidence varies, and those books, to which the strongest objections of unbelievers attach, are really the most dubious parts of the sacred canon.[28]

In other words, the infidel question was still uppermost in the reviewer's mind. The conclusion of that part of the review made a related point concerning the use of the Old Testament in the New, regretting that Marsh had been more unwilling than Michaelis to acknowledge the value of Dr A.A. Sykes's mode of interpretation of prophecy, since 'this, or something of the kind, is necessary to remove otherwise insuperable objections to revelation, and to prevent that latitude of explaining the O.T. [*sic*] by which visionaries and religious madmen would justify their wildest theories and conjectures'.[29] Again, what is interesting is as much the concern with 'visionaries and religious madmen' as the more technical point about the interpretation of scripture. In 1802 the *Monthly Review* welcomed Marsh's rejection of the inspiration of every word of scripture, but suggested that it was possible to understand inspiration as meaning that the writers 'were so far inspired as to relate, under the divine influence, whatever it was the will of Heaven that we should know through them, respecting the history and doctrine of Christ'; so no distinction was drawn between history and doctrine.[30]

Whatever the criticisms made of Marsh, it is necessary to remember that there is no sense in which, by mid-nineteenth-century standards, he was radical in his views. In fact, he published a defence of the Mosaic authorship of the Pentateuch in 1792, just before the edition of Michaelis appeared, which began as follows:

> Among the numerous attacks, that have been made on the truth of Christianity, one of the most formidable is that, which is directed against the authenticity of the sacred writings. It has been contended, that we derive a set of rules and opinions from a series of books, which were not written by the authors, to whom we ascribe them; and that the work, to which we give the title of divine, and which is the basis of our faith and manners, is a forgery of later ages.[31]

---

27 *British Critic*, iii (June 1794): 603; cf. Michaelis, *Introduction to the New Testament*, i, Preface, p. v.

28 *Monthly Review*, xvii (July 1795): 297.

29 Ibid.: 308. Dr A.A. Sykes was a follower of Newton and Hoadly against Waterland, who believed that the meaning of an Old Testament prophecy had to have the same meaning in both the Old and New Testaments. Marsh had, in fact, pointed out that George Benson had argued the same point in a prefatory essay to his *Paraphrase on St Paul's Epistles*, which was included in volume 4 of Watson's *Theological Tracts*: Michaelis, *Introduction to the New Testament*, i, 473.

30 *Monthly Review* xxvi (December 1801): 398.

31 H. Marsh, *The Authenticity of the Five Books of Moses considered* (Cambridge, 1792), p. 5.

Once again the deist attack on Christianity is at the heart of the matter; and for much of the nineteenth century it was impossible to detach critical study of the Bible from the memory of that attack.

What, therefore, was the significance of Marsh's own *Dissertation on the Origin and Composition of our first three Canonical Gospels*? The *British Critic* did not think that the question of the origin of the gospels was worth bothering with; we should be satisfied simply to receive them. But 'the German critics seem not to think so; and Mr Marsh, deeply versed in their writings, appears so far to have caught their spirit as to entertain no doubt that the solution is important, and even necessary'.[32] Why did Marsh think it was necessary, in view of his relatively conservative view of authenticity? The problem was the impossibility of reconciling the order of events in the four gospels. Michaelis explained this by saying that none of the first three gospel writers wrote in chronological order, and added that this was not surprising. Indeed events could be arranged by the historian to show the relation between cause and effect, rather than the chronological order. He then argued that, if the contradictions could not be reconciled, it followed that the writers were not infallible, though he did not believe that it therefore followed that the history itself was a forgery. In fact, Michaelis did 'not believe that the Evangelists were divinely inspired in matters of history'; nor did he believe that this impugned Lutheran doctrine. Not all contradictions were of equal importance, however, and the most significant were those concerning the resurrection: he did not feel that all of those had been satisfactorily resolved, but he had been stimulated to re-examine those questions by the *Wolfenbüttel Fragments*.[33] Marsh was clearly not satisfied by such an explanation.

One of his longest notes on any part of Michaelis's text gave Marsh's view. Without chronology 'a regular series of historical events will be converted into a rude mass of unconnected annecdotes [*sic*]'.[34] Nor was he impressed by the argument from cause and effect, since, although he conceded that there was a difference between immediate and mediate effects, 'whenever the order of time is neglected, [the reader] will be exposed to the danger of deducing a false inference'.[35] So he suggested an alternative possibility: instead of supposing that the Evangelists '*designedly* violated the order of time',

> may we not rather suppose, since inspiration does not produce omniscience, that, when the same facts are referred by one Evangelist to one period, by another to another period of Christ's life, they had a knowledge indeed of the facts themselves, but that not both of them had a knowledge of the particular period in which they happened?[36]

---

32   *British Critic*, xxii (February 1803): 178.
33   Michaelis, *Introduction to the New Testament*, iii-I, pp. 10, 13, 25, 27, 30–31 (quotation from p. 27).
34   Michaelis, *Introduction to the New Testament*, iii-II, p. 10.
35   Ibid., p. 12.
36   Ibid., p. 16.

Furthermore, since neither Mark nor Luke were eye-witnesses whereas Matthew was one of the twelve apostles, 'we must conclude that St Matthew's order is in general, I will not say without exception, chronological'.[37] Marsh's concession that inspiration does not produce omniscience was significant, but his hypothesis that only one Evangelist knew the chronological order of events had the merit, in Marsh's eyes, of preserving a clear evidential basis for the chronology of the gospel narratives. Yet the reason for his choice of Matthew was the traditional one that he was an Apostle, and had nothing to do with a comparison of the different chronologies.

The *Dissertation*, therefore, to use Newman's phrase in relation to a different problem, was a 'hypothesis to account for a difficulty'. In his opening chapter Marsh outlined the problems of harmonising the gospels and reduced them to a single dilemma: 'Either the succeeding Evangelists copied from the preceding; or, all the three drew from a common source'.[38] There were able advocates for both positions: it was impossible to prove that the gospels were written in the order they appear, but the opposite opinions were equally incapable of proof.[39] A careful review of all the eighteenth-century writers on the subject from Le Clerc to Herder followed; all of them in different ways postulated a common source.

Marsh has been said to have 'anticipated the "two-document" hypothesis, whereby Mark and [a] lost document were the sources for Matthew and Luke'.[40] This is misleading, since what he actually said was both simpler and more complicated than that. He had moved beyond the position suggested in his Notes, whereby Matthew's Gospel in its surviving form was the original source. Instead he followed Eichhorn's view that the original source was in Hebrew or Chaldee.[41] Nevertheless, as his diagram of the sources makes clear, he envisaged a single original, not two.[42] On the other hand, he postulated a complex process: first, there was a Hebrew document containing a narrative of facts; secondly, a Greek translation of the Hebrew; thirdly, copies of the Hebrew document with additions; fourthly, a Hebrew document with precepts, parables and discourses; fifthly, Matthew's Gospel in Hebrew; sixthly, Luke's Gospel; seventhly, Mark's Gospel; and lastly, the Greek translation of Matthew's Hebrew gospel, which is the first gospel in the canon, the translator of which consulted the Greek versions of Mark and Luke to help him.[43] Now the fourth stage is similar to what later critics called 'Q', though few, if any, have supposed that this was written in Hebrew; but this is hardly a ground for saying that Marsh adopted a 'two-document' hypothesis.

37    Ibid.
38    Marsh, 'Dissertation on the Origin and Composition of our three first Canonical Gospels' in Michaelis, *Introduction to the New Testament*, iii-II, p. 170. The Dissertation was also published separately.
39    Ibid., p. 176.
40    'Herbert Marsh', *ODNB*, xxxvi, p. 798.
41    Michaelis, *Introduction to the New Testament*, iii-II, pp. 191–2. The reference was to the *Allgemeine Bibliothek der biblischen Literatur*, v (1794): 759–996.
42    Michaelis, *Introduction to the New Testament*, iii-II, p. 367.
43    Ibid., pp. 362–76.

In any case Marsh deliberately rejected Herder's hypothesis that Mark's Gospel was closest to the original source.

At the end of the argument Marsh added a footnote that every step hypothesised was consistent with the doctrine of inspiration – not *verbal* inspiration, but partial inspiration as understood by Bishop Warburton.[44] This was designed to affirm the fundamental orthodoxy of his position. After a final chapter in which he examined the various examples of verbal harmony between the gospels, he concluded, 'It appears then, that the phaenomena of every description, observable in our three first Gospels, admit of an easy solution by the proposed hypothesis. And since no other hypothesis can solve them all, we may conclude that it is the true one'.[45]

Unfortunately this conclusion did not convince the reviewers. The *Monthly Review* hedged its bets by saying that readers would have to make up their own minds by reading the work in detail because 'the thread of the discussion is often very finely spun'.[46] More bluntly the *Critical Review*, having noted that Marsh exaggerated in saying that 'all possible' forms of the argument for a common Hebrew document had been considered, said that 'the algebraic form of argument adopted' suggested that he was really arguing in a circle and cited the conclusion as illustrating that.[47] The most hostile comment came from the *British Critic*:

> Supposing such a theory to be necessary for accounting for the verbal similarities and differences of the three first Evangelists, which we by no means admit, the obvious fault of this hypothesis is its extreme complexity ... Although no particular step may be in itself improbable, yet the discovery of ten different sources to certain works, by mere analysis, not one of them being clearly mentioned or alluded to in history, is altogether of the very highest improbability, and forms such a discovery as was never yet made in the world, and probably never will.[48]

The conclusion, therefore, that no other hypothesis could solve the problems was not extraordinary, since he had framed it for that very purpose. The emphasis on probability (and improbability) in these comments is interesting; so it is not surprising that the *British Critic* published an enthusiastic review of Paley's *Natural Theology* a few months later.[49] In fact, Marsh himself wrote, in a Note in Volume 1 on a disagreement between Michaelis and Semler, that the conjectures of all critics were sometimes ungrounded – 'a circumstance at which no one should be surprised, as the province of criticism is confined within the bounds

---

44    Ibid., p. 376. The reference was to W. Warburton, *The Doctrine of Grace; or the Office and Operations of the Holy Spirit* (2nd edn, London, 1763), pp. 34–8, summarised in the words: 'It imports us little to be solicitous about the Scriptural DELIVERY of Gospel Truth, whether they be conveyed to us by means merely human, or by the more powerful workings of the Holy Spirit, so long as we are assured that divine Providence guarded that delivery from all approach of error' (p. 37).

45    Michaelis, *Introduction to the New Testament*, iii-II, p. 409.

46    *Monthly Review*, xxvii (February 1802): 178.

47    *Critical Review*, xxxv (September 1802): 63.

48    *British Critic*, xxii (February 1803): 180.

49    *British Critic*, xxii (September 1803): 230.

of probability, and can seldom or never extend to absolute certainty'.[50] The Conclusion of his *Dissertation* lacked that tentativeness. Similarly the concern about complexity reflected a distaste for the kind of detailed analysis that was to become characteristic of biblical studies in the nineteenth century and beyond.

Marsh still had to wait some time for any kind of preferment. He was elected Lady Margaret's Professor without opposition in 1807, after canvassing privately for it during the previous year. Between 1688 and 1875 all the Lady Margaret's Professors came from St John's College.[51] Although St John's College had an advantage because of its size and its requirement that all Fellows in orders should take the BD, personal popularity nevertheless remained important. Thomas Kipling was said to have failed to secure the chair in 1788 because of his unpopularity in the University.[52] Holders of the chair also seem to have been long-lived: the average tenure in the period dominated by St John's was twenty-three years. The Regius Chair was still occupied by Watson, and the Norrisian Chair in 1795 went to another Fellow of St John's, James Fawcett. It is possible that Marsh was still regarded with some suspicion then in the aftermath of the Frend case (see below); he certainly suffered from the attack on him by the episcopal author of the *Caution to Students in Divinity* (probably Bishop Randolph of London).[53] So 1807 was his first opportunity for a theological chair.

Following his appointment Marsh broke with the custom of centuries by delivering lectures in English rather than Latin. He also gave them in the University in the Easter Term 1809, and following years, on the ground that the Divinity Schools were only suited for disputations and did not have sufficient seating for undergraduates.[54] Although in his opening lecture Marsh said that his lectures would relate to every branch of Theology, in fact they concentrated primarily upon the Bible. Nor did he have any hesitation about the system which should be the end of theological study at Cambridge: it was that of the Church of England, 'contained in our liturgy, our articles, and our homilies'.[55] Historical and critical arguments were the necessary basis for a sound theological knowledge, so he rejected the 'distinction between science and religion, that one is an object of reason, the other an object of faith': 'religion is an object of both'.[56] He rebuffed the notion that knowledge was dangerous to faith by suggesting doubts, saying

---

50  Michaelis, *Introduction to the New Testament*, i, p. 516.

51  D. Winstanley, *Unreformed Cambridge* (Cambridge, 1935), pp. 96–101.

52  'Thomas Kipling', *ODNB*, xxxi, p. 757.

53  See note 24 above; cf. H. Marsh, *A Reply to the Strictures of the Rev Isaac Milner* (Cambridge, 1813), pp. 6–7.

54  H. Marsh, *A Course of Lectures, containing a Description and Systematic Arrangement of the Several Branches of Divinity* (Cambridge, 1809). Part I appeared in 1809, Part II in 1810, Part III in 1813, Part IV in 1816, Part V in 1820, Part VI in 1822, and Part VII in 1823. The whole set was revised with additions and omissions and published in a new edition under the title, *Lectures on the Criticism and Interpretation of the Bible* (London, 1842).

55  Marsh, *Course of Lectures*, p. 10.

56  Ibid., p. 13. The use of 'science' as a synonym for knowledge here is worth noting.

that 'it is not learning, but want of learning, which leads to error in religion'.[57] Far from causing divisions in the church, theological learning was 'the only method of ensuring to us the advantages of the Reformation, by guarding against enthusiasm on the one hand, and infidelity on the other'.[58] Marsh's perception of where the crucial divisions in the church lay was significant. In his second lecture he discussed different ways in which the study of Theology could be arranged, suggesting that the best pattern was that long used in Germany: Expository Theology, Systematic Theology, Historical Theology and Pastoral Theology. But whilst it was clear that one should begin with scripture, there were many things to consider: its authenticity, credibility, divine authority, inspiration and doctrines. The foundation was the authenticity of the Bible, but that in turn depended on biblical interpretation; and the key to biblical interpretation was biblical criticism, by which he understood both the establishment of the correct text and also the genuineness of whole books.[59] He specifically argued that conjectural emendations were inadmissible in sacred criticism, because that opened the way to a party interpretation of scripture and then it would cease to be a common standard.[60] Consequently he proposed a sevenfold division: biblical criticism, biblical interpretation, biblical authenticity and credibility, the divine authority of the Bible and evidences for its divine origin, biblical inspiration, biblical doctrines, both those deduced by the Church of England and those of other Churches, and ecclesiastical history.[61] Marsh never made it to the study of ecclesiastical history!

The fundamental place given to biblical criticism is striking, and represents a significant shift in emphasis from Watson and Paley. The second edition added a section on the history of biblical interpretation, which was written during residence in Cambridge in 1827–28. But by then Marsh was a bishop, and quite an active one; and despite his declared intentions he did not avoid engagement in literary controversy. It was not surprising that Mark Pattison should write in *Essays and Reviews* that, 'Of an honest critical enquiry into the origin and composition of the canonical writings there is but one trace, Herbert Marsh's Lectures at Cambridge, and that was suggested from a foreign source, and died away without exciting imitators'.[62] Pattison also noted that it died away not because it was felt to be barren, but because of a fear that it might 'prove too fertile in results'. Nevertheless Marsh left a significant though ambiguous legacy. In his second lecture he had argued that it was impossible to appeal to inspiration in order to establish the truth of scripture. That had to be demonstrated by other means and therefore the credibility of the sacred writers had to be established in exactly the same way as for other writers. In this respect, Marsh followed the same line as Watson and

57    Ibid., p. 15.
58    Ibid., p. 16.
59    Ibid., pp. 18–25.
60    Ibid., p. 27.
61    Ibid., pp. 37–8.
62    M. Pattison, 'Tendencies of Religious Thought in England, 1688–1750' in *Essays and Reviews* (London, 1860), p. 262.

Paley. But in the next sentence he wrote, 'Nothing but either *divine* testimony, or prophecy, can confirm it'.[63] Both Marsh and later writers, therefore, attached special significance to the general question of the interpretation of prophecy and the particular question of whether certain texts could rightly be taken as being the *ipsissima verba* of God. Marsh's reduction of the grounds of inspiration to these two, whilst not unique to him, explains the importance which these two questions assumed.

Marsh's work on the New Testament therefore, notwithstanding some similarities in starting point to Watson and Paley, shows that he was a more conservative figure. That also sets some of the other events in his career in context. At the outset it was noted that he was cousin of William Frend (1757–1841), a Fellow of Jesus, who not only adopted Unitarian views but also supported the French Revolution. Early in 1793 he wrote a pamphlet entitled *Peace and Union*, which was essentially a manifesto for political reform, including parliamentary reform. When Louis XVI was executed in January, Frend wrote an appendix to his pamphlet condemning the British declaration of war on France. In February five Fellows of Jesus protested about his pamphlet to the Vice-Chancellor, who was Isaac Milner, President of Queens', and a doughty defender of the political status quo as well as a fervent evangelical. Subsequently twenty-seven Fellows of various colleges, headed by Dr Kipling formulated resolutions in favour of prosecuting the author of *Peace and Union*, at a meeting presided over by the Vice-Chancellor himself. The Fellows of Jesus resolved to deprive him of his Fellowship, but the implementation of this awaited proceedings in the Vice-Chancellor's Court, where Frend was charged with violating the University's statute, *De Concionibus*. The proceedings were something of a farce, and Marsh was involved in them because Dr Kipling wanted to call him as a witness. Marsh had apparently taken an advertisement for *Peace and Union* to be inserted in the *Cambridge Chronicle* at Frend's request, and would therefore be able to testify to the authorship of the pamphlet. Marsh protested against being asked to give evidence against a near relation and a friend. Milner ruled that Marsh should not be called unless Dr Kipling absolutely insisted, and so he was allowed to withdraw. Frend was banished from the University.[64]

Marsh's reaction was probably more due to family concern than political sympathy. There is no suggestion that he supported proposals for parliamentary reform. But he was a keen opponent of Milner's evangelicalism, and had disliked the machinations which lay behind this particular episode. He worried about evangelical tendencies towards enthusiasm, in a characteristically eighteenth-century way, and came to believe that what he regarded as the Calvinist tendencies of evangelicalism would lead inevitably to Dissent. Thus his loyalty to the established church was absolute.

It lay behind his involvement in two major controversies in the first decades of the new century. In 1808 a non-denominational school was opened in Cambridge,

---

63  Marsh, *Course of Lectures*, p. 36.

64  F. Knight, *University Rebel* (London, 1971), pp. 118–61; P. Searby, *A History of the University of Cambridge* (Cambridge, 1997), iii, pp. 414–21.

following the principles of Joseph Lancaster, who used Dr Bell's 'Madras system' of education of large classes through the use of monitors. Marsh believed that it was vital that children should be educated in the principles of the established church as well as being taught to read and write. On 13 June 1811 he preached a sermon at St Paul's Cathedral on the occasion of the annual gathering of children at charity schools in the Cities of London and Westminster, entitled 'The National Religion the Foundation of National Education', which was published by the SPCK. Pointing out that the canons required all schoolmasters to be licensed by the bishop and to educate children in the principles of the catechism, he criticised those churchmen who co-operated with Joseph Lancaster's British and Foreign Schools Society, on the grounds that religious neutrality was in effect 'a kind of hostility': 'It is *hostility* to the Establishment, to deprive our children of that *early* attachment to it, which an education in the Church cannot fail to inspire, and which, if lost in their *youth*, can never be recovered'.[65] Marsh hastened to say that he was not intending to limit the freedom of dissenters to educate their children in their own way, which indeed had specifically been permitted by the Act recognising dissenting schoolmasters in 1779. Nevertheless, Lancaster's basis of Christianity alone – 'Glory to God, and the increase of peace and good-will among men' – might be a basis for natural religion but not for the revealed doctrines of Christianity: it could be affirmed by 'a Deist, a Mahometan, or a Hindoo' as well as by a Christian.[66]

Marsh followed up his sermon with a series of six letters to the *Morning Post* in September 1811 defending Andrew Bell's system. Lancaster had written a letter to the paper, in which he claimed that Bell (who was a Church of England clergyman) stood for the 'universal limitation of knowledge', whereas he himself stood for the 'universal diffusion of knowledge'; Lancaster implied that Bell only wanted to teach reading, and not writing and arithmetic. This was based on a sentence included only in the third edition of Bell's *Elements of Tuition*. Marsh not only pointed out that Bell had always taught writing and arithmetic in Madras, but affirmed that it was 'a narrow and mistaken notion, that the learning to write and to cypher will raise the lower orders of society above their sphere'.[67] Thus Marsh became one of the principal movers behind the formation of the National Society for Promoting the Education of the Poor in the Principles of the Established Church in 1811, alongside the better known Hackney Phalanx – the London-based group of high churchmen.[68]

---

65    H. Marsh, *The National Religion the Foundation of National Education* (London, 1811), p. 11. The political atmosphere was somewhat tense following the defeat of Sidmouth's Bill to regulate Dissenting preachers in the House of Lords in May 1811.

66    Ibid., pp. 17–18, note 15.

67    H. Marsh, *A Vindication of Dr Bell's System of Tuition* (London, 1811), p. 14.

68    Alan Webster made no reference to Marsh's role in the formation of the National Society in his biography of Joshua Watson, the leader of the Hackney Phalanx: A.B. Webster, *Joshua Watson* (London, 1954), pp. 33–43.

The other campaign was less successful.[69] It was provoked by the proposal to set up an Auxiliary of the British and Foreign Bible Society in the University. Marsh clearly hoped to build on the success of his St Paul's sermon. At first his hopes seemed reasonable. Christopher Wordsworth, Domestic Chaplain to the Archbishop of Canterbury (and a future Master of Trinity), had already published a pamphlet in 1810, explaining why he as a churchman could not become a subscriber to the Society. The undergraduates, who wished to form the society, consulted William Farish, Professor of Chemistry and Vicar of St Giles, Joseph Jowett, Regius Professor of Civil Law and Isaac Milner, expecting support from these stalwarts of evangelicalism. Milner, clearly anxious about undergraduate initiatives of any kind, advised them to leave the matter to their superiors in the University. Although the embryonic committee decided to go ahead regardless, when they consulted Charles Simeon, he persuaded them not to follow a course of rebellion. But this left Simeon and others with the responsibility of carrying the matter forward. Farish approached the Vice-Chancellor, Dr Thomas Browne, Master of Christ's, who gave permission for a meeting to be held, but indicated his disapproval.

At this point Marsh circulated an Address to members of the Senate, in which he argued in favour of supporting the SPCK (which he described as 'the ancient Bible Society') in preference to the British and Foreign Bible Society, founded in 1804. His reason was that the SPCK in its circulation at home distributed the Liturgy of the Church of England as well as the Bible, whereas the BFBS used its funds to distribute Bibles only. The essence of his argument was the same as in his St Paul's sermon: religious dissent should be tolerated, but not encouraged. By contrast the principle of equality on which the modern Bible Society was formed entailed the danger that 'the preeminence of the *established religion* should be gradually forgotten, and finally lost'. This time he went further than he had at St Paul's, and suggested that, since religious and political dissension were closely conected, 'religious dissension therefore in this country becomes a *political* evil'.[70] Unfortunately for Marsh, despite the support for him from many strict churchmen in the University, the High Steward, Lord Hardwicke, agreed to take the chair at the meeting; the Duke of Gloucester, the recently appointed Chancellor, wrote a letter to say that he would subscribe fifty guineas and accept the Presidency of the branch society if that was the general wish; Milner decided to attend after all; and the Master of Trinity indicated his support, together with the Dukes of Bedford and Rutland, and the Rt Hon. Nicholas Vansittart. So on 12 December 1811 a Cambridge Branch of the Bible Society was founded. The President appointed was William Mansel, Master of Trinity and Bishop of Bristol, and Richard Watson, the Regius Professor, was a Vice-President. Milner spoke at the meeting, explaining his initial doubts, but saying that he was satisfied that there

---

69    See D. Winstanley, *Early Victorian Cambridge* (Cambridge, 1940), pp. 18–25; R. Hole, *Pulpits, Politics and Public Order, 1760–1832* (Cambridge, 1989), pp. 190–95.

70    H. Marsh, *An Address to the Members of the Senate of the University of Cambridge, occasioned by the Proposal to introduce into this Place an Auxiliary Bible Society* (Cambridge, 1811), p. 2.

was nothing like an improper combination among the undergraduates concerned. His main attack, however, was reserved for Marsh. Milner rejected 'the principle of a rooted aversion to any connection in religious concerns with Christians of any denomination, if they dissent from the Established Church'. 'I do not dread the dissenters, as if they were infected with a contagion,' he continued, 'but I cordially rejoice to shake hands with them on all points where we do agree.'[71]

The war of words then began in earnest, with Milner publishing an attack on Marsh in 1813, which broadened to include the whole of his work, including that on the New Testament, and Marsh replying. Simeon then joined in to 'congratulate' Marsh on acknowledging that members of the Bible Society did not neglect the liturgy; and Marsh responded, extending the attack to what he supposed to be Calvinism among the evangelicals, particularly in relation to baptismal regeneration.[72] This may be why Canon Overton regarded the baptismal controversy as part of the Calvinist controversy.[73] In fact, it is more plausible to suppose that this was part of Marsh's tendency to see Calvinists everywhere; and it also links with his later 'Trap for Calvinists', when Bishop of Peterborough. As far as the Bible Society was concerned, Simeon wrote:

> Of all the men in Britain that have done good to the Bible Society, there is scarcely one, except the Secretaries, that can vie with Dr Marsh. In doing all that man can do against it, he has advanced it a thousand times more than if he had written in its favour.[74]

What was more interesting about the Milner-Marsh controversy was that Milner revived the old issues of the 1790s, when Marsh criticised Archdeacon Travis in an attempt to demonstrate the inauthenticity of 1 John 5:7, and Marsh's own hypothesis about the origin of the synoptic gospels. He was sceptical of what he called 'Marsh's theorem' for judging the relative probability of different manuscript readings to be authentic. At the heart of Milner's criticism was a suspicion of algebra, relative to the certainties of geometry, and its significance was illustrated by the fact that Marsh devoted a complete Appendix in his *Reply* to a refutation.[75] Marsh's predecessor as Lady Margaret's Professor, John Mainwaring,

---

71   I. Milner, *Strictures on some of the Publications of the Rev. Herbert Marsh, DD, intended as a Reply to his Objections against the British and Foreign Bible Society* (London, 1813), pp. 411–12, 414–15.

72   Milner, *Strictures*; H. Marsh, *A Reply to the Strictures of the Rev Isaac Milner, DD* (Cambridge, 1813); C. Simeon, *Dr Marsh's Fact; or A Congratulatory Address to the Church-Members of the British and Foreign Bible Society* (Cambridge, 1813); H. Marsh, *A Letter to the Rev Charles Simeon, MA, in answer to his Pretended Congratulatory Address, in Confutation of his various Mis-Statements, and in Vindication of the Efficacy ascribed by our Church to the Sacrament of Baptism* (Cambridge, 1813).

73   J.H. Overton, *The English Church in the Nineteenth Century* (London, 1894), pp. 190–92. I have indicated why I do not share this view in D.M. Thompson, *Baptism, Church and Society in Modern Britain* (Bletchley, 2005), pp. 44–5.

74   W. Carus, *Memoirs of the Life of the Rev Charles Simeon, MA* (London, 1847), p. 373; cited in F.K. Brown, *Fathers of the Victorians* (Cambridge, 1961), pp. 310–11.

75   Milner, *Strictures*, pp. 238–55; Marsh, *Reply*, Appendix, pp. 3–28.

had complained in 1780 that too much emphasis was laid in the Senate House examination on 'the abstruser parts of algebra and mathematics', but the emphasis on geometry as the model for logical reasoning meant that the newer techniques in late eighteenth-century algebra tended to pass Cambridge by.[76] Paley's undesigned coincidences were more appealing than Marsh's hypotheses.

For more significant preferment in the church Marsh had to wait for Watson's death in 1816, when he was appointed Bishop of Llandaff. He was translated to Peterborough in 1819, and retained his chair until his death. At Peterborough he engaged in further controversy by requiring all candidates for incumbencies and curacies in the diocese to answer a series of questions, designed to discover whether they had evangelical sympathies. Marsh was attacked by Sydney Smith in the *Edinburgh Review*, in an article entitled, 'Persecuting Bishops', and did not win support from his episcopal colleagues. The number of questions asked was later reduced from 87 to 36, but Marsh's concern remained, even though he licensed some evangelicals.[77] In many ways he was a reforming bishop, but he had a knack of rubbing people up the wrong way, which obscured his better achievements. His later years were dogged by ill-health, but he never considered retiring from the Lady Margaret's chair. He was adding new parts to his *Lectures on the Criticism and Interpretation of the Bible* up to 1823, and revising them in the late 1820s. So what had begun as a career that opened up new initiatives for Cambridge theology tailed off with a twenty-year period as an only occasionally resident Professor. Meanwhile, alongside the continuing interest in the evidences of Christianity, so clearly articulated by Paley, there was an unexpected development: the appropriation of Paley by the increasingly influential Evangelical school.

---

76    J. Gascoigne, *Cambridge in the Age of the Enlightenment* (Cambridge, 1989), pp. 272–3.

77    C.Smyth, *Simeon and Church Order* (Cambridge, 1989), p. 245.

# Chapter 3

# Evangelicals, Protestants
# and Orthodox

He stood for many years alone – he was long opposed, ridiculed, shunned – his doctrines were misrepresented – his little peculiarities of voice and manner were satirized – disturbances were frequently raised in his Church – he was a person not taken into account, nor considered in the light of a regular Clergyman of the Church. Such was the beginning of things. But mark the close. For the last portion of his Ministry all was rapidly changing. He was invited repeatedly to take courses of Sermons before the University. The same great principles that he preached were avowed from almost every pulpit in Cambridge. His Church was crowded with young Students ... The Heads of Houses, the Doctors, the Masters of Arts, the Bachelors and the Undergraduates, the Congregation from the Town, seemed to vie with each other in eagerness to hear the aged and venerable man ... And at his death when did either of our Universities pay such marked honour to a private individual?[1]

Bishop Daniel Wilson's tribute to Charles Simeon in 1837, two years before the death of Herbert Marsh, marked the striking change that had come over Cambridge in the first thirty years of the nineteenth century.

Charles Simeon (1759–1836), however, was not the pioneer of the evangelical cause in Cambridge, and apart from his Fellowship at King's he never held any substantial college or University office. The first evangelical in a significant college position was probably Samuel Hey, Tutor and subsequently President of Magdalene from 1778, who was supported by William Farish, Professor of Chemistry (1794–1813) and Jacksonian Professor (1813–37), and Henry Jowett. Hey welcomed students supported by the Elland Society, a group of Yorkshire evangelical Anglicans, and by 1796–97 twelve Magdalene undergraduates were Elland pensioners. Peter Peckard, Master (1781–97), was described by Eamon Duffy as 'a man of decidedly liberal churchmanship', which in the light of his views of the trinity and original sin was an understatement. However, Peckard supported Hey's policy, and as Vice-Chancellor in 1784 set as the subject for the Latin prize-essay competition, 'The lawfulness of slavery'. Thomas Clarkson was the prize-winner, and as a result became involved in the abolitionist movement. In 1797 both the Master and President changed, and were replaced by men of

---

1     W. Carus (ed.), *Memoirs of the Life of the Rev Charles Simeon, MA* (London, 1847), pp. 837–8.

a decidedly non-evangelical stamp; and evangelical students were increasingly unwelcome.[2]

The chief beneficiary was Queens', whose President since 1788 had been Isaac Milner, Jacksonian Professor (1783–98) and Lucasian Professor (1798–1820). Milner achieved his goal of making Queens' into an evangelical college by appointing evangelical Tutors and making life difficult for Fellows who opposed him.[3] As important was the change in political direction: Gunning remarked that 'the College entirely changed its character, and … the Society, which, under the Presidentship of Dr Plumptre, had been distinguished for its attachment to Civil and Religious Liberty, became afterwards as remarkable for its opposition to liberal opinions'.[4] As Gunning implied, Milner was hostile to liberal opinions, whether religious or political, and the political element loomed larger in the febrile atmosphere of the 1790s. This has already been illustrated by the 'trial' of William Frend because, although Frend was a man of liberal religious views, it was his political pamphlet that was the subject of concern. Thus Milner's theological opinions were not so important or influential as his ability to secure positions for those of evangelical views. His most significant theological achievement may have been to introduce William Wilberforce to Philip Doddridge's *Rise and Progress of Religion*, which they read together on their journey from Nice to London in the winter of 1784–85.[5]

Charles Simeon was not a theological teacher in the academic sense. But his influence over several generations of undergraduates was probably more significant than that of the University professors. From Eton he entered King's on a scholarship in 1778. The peculiar constitution of the college meant that only Eton collegers were ever chosen as scholars; having been elected by the Provost and Fellows they were exempted from University examinations and entitled to proceed to a Life Fellowship upon graduation. This therefore was the path which Simeon followed. His conversion, as a result of reading *The Whole Duty of Man* and Bishop Wilson on the Lord's Supper, became the most significant point in his

---

2    P. Cunich, D. Hoyle, E. Duffy and R. Hyam, *A History of Magdalene College, Cambridge, 1428–1988* (Cambridge, 1994), pp. 185–93; cf. Searby, *History of the University*, iii, pp. 320–25.

3    J. Twigg, *A History of Queens' College, Cambridge, 1448–1986* (Woodbridge, 1987), p. 174. Twigg states that recalcitrant Fellows were forced into college livings, and this is repeated by Searby, *History of the University*, iii, p. 326. However, this is based on Gunning, a keen critic of Milner, who lists six Fellows who departed, two of whom took livings, and one who had a curacy at Eversden (itself formerly the parish of William Berridge, a noted evangelical) who was 'ordered into residence' in college, because of 'his irregularities in the country': Gunning, *Reminiscences*, i, pp. 263–4. So far as livings are concerned this was two out and one in.

4    Gunning, *Reminiscences*, i, p. 262.

5    The process continued with the study of the Greek New Testament on the journey to Genoa and back in the summer of 1785, and then by regular conversations with John Newton and the keeping of a spiritual diary. Wilberforce did not 'find peace' until Easter 1786: R. Furneaux, *William Wilberforce* (London, 1974), pp. 33–40; R.I. Wilberforce and S. Wilberforce, *Life of William Wilberforce* (London 1838), i, pp. 76–7, 81–2, 87–112.

undergraduate career.[6] A further stage came when he made up his mind on the nature of saving faith, rejecting the view of James Hervey as a result of reading Archbishop Shairp: 'I think it clear, even to demonstration, that *assurance* is not necessary to saving faith; a simple reliance on Christ for salvation is that faith which the word of God requires; assurance is a privilege, but not a duty.'[7] He was ordained by the Bishop of Ely on Trinity Sunday 1782 (26 May – some nine weeks before he graduated), and began his ministry by doing duty at St Edward's Church during the Long Vacation at the invitation of Christopher Atkinson, Fellow of Trinity Hall, who was in pastoral charge. Atkinson introduced him to John Venn, who subsequently took him home to Yelling to meet his father. By these means Simeon was drawn into the wider evangelical circles. In the course of the summer Simeon visited every house in the parish and filled St Edward's with hearers, 'a thing unknown there for near a century'.[8]

In November 1782 his father wrote to the Bishop of Ely urging him to present Charles to Holy Trinity Church, which had just fallen vacant. The parishioners wished for the previous curate, Mr Hammond, and not only wrote to the Bishop on his behalf but also elected him to the parish lectureship. The Bishop decided in favour of Simeon, and there was open warfare for several years, with the parishioners locking their pews when Simeon preached, and the churchwardens locking the church when Simeon proposed to give a Sunday evening lecture. Not only did Simeon persist without showing bitterness; he also preached in a variety of churches in Cambridge and the surrounding villages with great success. In many ways Simeon's greatest gift was not so much his theology as his preaching style, which was always effective and often moving. He was ordained priest by Bishop Hinchcliffe of Peterborough (Master of Trinity) in Trinity College chapel on 28 September 1783. Another key component of Simeon's ministry was also a result of the hostility of the Holy Trinity parishioners: he hired a room in the parish in order to hold bible studies and prayer meetings. Thus Simeon combined something of the peripatetic ministry of a Wesley in the Cambridge neighbourhood and also an equivalent of Wesley's class meetings, but all within the discipline of the Church of England. By 1790 he had secured the churchwardens' consent to the Sunday evening lecture and in 1794 Simeon was elected parish lecturer at Holy Trinity without opposition. His 'time of trial' was over.[9]

Simeon's preaching became legendary and had a lasting impact on undergraduate life. Probably sermons as a means of Christian communication became more popular than they had been for more than a century. Simeon was also chosen as University Select Preacher on a regular basis – his first sermon was in 1786 and many of the undergraduates who came to scoff were subdued and surprised by what they heard. When one said to another, 'Well! Simeon is no fool however', his companion replied, 'Fool! Did you ever hear such a sermon

6    Carus, *Memoirs of Simeon*, pp. 6–10.
7    Ibid., p. 15.
8    Ibid., pp. 21–7. The quotation comes from a letter by Henry Venn to the Revd J. Stillingfleet.
9    Ibid., pp. 40–138.

before?'[10] Theologically his evangelicalism was more moderate than that of Milner, especially in the refusal to attempt any systematisation of the doctrine of election. Simeon went as far as scripture went and no further, though he was still accused of Calvinism on several occasions.

Edward Pearson (1756–1811), Master of Sidney, criticised Simeon's University Sermon of 1 December 1805, entitled 'The Churchman's Confession', in a letter to the *Orthodox Churchman's Magazine*. Having acknowledged the importance of the sermon's theme (on the extent to which Christians fell short of their duty, as illustrated by the General Confession), Pearson suggested that its weakness was the

> evident design of supporting the unfounded notions, entertained by *Evangelical* or *Calvinistic* divines of the total corruption of human nature, and of justification or salvation by *faith only* as opposed to *obedience*, with which notions the *Confession* has just as much to do, as it has with the doctrine of *transubstantiation*, or *purgatory*.[11]

The comments showed the sensitivity to anything which detracted from obedience in this period. Pearson, by now Christian Advocate,[12] returned to the fray by publishing a pamphlet in January 1810, following Simeon's University sermon in November 1809 entitled 'Evangelical and Pharasaic Righteousness Compared' (Matthew 5.20). He admitted that there was much to be commended and little to be condemned in the sermon, but suggested that in speaking of those who now 'occupy the seat of Moses' Simeon could only have in mind his fellow Anglican clergy and when he referred to those 'who are in repute for wisdom and piety among us' as having 'a disapprobation of real piety lurking in their hearts' he must mean fellow members of the University. Pearson therefore regarded the sermon as 'a libel'.[13] Simeon prepared a reply entitled 'Fresh Cautions', but took the advice of Farish, who suggested that ridicule was inappropriate for a Christian. Instead he took the opportunity to affirm that he held up 'the standard of holiness very high', and noted that Pearson acknowledged that he was as strong an advocate of good works as Pearson was, and thus no one had any 'reason to fear an *Antinomian* spirit'. He therefore wondered what Pearson was cautioning the world against, since it 'would ill become a *Christian* Advocate' to caution people against placing the standard of morality too high.[14] Finally Herbert Marsh attacked Simeon's University sermons on 'The Excellence of the Liturgy', preached in November 1811, in the pamphlet war that followed the establishment of the Bible Society.

10    Ibid., p. 70.
11    E. Pearson, *Cautions to the hearers and readers of the Rev Mr Simeon's Sermon* (London, n.d.), p. 18; quoted in Carus, *Memoirs of Simeon*, p. 209.
12    This was the title first used for the position established under John Hulse's benefaction, when it was held for two years. In 1861 this was changed in into the Hulsean Professorship.
13    Pearson, *Cautions*, pp. 13–14, quoted in Carus, *Memoirs of Simeon*, pp. 277–8.
14    C. Simeon, *Fresh Cautions to the Public* (2nd edn, London, n.d.), pp. 14, 25; quoted in Carus *Memoirs of Simeon*, pp. 283–6. Pearson responded with *Remarks on the Revd Mr Simeon's 'Fresh Cautions to the Public'* (London, n.d.).

When Simeon published the sermons in 1812, he included a Letter to Professor Marsh, repudiating the view that supporters of the Bible Society neglected the Prayer Book. In particular he regretted that those who accused evangelicals of espousing Calvinism, such as Marsh and Pretyman-Tomline (Bishop of Lincoln and Pitt's close friend), would never quote the passages on which they based their charges.[15] Marsh's response did not answer Simeon's question.

Simeon also set great store by order. Carus commented that 'not only in later life was he singularly attentive to order himself, but was wont particularly to enforce upon his younger brethren the importance and duty of not indulging their zeal at the expense of regularity and discretion'.[16] Thus in the Bible Society controversy, he was the one who persuaded the undergraduates not to try to form a branch without the approval of their Seniors, even though it was eventually left to Farish to insist on going ahead. Obviously he was not unique among Anglican evangelicals in being concerned about order: the point is rather that he had the popular influence to ensure that orderliness prevailed. Nor were there manifestations of excessive enthusiasm in the services he conducted. Another contribution he made was to initiate support for overseas missions. Simeon had been one of those involved in the first discussions which eventually led to the formation of the Church Missionary Society in 1799. Two of his curates, Henry Martyn and Thomas Thomason, went out as missionaries to India in the first decade of the new century, but Martyn's brilliant career as a translator of the Bible was tragically cut short by his early death in 1812.

From the 1820s Simeon became an elder statesman and the sniping died away. Daniel Wilson could write in his tribute that

> Mr Simeon was more and more respected by the Senior part of the University - learning was observed not to be incompatible with his views of Scriptural piety – and many who were far from espousing those views themselves, were yet filled with respect for his consistent and striking character.[17]

He died on 13 November 1836, at the time he should have been preaching the University Sermon. King's College Chapel was filled for his funeral the following Saturday, when the town shops in the centre were closed and lectures were suspended. He was buried in the Fellows' Vault near the west door, and the memorial tablet in the chancel of Holy Trinity Church states that Simeon 'whether as the ground of his own hopes, or as the subject of all his ministrations determined to know nothing but Jesus Christ, and Him crucified (1 Cor II.2)'.[18]

However, the Simeonite influence only slowly affected the Professors of Divinity. Marsh remained determinedly hostile and outlived Simeon by three years. The same was true, though in a less public way, of John Kaye (1783–1853), who succeeded Watson in the Regius Chair in 1816. Kaye was a brilliant scholar.

---

15    Carus *Memoirs of Simeon*, pp. 293–304.
16    Ibid., p. 278.
17    Ibid., pp. 843–4.
18    Ibid., pp. 825–32.

He was born in Hammersmith, the only son of a City businessman, and was educated by a distinguished Greek scholar, Dr Charles Burney. In February 1800 he matriculated at Christ's and was soon elected a Foundation Scholar. He was Senior Wrangler and Senior Chancellor's Medallist in 1804, a rare double achievement.[19] His exact contemporary was James Monk of Trinity, later Regius Professor of Greek (1808), while Charles James Blomfield, also of Trinity, was four years younger; and the three became close friends. As bishops (Kaye at Bristol and Lincoln, Monk at Gloucester, and Blomfield at Chester and London), the trio were at the heart of the reform of the Church of England in the 1830s. Kaye was elected to a Fellowship at Christ's in 1804 and was Tutor until 1814, when at the age of thirty he was elected Master. In 1815–16 he was Vice-Chancellor, and as such ineligible for election to the Regius Chair when it became vacant. The electors to the Regius Chair therefore deferred the election until he had ceased to be Vice-Chancellor.

Like his contemporary at Oxford, Charles Lloyd, Kaye rekindled interest in the Fathers. He decided to follow Marsh's example by giving lectures and giving them in English. Interestingly in his Introductory Lecture on the study of the Fathers he suggested that the discontinuance of lectures was not due to 'any want of ability, or of zeal, or of industry, on the part of the Professors'.[20] Instead he surmised that, with the spread of printing, lectures had ceased to be the only or the most effective way of communicating information to theological students. But the temper of the present time once more insisted upon lectures being given, even though the substance of them might be 'communicated with less trouble to myself, and equal benefit to others, through the medium of the Press'.[21] Furthermore the University Statutes confined the Professor to 'the interpretation and explanation of the Holy Scriptures'. However, he intended to lecture on the Fathers, not only because knowledge of their writings was required of any candidate for the Chair, but also because of 'a conviction that by endeavouring to rescue them from the neglect and contempt into which they are fallen, and enabling the student to form a just estimate of their character and pretensions', he would render an important service to the cause of theological learning.[22] The reason was that in the seventeenth and early eighteenth centuries the credibility of the Fathers was attacked by a succession of writers, culminating in the *Free Inquiry* by Dr Conyers Middleton (1683–1750) in 1749.[23] Middleton had accused the Fathers of unsound reasoning and a credulous attitude to miracles. Kaye set out to defend them, just as Watson had in his *Apology for Christianity* some

---

19    W.J.J. Kaye (ed.), *The Works of John Kaye* (London, n.d.), pp. viii, 1.

20    Ibid., pp. 7–8.

21    Ibid., p. 10.

22    Ibid., pp. 11–12.

23    The full title was *A free inquiry into the miraculous powers, which are supposed to have subsisted in the Christian church, from the earliest ages through several successive centuries: By which is shewn, that we have no sufficient reason to believe, upon the authority of the primitive fathers, that any such powers were continued to the church, after the days of the apostles.*

forty years earlier. The question, as Kaye saw it, was whether the Fathers could be relied on as guides to moral truth – and he suggested that it was wrong to compare them with Locke and Butler, and perhaps better to compare them with heathen philosophers such as Plato. Against Bishop Warburton he suggested that the allegorical mode of interpretation favoured by the Fathers did not come from heathen philosophy but from Jewish tradition. Nor were the Fathers any more credulous than the heathen philosophers of the age; they were simply human. More significant was the fact that miracles did not figure largely in the writings of the Apostolic Fathers, but rather in the writings of the Fathers of the fourth and fifth centuries. Even the pious frauds, which Kaye admitted existed in the later Fathers, were characteristic of the age. Instead he chose to concentrate upon the positive value which Middleton saw in their work: the transmission and attestation of the genuine books of the holy scriptures, and their account of the doctrines, rites, manners and learning of the ages in which they lived. This had already been demonstrated by the work of Dr Lardner. So he intended to concentrate upon the way in which the Fathers threw light upon the articles of the Church of England which, he said,

> can never be perfectly understood, but by those who have traced the gradual development of the doctines contained in them, from the unconnected and incidental notices scattered over the writings of the Primitive Fathers to the regular and systematic form, in which they were at length embodied by the Founders of our Church at the time of the Reformation.[24]

Kaye's subsequent works on Tertullian, Justin Martyr, Clement of Alexandria, and Athanasius and the Council of Nicaea, all of which were published after he became a bishop, set out to fulfil this programme. An interesting illustration of his style of argument is given in the first chapter of his book on Justin Martyr. Whereas in human science there was a progression from less to greater degrees of knowledge so that 'the most recent opinions are those which are most likely to be correct', in relation to Divine Revelation the opposite was the case and 'the greater the distance from the fountain-head, the greater the chance that the stream will be polluted'. This was why all parties in religion were anxious to show that Christian antiquity – the authority of those who lived nearest to their times – was on their side. Justin Martyr was therefore important because some appealed to him as representing the view of primitive Christians on some of the fundamental articles of faith, whereas others thought that he had a fatal influence because of 'introducing into the Church a confused medley of Christianity and Platonism, to the exclusion of the pure and simple truths of the Gospel'.[25] There then followed a detailed discussion not only of what Justin said but also of the texts and versions available. In discussing Justin's arguments for the truth of the Christian Revelation, Kaye reiterated his observation in his volume on Tertullian that it was unreasonable to censure the Fathers for not

---

24   Ibid., p. 29.
25   J. Kaye, *Justin Martyr* in *Works*, iii, pp. 2–3.

providing 'a regular exposition of the Evidences of Christianity', since they wrote to remove the prejudices of Christianity's opponents. The essential distinction between the incredulity of the Fathers and modern sceptics was that the former admitted that an extraordinary event had occurred 'but denied that it afforded conclusive proof of the Divine Mission of Him, through whose agency it was brought to pass'; the modern sceptic simply asserted 'that no testimony whatever can outweigh the antecedent incredibility of the event'.[26] In his final chapter he criticised Herbert Marsh's view that 'Justin did not quote our Gospels', because he did not find Marsh's arguments convincing.[27] Kaye cited the arguments of the American scholar Edward Everett's *Defence of Christianity* (1814): the verbal coincidence was sometimes exact; Justin called the books gospels, and said that 'they were written by Apostles and Apostolick men'; and Irenaeus did not refer to any other books so similar to ours as Justin's were. Thus 'we shall find it hard to believe that Justin quoted any other Gospels than ours'. In any case, if there were another set of books different from ours that testified to the truth of the same facts, that would still favour Christianity.[28] The essential difference between Kaye and Marsh was that Marsh sought to defend the authenticity and credibility of the New Testament independently of subsequent testimony, whereas Kaye sought to show that the patristic testimony could be trusted, notwithstanding some of its recognised problems. But for both of them the apologetic agenda remained paramount.

Both Kaye and Marsh have been described as high churchmen, though clearly they were not the same. One Cambridge man in this period who can unequivocally be called a high churchman is Hugh James Rose (1795–1838). His life was unusually short, even for the early nineteenth century. Rose was the elder son of a Church of England clergyman in Sussex. As a result of an attack of croup at the age of five he was left permanently subject to frequent inflammation of the lungs. He went up to Trinity in October 1813, where his Tutor was Dr Monk; and in 1817 he graduated as fourteenth wrangler and first Chancellor's medallist. Having failed to gain a Trinity Fellowship, he returned to Sussex as a curate, becoming associated with the 'Hackney Phalanx'.[29] Thereafter his involvement with the University was as a Select Preacher from time to time and as Christian Advocate from 1829 to 1833 (though he was not permanently resident for this period, and was presented with the Rectory of Hadleigh in Suffolk by the Archbishop of Canterbury in 1830). He served as Professor of Theology at Durham from 1833 to 1834, and then was appointed Principal of King's College, London in 1836.

Dean Burgon gave a eulogistic account of Rose (who was his brother-in-law) in his *Lives of Twelve Good Men*, calling him 'The Restorer of the Old Paths'.[30] Rose preached several notable series of sermons in Cambridge. The first and best known were the *Discourses on the state of the Protestant Religion in Germany*,

---

26    Ibid., iii, pp. 96–8: quotations from p. 98.
27    Ibid., iii, p. 105.
28    Ibid., iii, p. 120.
29    A.B. Webster, *Joshua Watson* (London, 1954), p. 27.
30    See J.W. Burgon, *Lives of Twelve Good Men* (London, 1888), i, pp. 116–283.

delivered in May 1825 and dedicated to Charles Sumner, Bishop of Chester, which were ostensibly prompted by a European tour (including Germany) in the previous twelve months. The one-sided character of his representation of German theology was criticised by Edward Pusey in 1828: Rose responded with a second, enlarged edition of his *Discourses* in 1829.[31] In April 1826 he preached four sermons *On the Commission and consequent Duties of the Clergy*, which were published in 1828, with an enlarged second edition in 1831. During his period as Christian Advocate he preached *Eight Sermons before the University of Cambridge* in 1830 and 1831, which were published with his Commencement Sermon of 1826 and dedicated to Joshua Watson of Hackney. In 1831 Rose also allowed himself to be persuaded to edit a new periodical, *The British Magazine*, intended to provide ecclesiastical information and to defend the institutions and doctrines of the church: the first issue was published on 1 March 1832.[32] It was, in a sense, his equivalent to the *Tracts for the Times*, which appeared in the following year; Newman was an early contributor, and the papers which were eventually published as *The Church of the Fathers* in 1840 appeared first in the *British Magazine*.[33] Rose's alarm at Lord Grey's belief in the need to reform the Church of England is well known, and explains the meeting he hosted at Hadleigh Rectory on 25 July 1833, attended by Richard Hurrell Froude, Arthur Perceval and William Palmer, eleven days after John Keble's famous Assize Sermon in Oxford. (Newman and Keble were not there, according to Webster because they distrusted committees.)[34] Just over a month earlier Rose had written to Joshua Watson, '*I get no help whatever* from Cambridge. What help could I get equal to Keble, Miller, Palmer, Newman, Froude, Hook, Ogilvie? I love Cambridge to my heart: but Divinity is not her tower of strength just now'.[35] These words have often been quoted, but their fairness is less frequently assessed. Why should Rose's understanding of Divinity be regarded as definitive? Rose chose to make his own plea in Cambridge in a sermon preached on Whitsunday 1834, 'On the duty of maintaining the Truth', which made a great impression.

An explanation of the high church thread running through all Rose's works illuminates both the character of high churchmanship and the reasons why Burgon regarded Rose as the one who inspired the Oxford Movement. His *Protestant Religion in Germany* expressed concerns, regularly repeated before and since, that it was possible without rebuke to espouse opinions of a rationalising character, which rejected the necessity of a divine revelation and viewed the Bible simply as a historical document. Although criticism of Rose's *Discourses* concentrated on

---

31   Pusey amplified his original work in 1830, but subsequently changed his mind and forbade any reprint of either of his volumes, which has made them very rare items.

32   Burgon, *Twelve Good Men*, i, pp. 145–50. Webster wrote that the *British Magazine* was 'committed to an intransigent defence of every ecclesiastical abuse', *Joshua Watson*, p. 87.

33   The fact that Newman became editor of *The British Critic* may imply that Rose's magazine was not thought to be adequate to the task.

34   Webster, *Joshua Watson*, p. 101.

35   Rose to Watson, 19 June 1833, quoted in Burgon, *Twelve Good Men*, i, p. 163.

whether he had given a fair account of German theology, his main point was rather different. He began by noting that 'a very remarkable characteristic of the age in which we live, is its tendency to exalt and exaggerate the power and capacities of the human mind', and then observed that 'the preliminary condition indeed at present of any consideration of a religious subject, is not only the *moral right*, but the *full capacity* of each individual to judge of it'.[36] Whilst a large portion of the Protestant churches of Germany hailed these principles with delight, including the occupants of pulpits and professorial chairs, he argued that this was bound to be so in view of 'the entire want of controul [*sic*] in them over the opinions of their own ministers, and the consequent wild and licentious exercise of what was deemed not the base merely, but the essence of Protestantism, the right of private judgment on every question however difficult or however momentous'.[37] For the same reasons he rejected the right claimed by Reformed churches to change their confessions in the light of scripture: 'if then it be an essential principle of a Protestant church that she possess a constant power of varying her belief, let us remember that we are assuredly no Protestant church'.[38] The Church of England had not separated from the Church of Rome because it had discovered any new views of scripture doctrine, but because it wished to return to 'the primitive confession, and the views held by the apostles and early fathers of the church'.[39]

In his final address, Rose affirmed that 'common sense has shown the utter hopelessness of a church existing without making a declaration of faith and requiring her ministers to subscribe to it, and common honesty and honour have pointed out the disgrace of countenancing subscription to that declaration in any but its literal, and obvious sense'.[40] He continued:

> [A minister] is therefore now become the minister *of a church*, and as such, must pursue the road which that church dictates. He must no longer think his own thoughts, or form his own plans, but he must teach what the church commands in the sphere which she assigns. He may think that at some time, something is left in that church undone, which should be done, something done, which should be undone – but he will know also that it belongs not to him to remedy the error or supply the deficiency … His own aim will therefore be to understand fully what the spirit of the church is, to fulfil it, to unite with, not to separate from his brethren, to yield a ready and cheerful obedience to his superiors, not to endeavour to escape from it.[41]

Rose believed that God would correct things in his own time and in his own way, though he did not suggest how. In effect Rose was presenting an argument for the necessity of subscription to the Thirty-Nine Articles and against any form of

---

36    H.J. Rose, *The state of the Protestant religion in Germany; in a series of discourses preached before the University of Cambridge* (Cambridge, 1825), pp. 1, 2.
37    Ibid., p. 10.
38    Ibid., p. 21.
39    Ibid.
40    Ibid., pp. 104–5.
41    Ibid., p. 108.

dissent; and the reason the focus of the *Discourses* was the Church in Germany was that he did not believe that English Dissent posed any significant theological threat, whereas the ideas of German theology did.

Thus it was quite natural to take the theme of Apostolic Order and Church Principles in the next year. Noting in his 'Advertisement' that sermons on church discipline had been condemned from the University Pulpit in James I's reign, he nevertheless castigated the limited nature of the understanding of the church, which saw it primarily as a means of social control (as Marxists would later put it). The idea that God had created the church as a means of grace scarcely existed, and the efficacy of the Christian Sacraments was 'not only practically despised ... but passed by with contempt', not only by the laity but by many of the clergy: 'still more contemptuous would be the rejection of all belief in the notion that they who are really ministers of the living God, possess in that character any powers beyond other men, and that the means of grace, offered through them, in the Gospel, must, to obtain their full effect, be received through them by the Christian world'.[42] Rose set himself a challenging agenda and applied himself to it vigorously. Once more the theme was the divinely-based authority of the clergy, not dependent on the will of some secular power, and Rose presented a carefully nuanced defence of high church Anglicanism, not, for example, arguing for an *ex opere operato* view of the sacraments, but emphasising that the Prayer Book made it clear that the sacraments did not convey an infallible grace, since 'it depends on the heart of the receiver, whether the grace they may convey be conveyed or not'.[43] The clergy had a duty to teach the faith, so they needed minds to study, particularly the interpretation of scripture; and Rose recommended the study of ecclesiastical history as particularly suited to explain the ways of God to his people. Such a responsibility had inevitable consequences for the conduct of the clergy, and he spoke in language that could almost have come from Simeon when he asked rhetorically, 'what besides satisfaction and joy can he feel, whose duty and whose glory it is to preach Christ crucified, and who directs every thought, wish, and desire, to the purity, perfection, and happiness of immortal beings'.[44] His conclusion was a comparison of the thoughts of a worthless and negligent priest on his deathbed with those of a faithful one. Burgon, in making his case that Rose was 'the true moving cause of that stirring of the waters which made an indelible impress on the Church of England ... and which it is customary to date from the Autumn of 1833', picked out the sermons on the Commission of the Clergy as being the first to recall attention to neglected church principles and to warn against the coming danger.[45]

Rose's sermons as Christian Advocate in 1830–31 were more directed at the laity than those who were intending to be ordained, and could be regarded as an alternative to the evangelical agenda. For example, they emphasised the sanctifying

---

42    H.J. Rose, *The Commission and consequent Duties of the Clergy* (Cambridge, 1828), pp. 5–7.

43    Ibid., p. 44.

44    Ibid., pp. 97–8.

45    Burgon, *Twelve Good Men*, i, pp. 158–9.

power of God's grace, rather than its saving power; but presented the same duty to resist evil and considered the difference made by faith to the way in which moral and intellectual issues were considered. His controversial sermon on *The Duty of Maintaining the Truth* was preached on Whitsunday 1834, just about the time he finished his duties as Professor of Theology at Durham. Its character is aptly summarised in the following paragraph:

> Short therefore of the fanaticism so guarded against, the first duty of a Christian to Christian Truth, is to proclaim and maintain it at all times, and in all places, against all opposition; in spite of all persons, in spite of public opinion, in spite of the fashion of the day, in spite of changed and changing circumstances, in spite of expediency, real or fancied, in spite of all the usual cry of bigotry, and intolerance, and ignorance.[46]

Even when read more than 150 years later, it is easy to see how the rhetoric might carry the congregation along, just as it is never exactly clear what the truth which had to be defended at such cost was. Rose used material from a recent lecture at Durham on the value of Church History to argue that it was necessary to recognise the value of other ages as well as the present: thus he noted that 'the *dark* ages created the great institutions of this country in politics, religion and literature'.[47] Joseph Romilly, Registrary from 1832, commented rather grumpily in his diary that 'The curiosity of it was his eulogising most warmly the dark ages: the only thing he made out to my mind in their favor [*sic*] was their having built noble churches'.[48]

Rose concluded in a way that is now familiar: 'Learn here to despise, as ye ought, the solemn mockeries which tell you that Truth changes with times, and that principles must be altered to meet altered circumstances, that you must bow to the voice of the million, and hold public opinion for truth.'[49] In his Durham lecture he had been more explicit in arguing that history was a better guide to public opinion than the opinion of the day, where 'the loudest voices usually come from the weakest heads'; and that it was particularly important in an age when everyone believed that he was competent to decide all the great questions of religion and philosophy for himself, that one should be aware of what is taught by the Universal Church.[50] In other words, the message was the same as it had been in relation to the German churches: beware of private judgement. From this point of view Rose was offering the Cambridge equivalent of Newman's protest about liberalism, perhaps even in terminology that was easier to grasp; and like Newman, Rose saw a church that clearly recognised that its teaching office did not

---

46   H.J. Rose, *The Duty of Maintaining the Truth* (Cambridge 1834), p. 8; also quoted in Burgon, *Twelve Good Men*, p. 142.

47   H.J. Rose, *The Study of Church History Recommended* (London, 1834), p. 16; cf. *Maintaining the Truth*, p. 22. By 'the dark ages' Rose clearly meant what would now be called the Middle Ages.

48   J.P.T. Bury (ed.), *Romilly's Cambridge Diary, 1832–42* (Cambridge, 1967), p. 58.

49   Rose, *Maintaining the Truth*, pp. 24–5.

50   Rose, *Study of Church History*, pp. 23, 28.

depend on Act of Parliament as the only remedy for the theological problem that such claims to freedom of thought posed. Consequently for Rose the apologetic problem was simple: indeed technically it did not exist. 'The gates of hell shall not prevail against it' was a text he quoted often in defending the church and the truth which the church taught.

So what was the 1834 sermon about? Burgon quoted the view of Henry Bradshaw (later University Librarian) that Rose's influence was even deeper than that of Simeon. Since Bradshaw was a high churchman and only born in 1831, this must have been a retrospective assessment based on reading, rather than hearing, Rose's sermons. The basis seems to have been the testimony of Bradshaw's mentor, George Williams, also a high churchman.[51] Among Rose's congregation was George Selwyn, future Bishop of New Zealand, who testified to Rose's influence in a University sermon of 1854.[52] By contrast Joseph Romilly described the 1834 sermon as 'an intemperate, uncompromising, High Church sermon' and added, 'I think a more inflammatory party Sermon has hardly been preached since the days of Sacheverel (sic)'.[53] The explanation was that the University was already vexed by the issue of admitting dissenters, and therefore by relaxing or abolishing the religious tests at graduation; that makes Romilly's comparison with Sacheverell more relevant. Whether this was intended by Rose or not, he was understood to be reaffirming his opposition to any compromise, thereby raising the moral and religious stakes involved.

By the 1830s there was little difference on religious tests between Rose and the Theology Professors, who if anything were more inclined to sympathise with the kind of evangelicalism represented by Charles Simeon. Samuel Lee, Regius Professor of Hebrew (1831–48), who did not matriculate until he was 31, by which time he already knew seven languages, had been Professor of Arabic since 1819; he engaged in controversy both with Dr John Pye Smith on Dissent and Dr Pusey on the eucharist from an evangelical standpoint. George Corrie, Norrisian Professor (1838–54), was a Wrangler just below Rose in the class list; he was the youngest brother of Daniel Corrie who became first Bishop of Madras in 1835. John Blunt, Lady Margaret's Professor (1839–55), was a curate to Reginald Heber, who became Bishop of Calcutta in 1823. W.H. Mill was the first Principal of Bishops College, Calcutta from 1820 until his return to England on health grounds in 1838, where he became chaplain to Archbishop Howley, Christian Advocate in 1839 and Regius Professor of Hebrew in 1848. Alfred Ollivant, Regius Professor of Divinity (1843–49), had been influenced by Simeon as an undergraduate and reflected that both as Professor and as Bishop of Llandaff (1849–82). The exception in the list is Thomas Turton, Regius Professor (1827–42), who reflected an older set of concerns, more like those of Watson. Thus he engaged

---

51    Burgon, *Twelve Good Men*, i, pp. 141–2. Burgon refers to having received the paper containing this statement from H.R. Luard, Romilly's successor as Registrary in 1862, who found it among Bradshaw's papers. (Bradshaw died in 1886.)

52    Ibid. pp. 142–3. Burgon also implies that Bishop Patteson was in the congregation, but this is implausible, given that he was only seven years old.

53    Bury, *Romilly's Cambridge Diary, 1832–42*, pp. 57–8.

in controversy with Lord Brougham over natural theology, with Wiseman over the Roman Catholic doctrine of the eucharist, and edited John Hey's *Lectures on Divinity*. But all were Conservative in politics, and none favoured the admission of dissenters to the University.

What characterises this generation is their commitment to the reformed character of the Church of England. Corrie's description of himself was that he 'desired to be represented as of the old Evangelical party as vindicated by Overton in his *True Churchman Described*'.[54] But he was also a founder member of the Cambridge Ecclesiological Society, the Cambridge Antiquarian Society and the Parker Society. For the last he edited Latimer's *Sermons and Remains* and *The Homiles*, Nowell's *Catchism*, Twysden's *Historical Vindication*, Burnet's *History of the Reformation*, and Wheatly's *Common Prayer*. His interests also extended back to the Fathers; thus in 1840 he was verifying references to the Fathers in Bullinger's *Decades*.[55] Moreover, his biography contains a number of letters written to an anonymous clergyman on baptism, where he was anxious to defend its significance. 'It is of great importance', he wrote in 1841, 'to make an enduring effort to give more sacred character to Baptism than our people (under the blight of dissenting influence) are wont to give it.'[56] Obviously Corrie did not support the Tractarians, but it is not easy to imagine him taking the side of those who challenged baptismal regeneration. This letter, and others later, are significant precisely because the Tractarian challenge in Pusey's tracts on Baptism had already been made. Corrie had little respect for the learning or honesty of the Tractarians. A friend recalled him saying 'that the most charitable view was that they had read their authorities by indexes and picked out what suited their purposes without regard to the context'.[57] Yet Corrie also believed that Charles I 'was as really a martyr as those of any age who beforehand had suffered for God's truth. He died for the Church of England'.[58] If these sentiments are not usually associated with evangelicals, then the definition at least of Anglican evangelicalism ought to change; if it did, the precise differences between it and Tractarianism could be more tightly defined. What stands out most about Corrie is that he was a Tory: his role in conservative politics inside and outside the University was clear – and indeed the majority of the Divinity Professors in the nineteenth century were of solid Tory views. Thus Corrie was involved in backing the election of Lord Powis as Chancellor in 1847 – when

---

54    M. Holroyd, *Memoirs of the Life of George Elwes Corrie* (Cambridge, 1890), p. 330. Holroyd did not check the title of John Overton's book, which was *The true churchmen ascertained, or, An apology for those of the regular clergy of the establishment who are sometimes called evangelical ministers* (London, 1801). Overton defended the need to take the Thirty-Nine Articles in their literal and grammatical sense, and rejected the aspersions cast on evangelicals by high churchmen such as Bishop Porteous, Charles Daubeney and Thomas Ludlam. He was also highly critical of Cambridge divines like Watson, Paley and Hey.

55    Ibid., p. 138.

56    Ibid., p. 166.

57    Ibid., p. 326.

58    Ibid., p. 170.

Prince Albert was elected. The point is significant since the Powis supporters have often been described as Tractarians.[59] Corrie told Beresford Hope that it was Powis's support for the integrity of the Episcopate which led him to back him – though he commented on Beresford Hope's proposal for an episcopal Chancellor (Blomfield, Kaye and Thirwall were mentioned) that it was a matter of deep regret to him 'that some of the most threatening innovations on our Ecclesiastical institutions had originated with and are patronised by some of our present bishops'.[60]

Blunt is even more interesting. Before he became Lady Margaret's Professor in 1839 he wrote several articles for the *Quarterly Review* – one of the few Cambridge professors to write for the quarterlies. Westcott, Lightfoot and Browne wrote more – but for the *Contemporary*, a later magazine of a different colour. Blunt probably was introduced to the *Quarterly* by Reginald Heber, who was one of the original staff. The range of articles is interesting: they include one on Robert Hall the Baptist and Adam Clarke the Methodist, and there are two articles on Bishop Butler (one on the *Works* and one on the *Memoirs*) and one on Paley (review of the *Collected Works* in October 1828). A clue to Blunt's approach lies in a sentence from his article on Paley. 'The truth of Christianity depends upon the truth of its leading facts.'[61] But although Blunt wrote on Paley, the *Horae Paulinae* interested him more than the *Natural Theology*. From a philosophical point of view Blunt admired Butler much more than Paley. William Selwyn in his 'Memoir of Blunt' said that his early friends remembered that he knew Butler's *Analogy* and *Paradise Lost* almost by heart.[62] Blunt's argument in 1826–27 was very similar to Newman's – Butler eschewed demonstrative proof and concentrated on probability.[63] Thus revelation, rather than nature, was the key to understanding God: and Butler was a moderate guide against the temptations of fanaticism. Hence what he drew from Paley was the argument that the coincidences in scripture which could not have been expected were evidence of its authenticity.

Blunt wrote several books on the undesigned coincidences. His Hulsean Lectures for 1831 were entitled *The Veracity of the Historical Books of the Old Testament, from the conclusion of the Pentateuch, to the opening of the prophets, argued from the Undesigned Coincidences to be found in them, when compared in their several parts: being a continuation of the argument for the veracity of the Five Books of Moses.* He began with Butler's comment that the 'credibility of the common scripture history gives some credibility to its miraculous history';[64] and

59    The fullest account of the election is in D.A. Winstanley, *Early Victorian Cambridge* (Cambridge 1940), pp. 106–21.

60    Holroyd, *Corrie*, p. 247.

61    J.J. Blunt, *Essays contributed to the Quarterly Review* (London, 1860), p. 147.

62    W. Selwyn 'Memoir', in J.J. Blunt, *Two Introductory Lectures on the Study of the Early Fathers* (2nd edn, Cambridge, 1856), p. vi.

63    Blunt, *Essays*, pp. 273–4.

64    J.J. Blunt, *The Veracity of the Historical Books of the Old Testament* (London 1832), pp. 2–3, quoting J. Butler, *Analogy of Religion* (London, 1788), p. 368; also in J.J. Blunt, *Undesigned Coincidences* (London, 1847), p. 108.

he went on to comment that the undesignedness of the history was testimony to the *general* truth of scripture, thereby assisting the resolution of critical difficulties. For example: Joshua took his armies over Jordan at the time of the barley harvest, when it was flooded. That coincided with the flax harvest; and the spies sent to Jericho who were given hospitality by Rahab were hidden with stalks of flax – 'the stalks of flax no doubt just cut down which she had spread upon the roof of her house to steep and to season'. 'Here I see truth', he wrote. 'Could the historian have contemplated for one moment the effect which a trifle about a flax stalk might have in corroboration of his account of the passage of the Jordan?'[65] A modern critical scholar might smile – but the assumption about the significance of unimportant details has remained common ground for historians in testing the authenticity of documents since. In 1847 Blunt put together all the books he had written on this theme into a single volume, containing the Pentateuch, the other historical books of the Old Testament, the prophetical books, and the gospels and Acts. In the introduction he noted that Professor Turton had pointed out that this principle, usually attributed to Paley, had actually first been used by Philip Doddridge in his *General Introduction ... to the First Epistle to the Thessalonians*.[66] (This is an interesting indication of the way in which Anglicans in this period continued to use the works of nonconformist divines.) However, the publication of several of Paley's books by the Religious Tract Society at end of the 1840s illustrates the shift in opinion since the 1790s. Whereas John Overton saw Paley as a threat to evangelical religion, men like Blunt saw Paley's approach to the Bible as a help in the face of more serious threats.

Blunt also gave attention to the study of the Fathers. Selwyn wrote that 'He enjoined his hearers to study the early Fathers, not with blind allegiance, as authorities to be followed in all things; but as the only witnesses to the belief and constitution of the Church immediately after the Apostolic times; and thus to see for themselves, by the evidence of these ancient records, that the Church of England is truly, as her formularies assert, *based upon Scripture and primitive antiquity*'.[67] In his Introductory Lecture he wrote:

> If therefore there are any who look with jealousy on the Fathers as abettors of *high church* principles as they are now called (I have no delight in the phraseology, but it saves circumlocution), which they partly may be; let them forgive the wrong when they contemplate them as abettors of *Gospel* principles too, which is undoubtedly true of them – and I feel confident ... that these two results would be found generally to follow from a study of the Fathers: namely an increased reverence, certainly, for ecclesiastical institutions and ordinances, as having in them a great mystery; but an

---

65 Blunt, *Veracity of Historical Books*, p. 11; cf. *Undesigned Coincidences*, pp. 110–11.

66 Blunt, *Undesigned Coincidences*, pp. vi–vii, quoting T. Turton, *Natural Theology considered with reference to Lord Brougham's Discourse* (Cambridge, 1836), p. 23; *The Works of Philip Doddridge, DD* (Leeds, 1805), ix, p. 504.

67 Blunt, *Two Introductory Lectures*.

increased conviction also that the only sound and apostolical divinity is that, which '*ceases not* to teach and preach Jesus Christ'.[68]

As he said a little later, 'the Old Fathers were at one and the same time zealous *Churchmen ...* and *Evangelical Teachers*'.[69] Thus he was able to quote Bishop Ken: 'I die in the communion of the Church of England as it stands distinguished from all Papal and Puritan innovations and as it *adheres to the doctrine of the Cross*.'[70] Selwyn's verdict was that

> it would be difficult to name any one who has been more generally honoured and loved, or whose memory will be more reverently cherished, in the University of Cambridge, than Professor Blunt. Amid the many changes and perplexities of the times – which grieved his spirit but could not 'change his constant mind' – he remained unshaken; his foundations (to use his own words) were '1800 years deep': he delighted to stand in the old ways and seek for the old paths; living in communion with the Fathers of the Primitive Church and with the great spirits of our own reformed branch of the Church Catholic.[71]

These then were the men who guided Cambridge theology during the period of the Tractarian explosion at Oxford. By contrast with that they were eminently safe – though apart from Pusey, the Oxford Movement was not led by professors. William Whewell's somewhat dismissive verdict on the theology professors at the beginning of the 1840s as not the 'men to create a new system' was noted in the Introduction, but it was Cambridge, rather than Oxford, which produced the trio of bishops – Blomfield, Monk and Kaye – who were behind the reform of the Church of England in the 1830s.

How important are the distinctions between party, whether political or ecclesiastical? And how should they be defined? From some points of view the moderate evangelicals are easiest to classify. Their primary emphasis was on the Bible, even following Simeon in being free from enslavement to any religious system. But it is often forgotten that they also emphasised the significance of the Fathers, and in this sense stood for the truth of tradition. Thus they articulated the issue of authority in a similar way to the Tractarians, but they placed the priority differently. There was also greater potential for movement, since, if critical views of scripture were accepted, the whole structure could shift.

The problems of interpretation have arisen over the nature of high churchmanship. In rather different ways both Jonathan Clark and Boyd Hilton have merged the ecclesiastical and theological divisions into political ones. Clark emphasised the belief in establishment and opposition to dissent; a passing reference to Richard Watson's apologetic works avoided any reference of the value he attached to Locke and his decidedly Whig politics.[72] Hilton has been more

---

68    Ibid., p. 44.
69    Ibid., p. 46.
70    Ibid., pp. xi–xii. The quotation from Ken comes from his will.
71    Ibid., p. xi.
72    J. Clark, *English Society 1688–1832* (Cambridge, 1985), p. 220.

concerned with political economy and attitudes to providence and utilitarianism, and found his archetypical evangelical in the Scot, Thomas Chalmers.[73]

But when the labels are applied to people, it becomes more difficult. Thus Nockles regards Marsh as a high churchman, principally because of his role in the National Society and support of the Prayer Book, but also notes his eulogies of Laud.[74] Marsh certainly believed in establishment (what Anglican did not at this time?) and supported the Hackney Phalanx for his own reasons. Yet theologically Marsh had no time for the Councils and Fathers, placing his confidence in scripture (like Isaac Milner). He was not in other ways high church in either the pre- or post-Oxford Movement sense. On the other hand, Milner was opposed to Marsh theologically, but politically he was even more Tory. Kaye studied the Fathers, but this was the standard Reformation defence of the Church of England against the Church of Rome: in fact, he pursued the same agenda as Watson's *Apology for Christianity*, by defending the Fathers against the accusations of Conyers Middleton and others that they had discredited Christianity by their credulity. Marsh defended the establishment on the grounds of utility, as did Sumner (evangelical), Blomfield (high church) and Paley – and in this respect all went back to Warburton.

Does not this suggest that there is no consistent relationship between the views taken of first, scripture and the Fathers, secondly, the church as an establishment based on utility and as a *iure divino* institution, and thirdly, the readiness to defend the right of political resistance against arbitrary monarchy in defined circumstances? In other words to use high/orthodox and low/liberal as a single catch-all division in which all will turn out on the same side on each view does not work.

The one person to score most consistently as a high churchman – theologically, ecclesiastically and politically – was Rose. Romilly's comparison of his 1834 sermon to Sacheverell has already been noted; perhaps even more significant is a comment in his diary two days later when he referred to William Smyth (Regius Professor of Modern History 1807–49 and a Fellow of Peterhouse),

---

73   B. Hilton, *The Age of Atonement* (Oxford, 1988), pp. 20–21, 32–3, where similarities are discerned between evangelicals and Anglican utilitarians, such as Paley. The observation is acute, but it does undermine a coherent theological understanding of evangelicalism: cf. B. Hilton, *A Mad, Bad, and Dangerous People: England 1783–1846* (Oxford, 2006), p. 313, where the Atonement is seen as the '*hinge* of Christian truth' in a way which applies to all theological strands. 'The Age of Atonement' might have been better described as 'the Age of Providence'.

74   P. Nockles, *The Oxford Movement in Context* (Cambridge, 1994), p. 108. I have failed to find any eulogy of Laud in Marsh's *Comparative View of the Churches of England and Rome* (2nd edn., London, 1816), to which Nockles refers. His discussion of Marsh's views on Tradition is unconvincing. There is nothing in the Appendix to the *Comparative View*, cited by Nockles, which retracts his firm distinction in the opening chapters between the written Word of God, the unwritten Word of God, and ceremonies of human origin (taken from Bellarmine). Marsh rejects the Roman view of an unwritten Word of God on the basis on the Thirty-Nine Articles, and particularly Article VI. This was the classic Anglican position and Laud's belief in ceremonies is irrelevant to it.

who was warm in his praise of Rose. Romilly responded that 'I knew from the Prayer what sort of a Serm. it would be, as he said 'pure and *apostolical*' instead of *reformed*, and called the King *sacred*'.[75] That use of the term 'apostolical' a year or so after the Oxford Tracts (to which Rose did not contribute) began, and four years before Newman published Hurrell Froude's *Remains*, with their explicit condemnation of the Reformation, is a significant indicator of the shift in emphasis in the nature of Anglican high churchmanship. For his part, however, Rose was worried by the direction, which the Tracts were taking, particularly in their attitude towards Rome. His belief in the value of Church History did not mean an uncritical acceptance of every patristic practice; and he characteristically objected to the tone of the Tracts, which implied that in exploring antiquity the Church of England was discovering new truths. On the contrary Rose held that all the significant treasures of antiquity were already present in the Church of England; but they had been neglected. Rose has been criticised for being 'unimaginative and static' by comparison with Newman, who was 'on a voyage of discovery'.[76] This substitutes attractive and unattractive metaphors for argument. Webster rightly noted Newman's view that 'if [history] assumes to be the sole means of gaining Religious Truth, it goes beyond its place';[77] but Rose never argued that. Rose wanted a recognition of the significance of history, both for the forgotten truths that lay hidden, and for the rectification of abuses which needed attention. In a letter to Newman in May 1836, he wrote: 'I will not *talk* of the *glorious* Reformation [you forbid me]; – but *deliverance is deliverance*. And though we may deplore that there were evils to be delivered from, *that* was not *our* fault. And we must bless GOD for rescuing us from them.'[78] Rose also produced the clearest critique of rational divinity, which is more effective than the usual disparagement of rationalism as 'dry' or 'arid' by most writers. In his Durham lecture he acknowledged the invaluable succession of works in reply to the deists, but then he added: 'The perpetual weighing of evidences, the consideration of sophistry, the replying to fallacies, is any thing but a favourable employment for purifying and exalting the heart.'[79] In Rose's view, the consequence was that arguments were reduced to the lowest ground, whereas church history had to be read not with a sceptical eye, but in faith. Rose's point is sound, but the alternative view which was developing in Cambridge was not faithless.

---

75   Bury, *Romilly's Cambridge Diary, 1832–42*, p. 58.
76   Webster, *Joshua Watson*, p. 106, citing A.C. Headlam, 'Hugh James Rose and the Oxford Movement', *Church Quarterly Review*, xciii (Oct 1921): 99.
77   Ibid., 106. The reference is to J.H. Newman, *The Idea of a University*, ed. I.T. Ker (Oxford, 1976), p. 90.
78   Quoted in Burgon, *Twelve Good Men*, i, pp. 218–19.
79   Rose, *Study of Church History*, pp. 48–9.

# Chapter 4

# The Coleridgean Inheritance

'Evidences of Christianity! I am weary of the word. Make a man feel the need of it … and you can safely trust to its own evidence.'[1] Coleridge's well-known words have often been used to illustrate his rejection of eighteenth-century theology; yet he had not always taken this view. In the fourth of his *Lectures on Revealed Religion* of 1795, he referred approvingly to Paley's *Evidences* in general and to his *Horae Paulinae* in particular.[2] By the time of *The Statesman's Manual* (1816) he had changed his mind. Now the theological villain of the piece was 'MR LOCKE'. Hence he was convinced that the principles of taste, morals and religion 'taught in our most popular compendia of moral and political philosophy, natural theology, evidences of Christianity, etc are false, injurious, and debasing'. More significantly he continued that

> all the well-meant attacks on the writings of modern infidels and heretics, in support of either the miracles or of the mysteries of the Christian religion, can be of no permanent utility, while the authors join in the vulgar appeal to common sense as the one infallible judge in matters, which become subjects of philosophy only, because they involve a contradiction between this common sense and our *moral* instincts, and require therefore an arbiter, which containing both (*eminenter*) must be higher than either.'[3]

The rejection both of Lockean-based argument and its counterpoise marks out Coleridge's distinctiveness. *The Statesman's Manual* was subtitled 'The Bible the best guide to Political Skill and Foresight'. Although Coleridge was never a teacher in the University, his influence was significant, and ultimately it was the inspiration for 'the alternative conservatism' of early nineteenth-century Cambridge.

Samuel Taylor Coleridge (1772–1834) came up to Jesus College in 1791, and was converted to Unitarianism by his tutor, William Frend; hence he never took his degree. After going down in December 1794 he gave occasional lectures in

---

1 S.T. Coleridge, *Aids to Reflection*, ed. J. Beer (Princeton, 1993), pp. 405–6. The passage is discussed in D. Hedley, *Coleridge, Philosophy and Religion* (Cambridge, 2000), pp. 230–36, cf. pp. 45–50, where Dr Hedley argues that the Christology of Locke and others, including Paley, was essentially Socinian. The word is often taken in a pejorative, non-trinitarian sense and, in view of its religiously and politically loaded character in the period of the American and French Revolutions, I think that its use does not assist clear historical, as distinct from philosophical, judgement.

2 L. Patton and P. Mann, *Lectures 1795 on Politics and Revealed Religion* (Princeton, 1971), pp. 169–91, especially p. 186. Coleridge also used Marsh's translation of Michaelis.

3 S.T. Coleridge, *Lay Sermons*, ed. R.J. White (Princeton, 1972), p. 110.

Bristol. He had intended to become a Unitarian minister, but an annuity from Josiah Wedgwood rendered that unnecessary. He had met Robert Southey in Oxford while an undergraduate, and they became firm friends. Coleridge met Wordsworth in September 1795 and in 1798 they published *Lyrical Ballads*. All three supported the French Revolution and opposed Pitt's government. The revolutionary enthusiasm was captured in Wordsworth's lines of 1805 about his visit to France in 1791–92:

> Bliss was it in that dawn to be alive
> And to be young was very heaven.[4]

Yet the first publication of those lines itself illustrated the fading of the initial enthusiasm. Coleridge published them in his journal *The Friend* in 1809 in an article significantly entitled 'On the errors of Party Spirit: or Extremes Meet'. He argued that the anti-Jacobins had overreacted to the French Revolution and had sought to defend the indefensible in the British constitution: 'If the Jacobins ran wild with the Rights of Man, and the abstract Sovereignty of the People, their Antagonists flew off as extravagantly from the sober good sense of our Forefathers and idolized as pure an abstraction in the Rights of *Sovereigns*'.[5] Coleridge reckoned that thousands as young and innocent as himself were driven along with the general current. Thus the sentence which introduced Wordsworth's verse was:

> I trust there are many of my Readers of the same Age with myself, who will throw themselves back into the state of thought and feeling, in which they were when France was reported to have solmnized her first sacrifice of error and prejudice on the bloodless altar of Freedom, by an Oath of Peace and Good-will to all Mankind.[6]

He argued that 'every speculative Error, which boasts a multitude of Advocates, has its *golden* as well as its dark side' and that 'no Assailant of an Error can reasonably hope to be listened to by its Advocates, who has not proved to them that he has seen the disputed Subject in the same point of view, and is capable of contemplating it with the same feelings as themselves'.[7]

---

4    W. Wordsworth, 'The French revolution as it appeared to enthusiasts at its commencement' (1805), included in *The Prelude* (1805 version, x, pp. 693–4; 1850 version, xi, pp. 108–9; ed. E. de Selincourt (Oxford, 1926), pp. 400–401). This was first published in *The Friend*, 26 October 1809: see B.E. Rooke (ed.), *The Friend* (Princeton, 1969), ii, pp. 147–8. Wordsworth's reaction to the French revolution was at odds with the conservatism of his family, represented by John and the two Christophers. (Robert Southey was equally enthusiastic originally, and also someone who believed in the national church, yet did not personally accept its doctrines and thus did not become a clergyman: see E.R. Conder, *Josiah Conder: A Memoir* (London, 1857), pp. 192–4, 199).

5    *The Friend*, 19 October 1809, in Rooke, *The Friend*, ii, p. 141.

6    Ibid., p. 147.

7    Ibid., p. 149.

The other aspect of Coleridge's thought, which was important for his Cambridge disciples, was his view of the relationship between church and state. Here the primary text was *On the Constitution of the Church and State* (1829). It was provoked by the Catholic Emancipation Act, which effectively removed the confessional basis of the English state; but it drew together thoughts that Coleridge had been maturing at least since the Act of Union with Ireland in 1800 and Napoleon's Concordat with the French Church in 1801. He began to write after the unsuccessful campaign for emancipation in 1825, intending to set out principles rather than political expediency. Coleridge distinguished the idea of a National Church (or clerisy) from the Church of England as it currently existed, and he distinguished both from the Church of Christ, the universal fellowship of all true believers.[8] The clerisy comprised the learned of all denominations and included all branches of knowledge: the theologians took the lead because theology was the root and trunk of all knowledge, alone possessing the capacity to train people as free citizens or subjects of the realm.[9] Hence the function of the national church after the reform of Henry VIII was to maintain the universities, and a pastor and a schoolmaster in every parish.[10] Furthermore 'in relation to the National Church, Christianity, or the Church of Christ, is a blessed accident, a providential boon, a grace of God'.[11] Thus the national church need not be Christian, and Coleridge cited the Levites in Judaism or the Druids in Celtic Britain as examples. The primary condition of belonging to the national church was that the clergy should acknowledge no 'other earthly sovereign or visible head but the king'.[12] Similarly Coleridge believed that the articles of faith, which the sovereign undertook to maintain by the Coronation Oath, were those which required resistance to the characteristic positions of the Roman Catholic Church.[13] Although Coleridge's distinctions were not always easy to grasp, he was a fertile source for subsequent thinkers as diverse as W.E. Gladstone, Thomas Arnold and F.D. Maurice.

Coleridge's attitude to dissent was influenced by his own experience of Unitarianism. In his Notebook he wrote of his dissatisfaction with Unitarianism as 'a Creed of Negatives', and as a result of his determination to make 'a Creed of Positives', he returned to the doctrines of the Catechism he had learned as a child.[14] He disliked Methodism and also what he called 'the modern Calvinists', principally it seems because he associated them with a distinction between the visible and the invisible church, which he recognised would not have appealed to Calvin himself.[15] There is no *Table Talk* for the time when the Test and Corporation

---

8    S.T. Coleridge, *On the Constitution of the Church and State*, ed. J. Colmer (Princeton, 1976), pp. lviii–lx.

9    Ibid., pp. 46–8.

10    Ibid., pp. 52–3.

11    Ibid., p. 55.

12    Ibid., p. 77.

13    Ibid., pp. 104–6, cf. pp. 120–21.

14    Ibid., p. 135, note 3.

15    Ibid., p. 135.

Acts were repealed in 1828, but he was vitriolic about the proposal to admit Dissenters to Cambridge degrees, because he regarded it as a political cover for an attack on the Church of England.[16]

The principal champions of Coleridge at Cambridge in the 1820s were J.C. Hare (1795–1855) and Connop Thirlwall (1797–1875). Neither was a professor, but as Fellows of Trinity their influence on a whole generation was profound. To them may be attributed a greater awareness of German scholarship and as a result of that a new emphasis on philology in classical learning. This had implications for biblical scholarship, but for the moment these were not drawn out. Julius Hare had been brought up in Italy, to which his parents had eloped, and he learned German while they were in Weimar in 1804. Rather like Herbert Marsh, therefore, Hare had an unusual exposure to wider European literature and culture generally. His parents were enthusiastic about the French revolution, though Hare's own political views later were less radical. Thirlwall by contrast was the son of a London clergyman and did not learn German until he was an undergraduate. Hare and Thirlwall became friends at Charterhouse, and both went to Trinity as undergraduates, Hare two years before Thirlwall. Their circle of friends included William Whewell (1794–1866), Knightbridge Professor and Master of Trinity; Richard Sheepshanks (1794–1855), one of the founders of the University Observatory; Charles Babbage (1792–1871), the mathematician; and George Peacock (1791–1858), Lowndean Professor of Astronomy and Dean of Ely, besides two alumni of St John's, the astronomer J.F.W. Herschel (1792–1871) and J.S. Henslow (1796–1861), Professor of Mineralogy and later of Botany, who taught Charles Darwin. Hugh James Rose was also a friend. Hare was an early member of the Cambridge Union Society, founded in 1815: when it was personally closed down by the Vice-Chancellor in March 1817 because he feared political radicalism, Hare led a small group, including Whewell, Thirlwall and Rose, in the study of German. Both Hare and Thirlwall were taught by Monk, Regius Profesor of Greek. Hare's lack of interest in Mathematics meant that he did not do the Tripos or compete for University prizes; but he competed successfully for a Trinity Fellowship in 1818, being elected at the same time as Whewell and Thirlwall. However, he and Thirlwall went to London to study for the Bar, since neither at that stage envisaged ordination. Hare used the time to begin his translations from German, and he also became a regular visitor to Coleridge's Thursday soirées at Dr Gillman's house in Highgate.[17]

In 1822 Hare was appointed to a Classical Lectureship at Trinity, and over the next ten years he influenced a generation of undergraduates. W.C. Lubernow has drawn attention to the significance of the changes in the size and age structure of the ancient universities in the first quarter of the nineteenth century: both Oxford and Cambridge began to expand and the proportion of students under sixteen declined sharply, being only 2 per cent at Cambridge in the 1820s and

---

16    S.T. Coleridge, *Table Talk*, ed. C. Woodring (Princeton, 1990), i, p. 475. See below pp. 80–82.

17    N.M. Distad, *Guessing at Truth* (Shepherdstown, West Virginia, 1979), pp. 23–5, 32–4; J.C. Thirlwall, *Connop Thirlwall* (London, 1936), pp. 8–9, 12–17.

nil at Oxford in the 1830s.[18] The older age-group of undergraduates wanted new kinds of activity, symbolised by the foundation of the Cambridge Union Society in 1815. A different group was 'The Apostles', so called because its membership was restricted to twelve. They began as the Cambridge Conversazione Society in 1820, consisting of members of St John's, principally men who did not come from well-established families; several were evangelicals.

By 1823 the Apostles had moved to Trinity and for the next thirty years nearly all the members were Trinity men. Under F.D. Maurice's leadership in 1823–24, the society was reconstituted and became much more intellectually focussed. It met weekly to discuss a paper by a member on a social or moral topic.[19] Though not directly involved in the Apostles, Hare was greatly admired by them. Maurice later said that he could trace to Hare's lectures on Sophocles and Plato of 1823–24 'the most permanent effect upon my character, and on all my modes of contemplating subjects, natural, human, and divine'.[20] Another Apostle, Charles Merivale, wrote 'Coleridge and Wordsworth were our principal divinities, and Hare and Thirlwall were regarded as their prophets'.[21] However, this was probably a retrospective exaggeration. The more popular kind of forward thinking in the 1820s was utilitarian: Arthur Hallam wrote to Gladstone in 1828, on the basis of his assessment of the Union, that 'the ascendant politics are *Utilitarian*, seasoned with a plentiful seasoning of heterogeneous Metaphysics'.[22] Maurice and John Sterling, who was elected an Apostle in 1825, were actually a minority in following the then unfashionable Coleridge and Wordsworth.

Hare was one in a network of friendship and marriage links that drew together a number of progressive figures in the Church of England in the second quarter of the nineteenth century. He was an unsuccessful candidate for the Regius Professorship of Greek in 1825. James Scholefield won because the electors were divided between Scholefield and Rose, and John Croft, deputy for the Master of Christ's, who had voted for Hare, decided to back Scholefield to keep Rose out. As Scholefield was Regius Professor until 1853, that eliminated Hare's chance of a chair.[23] Hare did not leave Cambridge, like so many, in order to marry, but to take the family living at Herstmonceux in Sussex in 1832, when his elder brother decided to remain in his parish of Alton Barnes in Wiltshire. One of Hare's most brilliant pupils was James Prince Lee (1804–69), recruited by Arnold to the staff of Rugby in 1830, appointed Head of King Edward's Birmingham in 1838, and

---

18    W.C. Lubenow, *The Cambridge Apostles, 1820–1914* (Cambridge, 1998), pp. 28–9.

19    P. Allen, *The Cambridge Apostles: The Early Years* (Cambridge, 1978), pp. 1–4.

20    Quoted in Distad, *Guessing at Truth*, p. 44, from Maurice's Introduction to the *Charges of Archdeacon Hare* (London, 1856), reprinted in J.C. Hare, *The Victory of Faith* (London, 1874), pp. xxiv–xxv.

21    J.B. Merivale, *Autobiography and Letters of Charles Merivale* (Oxford, 1898), p. 98; quoted in Distad, *Guessing at Truth*, p. 46.

22    Quoted in Allen, *Cambridge Apostles*, p. 45.

23    Distad, *Guessing at Truth*, pp. 49–51. The Kennedy Professorship of Latin was not established until 1869, and there was no chair in Philology.

a profound influence on Westcott, Lightfoot and Benson. Arthur Stanley (who wrote *The Life of Dr Arnold*) was a pupil of Hare's at Herstmonceux in 1834. John Sterling, who had been his pupil at Cambridge, became Hare's curate at the same time. Maria Hare (Hare's sister-in-law who used to visit him every year) became a friend of Priscilla, F.D. Maurice's sister; in 1837 Maria brought Priscilla's younger sister, Esther, and in 1844 Esther and Julius became engaged. They were married in the same year by Maurice, who had married Sterling's sister-in-law as a result of Sterling engineering their meeting at Herstmonceux in 1837.[24] A final link was to Baron Bunsen, whom Hare met on his visit to Rome in 1832. Bunsen marrried Frances Waddington, cousin of James Monk, and she introduced Thirlwall to Bunsen, who was B.G. Niebuhr's secretary when the latter was ambassador in Rome.

As a mediator of Coleridge, Hare was concerned to demonstrate the significance of the learning of the past. His first University Sermon in Great St Mary's on Advent Sunday 1828, entitled 'The Children of Light', was printed as a result of student demand. It was later described by E.H. Plumptre as 'a strong blow aimed at the despotic exclusiveness of a purely scientific course of studies, and at the narrowness of the Paley utilitarianism and Simeon evangelicalism which were then the chief nurture of Cambridge religious life'.[25] His text was Ephesians 5:8: 'For ye were sometimes darkness, but now are ye light in the Lord: walk as children of light'. The confining of the understanding of reason to 'the logical faculty or the power of drawing inferences' made it 'so fruitful a parent of errour and mischief'. In a characteristically Coleridgean way he affirmed that imagination, reason and understanding had to act together.[26] 'Everywhere it has been asserted, that we are not only wiser than our ancestors,' he said, 'but that, while we are all wise and clearsighted, our ancestors were all ignorant and blind.' This was not what was meant by saying that Christ had brought us from darkness to light: on the contrary the coming of Christ had unfolded what God had done for us and what he designed us for, and it had told us what we ought to do to testify our thankfulness for his mercies. Hence 'the office of Reason is not so much to divine what is not shewn, as to understand what is shewn'.[27] The critique of evangelicalism came in Hare's rejection of any idea that human nature was totally bad. 'Christ came not to contend with mankind as with an adversary; he came only to contend with that which is bad in human nature; he came to succour and encourage and foster whatever is good in it.' The Gospel provided the assurance of our immortality, our faith in God and our knowledge of God, and from the Gospel we had to learn to 'mould the heart and to sway the will' – which only made sense if it was possible to do it. In conclusion he outlined the characteristics of the children of light, ending with love – which he

---

24    Distad, *Guessing at Truth*, pp. 116–19, 125–32; F. Maurice, *The Life of Frederick Denison Maurice* (London 1884), i, pp. 227–8.

25    Memoir by E.H.P[lumptre], *Guesses at Truth, by Two Brothers* [A.W. & J.C. Hare] (London, 1867), p. xxvii; cf. Distad, *Guessing at Truth*, pp. 47–8.

26    J.C. Hare, *The Children of Light* (Cambridge, 1828), pp. iv–v.

27    Ibid., pp. 17–18.

took to be the same thing as light.[28] It is easy to see from this sermon that Hare had something in common with Rose, but the thrust of his thought was in the opposite direction.

The interest in German, which Hare and Thirlwall began in London, continued after Hare's return to Cambridge, and he continued to supply Thirlwall with the latest products of German theology. Hare suggested that Thirlwall translate Schleiermacher's *Critical Essay on the Gospel of St Luke*, and it was published in 1825. Thirlwall's letters to Hare in the second half of 1824 show how much Hare's own thinking was reflected in the Translator's Introduction, and they also illustrate Hare's nervousness that Schleiermacher's doubts concerning the authenticity of Matthew's Gospel might worry some readers. Thirlwall bluntly stated that he was 'not disposed to undertake the vindication of Matthew's Gospel, nor would that be the way to save Schleiermacher's credit'.[29] The Introduction first defended the view that tracing the development of gospel criticism was 'neither dangerous nor useless'. J.J. Conybeare's Bampton Lectures for 1824 on the 'history and limits of the secondary and spiritual interpretation of Scripture' had included a warning against the scepticism of the system of biblical criticism, which had spread through the protestant churches of continental Europe.[30] In a sharp footnote on them Thirlwall, noting 'the candour and earnestness displayed by the author', regretted 'that his studies had not led him to feel the necessity of acquiring the German language before he undertook that work, and that he was snatched away before he had an opportunity of enlarging and correcting his views'.[31]

For Thirlwall the discussion of hypotheses about the composition of the gospels did not affect the question of inspiration. Such hypotheses were irreconcilable with the doctrine of inspiration formerly universal, whereby 'the sacred writers were merely passive organs or instruments of the Holy Spirit' (the view condemned by Coleridge in *Confessions of an Inquiring Spirit*). But Thirlwall felt that this doctrine had been 'so long abandoned that it would now be a waste of time to attack it'.[32] Instead two alternative views had been accepted – the inspiration of suggestion and that of superintendence – which had enabled the Church of England to insist on the inspiration of scripture as a fundamental tenet, while allowing her members full liberty of private judgement on the nature and mode of that inspiration. In

---

28    Ibid., pp. 20, 23, 30–31. Significantly the sermon he preached at Thirlwall's consecration as Bishop of St David's in Lambeth Palace in August 1840 was entitled, 'The Church the Light of the world'.

29    Thirlwall to Hare, 29 Nov 1824: J.J.S. Perowne and L. Stokes (eds), *Letters Literary and Theological of Connop Thirlwall* (London, 1881), p. 83; for the letters generally, see pp. 71–83. Thirlwall at this stage was not ordained.

30    F. Schleiermacher, *A Critical Essay on the Gospel of St Luke* (London, 1825), p. viii; J.J. Conybeare, *Bampton Lectures for the year MDCCCXXIV* (Oxford, 1824), p. 8.

31    Schleiermacher, *St Luke*, p. ix. J.C. Thirlwall suggested that this note was a response to Conybeare's wish that 'all your German theology might be buried at the bottom of the German Ocean', but I have been unable to trace this quotation; it is not in his Bampton Lectures: Thirlwall, *Connop Thirlwall*, p. 31.

32    Thirlwall, *Connop Thirlwall*, p. xi.

practice, the idea of suggestion was no better defence against the discrepancies in the gospels than the original view, and without it the idea of superintendence ceased to be anything more than 'an ordinary dispensation of divine providence, which might have been equally granted to a heathen historian of Christianity'.[33] Therefore Thirlwall suggested a return to the old idea, stripped of its exaggerations, so that the operation of the Spirit was sought 'not in any temporary, physical or even intellectual changes wrought in its subjects, but in the continual presence and action of what is most vital and essential in Christianity itself'.[34] The *British Critic* reviewer felt that this was a distinction without a difference, since it was the end rather than the means that was at issue in inspiration. For the reviewer, 'our faith in the Gospels, as a book for the guidance of our belief, was gone at once, if we could persuade ourselves that the writers admitted poetic fictions, and symbolical narratives, into their history'.[35]

Thirlwall argued that the fundamental difficulty with Marsh's hypothesis, and that of Eichhorn upon which it was based, was that it was unnecessary to postulate a single common source for the first three gospels. Indeed if there had been one, it was surprising that it should have so soon been lost. There followed a detailed examination of the issues, particularly as discussed by Professor P.A. Gratz (1769–1849) of Bonn, Professor J.L. von Hug (1765–1846) of Freyburg (both Catholics), Professor H.E.G. Paulus (1761–1851) of Heidelberg, and Professor J.K.L. Gieseler (1792–1854) of Bonn and Göttingen (both Protestants). Thirlwall used Gieseler's conclusion that the appeal to the canonical gospels dated from the church's attempts to combat heresy from the mid-second century to argue that 'the *regula fidei*, which both in its origin and in its subsequent enlargements and modifications was independent of scripture, always constituted the principal and only essential part of the catechumen's religious education'.[36] Thus both Tertullian and Ignatius appealed to the *regula fidei* rather than scripture, and Thirlwall commented that

> as the doctrinal tradition was in the time of Ignatius more fresh, and more vividly impressed on the minds of those whom he addressed, we cannot be surprized that whatever degree of circulation and authority the sacred writings had then acquired, he should have preferred appealing to the former, and to the teachers of the church, its guardians and expounders.[37]

But in order to avoid being thought to be backing the Roman Catholic rather than the Protestant side on the relative authority of scripture and tradition, Thirlwall added a footnote that to take the Catholic positon now would confound 'different ideas and distinct epochs of ecclesiastical history'. In Tertullian's time an orthodox polemic had 'to appeal to an authority paramount to all scripture – the

---

33   Ibid., p. xvi.
34   Ibid., p. xix.
35   *British Critic*, ii, 4 (October 1827): 387–8.
36   Schleiermacher, *St Luke*, p. cxxxvi.
37   Ibid., p. cxxxvii.

testimony of the apostolical churches, which had preserved at once the canonical scriptures and the unwritten *regula fidei'*; and this was consistent with Protestant principles, because there was a difference between asserting 'that all the articles of Protestant faith are contained in Scripture', and 'that they were originally deduced from it'. Rome did not attach particular significance to the records of the primitive church because it thought it was identical to it; 'the Protestant church, which arose out of a reflexion on the alterations that the primitive church had undergone and the desire of restoring its ancient purity, naturally and wisely keeps constantly in the view of its members the image of original Christianity contained in the sacred writings'.[38]

The significance of Schleiermacher's *Essay* for Thirlwall was as a critical inquiry rather than as a new hypothesis. It did not offer a complete solution of the difficulties which it discussed, but it proposed a new method for approaching them. Although it was intended as a discussion of the origins of Luke's Gospel rather than a commentary upon it, some important points relating to its content had emerged. Readers were invited to suspend judgement until they had compared the views with those to which they were accustomed. 'But the end of the author's labours will have been equally attained, if his opinions shall only be rejected in the same spirit of impartial criticism in which he has himself adopted and endeavoured to establish them.'[39]

Schleiermacher's *Essay* distinguished between the work of the Spirit in those who were witnesses to the original events in faithfully reporting and interpreting what they had seen and heard, and in those who collected and digested the work of those witnesses. He challenged Eichhorn's theory of a single original as improbable on the basis of human experience, and argued that it was not sufficient simply to compare the sections of the gospels which were either common or peculiar to them, since that diverted attention from the way in which they were connected together.[40] He divided Luke's Gospel into four main parts, the first on Jesus' birth covering the same material as Matthew but not Mark, the second based in Galilee, which was shared with Matthew and Mark, the third relating to the journey to Jerusalem being almost entirely Lucan, and the final account of the Passion being shared with both the others, though not in detail to the same extent as the second. Schleiermacher's approach was well illustrated by the conclusion of the first part:

> Now if we compare, without any prepossession, this and the corresponding portion in Matthew, we have two parallel successions of narratives, parallel in the strict sense of the word, inasmuch as they have no single point, that is in this case no entire fact, in common, and also inasmuch as they are not at all supplemental to each other, but, on the contrary, the corresponding members of the two successions almost entirely

---

38    Ibid., p. cxxvii–cxxxix.
39    Ibid., p. cliii.
40    Kümmel noted that he failed to appreciate the extent to which the Synoptic Gospels exhibited a remarkable agreement in sequence and actual wording: W.G. Kümmel, *The New Testament: The History of the Investigation of its Problems* (London, 1973), p. 84.

exclude each other. Hence then if in any one point the narrative of the one evangelist is correct, that of the other, so far as it relates to the same epoch, cannot be so.[41]

Thus 'in these books poetry and history are nowhere kept quite distinct'.[42] The conclusion of the whole essay was that Luke 'is from beginning to end no more than the compiler and arranger of documents which he found in existence, and which he allows to pass unaltered through his hands'.[43] His chief merit was to have included little that was not 'genuine and good' – 'for this was certainly not the effect of accident, but the fruit of a judiciously instituted investigation, and a well weighed choice'.[44]

The immediate impact of the publication of Thirlwall's translation is unclear. It has been claimed that it provoked Hugh James Rose's Cambridge sermons on German theology, but this is unlikely. The book was not published until after Easter[45] and Rose's sermons were given in May 1825. Nowhere in his very detailed notes did Rose refer to Schleiermacher's *Essay on St Luke*, nor in his subsequent response to criticisms, published in 1828. He criticised Schleiermacher's *Christian Faith* and the *Speeches on Religion*, but said that he was the only divine in Germany who was also a great scholar.[46] Ironically the Advertisement at the beginning of these sermons referred to an article (by Thomas Arnold) in the *Quarterly Review* on Niebuhr, which disavowed any general charge of German folly and infidelity and specifically exempted Niebuhr from any such criticism.[47] On the other hand, the book was reviewed in few of the religious or secular journals; however, the *British Critic* published a notice which, whilst critical of Schleiermacher's views, praised the translator, apart from his views on inspiration.[48] Two points should be emphasised: one is that a decade later, after the publication of David Strauss's *Life of Jesus*, it became easier to see this as one stage along a road to inevitable scepticism; the other is the opposite, that Schleiermacher was actually taking on the Enlightenment sceptics about the internal coherence of scripture by arguing that it was neither necessary nor reasonable to defend that particular ground in order to establish the truth of Christianity. In the long run this changed the agenda for biblical criticism.

In 1827 Thirlwall returned to Trinity, and was ordained in the same year. Almost immediately he began work with Hare on the translation of B.G. Niebuhr's *History of Rome*, the first two volumes of which had been published in 1812. Niebuhr's work marked a revolution in the writing of history, with extensive critical evaluation

41   Schleiermacher, *St Luke*, pp. 44–5.

42   Ibid., p. 51.

43   Ibid., p. 313.

44   Ibid., p. 314.

45   Perowne and Stokes, *Letters of Thirlwall*, p. 84.

46   H.J. Rose, *The state of the Protestant Religion in Germany* (Cambridge, 1825), pp. 136–7, 145.

47   Ibid., p. xiii; A.P. Stanley, *Life and Correspondence of Thomas Arnold* (London, n.d.), p. 45.

48   *British Critic*, ii, 4 (October 1827): 351–2, 388; Thirlwall, *Connop Thirlwall*, pp. 32–4; Distad, *Guessing at Truth*, p. 89.

of sources, including traditional works such as Livy's *History*; but in particular it utilised philology to see what light language itself could shed on history, and the idea of the evolutionary development of society. Hare had already written that 'the idea of the progressiveness of mankind first revealed itself' in Germany, but suggested that it was not explicitly enunciated before Hegel. In the previous fifty years it had been applied to the history of religion, philosophy, poetry and the arts. 'In each it has been attempted to arrange and exhibit the various phenomena which are the subjects of history, not in a mere accidental sequence, after the practice of former times and of other countries, but as connected parts of a great whole.' But the progress of mankind was not therefore 'in a straight line, uniform and unbroken'. Rather it was subject to periodic interruptions and delays, and even reverses. It was more like the cycle of the seasons with growth and decay, or the life of an individual 'in which every day adds something, and every day takes away something'.[49] Such a view enabled Hare to retain a place for God's providence; indeed it had some of the same characteristics, which enabled Francis Bacon to reconcile the analysis of secondary causes with an over-arching providence, but it differed crucially from the more confident assumptions of the Enlightenment about steady and uniform progress. Here there was a difference between Arnold and the two Cambridge scholars, because Arnold was worried by Niebuhr's 'veneration for a remote antiquity'; by contrast, Hare and Thirlwall believed that the translation of Niebuhr was 'scarcely less valuable as a moral than as an intellectual discipline'.[50]

The translation of Niebuhr was therefore more than a study in ancient history. In effect Thomas Arnold's article on the German edition in the *Quarterly Review* had already suggested that a German scholar might be a sincere believer in the Gospel 'without having fully considered how closely the truth of the Jewish revelation is connected with that of the Christian, and even without allowing the inspiration of Scripture in a sense so universal as that in which we ourselves take it'. It was Arnold's suggestion that the 'wildness of criticism on theological subjects which is too prevalent in Germany' could only be restrained 'by learning to tolerate among ourselves a sober freedom of honest and humble inquiry' that had aroused Rose's ire in 1825.[51]

The modern reader is bound to catch the broader implications for biblical scholarship, however anachronistic these are. Thus the Preface began:

> The History of Rome was treated, during the first two centuries after the revival of letters, with the same prostration of the understanding and judgement to the written letter that had been handed down, and with the same fearfulness of going beyond it, which prevailed in all the other branches of knowledge. If any one had asserted a right of examining the credibility of the ancient writers and the value of their testimony, an outcry would have been raised against his atrocious presumption: the object aimed at was, in spite of all internal evidence, to combine what was related by them. At the

---

49    Distad, *Guessing at Truth*, pp. 93–4; *Guesses at Truth*, pp. 333, 335, 337, 338.

50    D. Forbes, *The Liberal Anglican Idea of History* (Cambridge, 1952), p. 19; J.C. Hare, *Vindication of Luther against his recent assailants* (London, 1855), p. 201.

51    *Quarterly Review*, xxxii, 63 (June 1825): 87.

utmost one authority was in some one particular instance postponed to another, as gently as possible, and without inducing any further results.[52]

Bentley's philology had rescued scholars from this plight.

To take some examples at random, Niebuhr illustrated the 'very erroneous suppositions' in the various Roman genealogies by comparison with the Mosaical, 'which represents races, belonging unquestionably to entirely different families, as connected'. The Etruscan ritual books 'like the Mosaical ... prescribed, under the form of divine law, the civil polity'. A comment on what could be learned from archaeology led to the observation that the creation of mankind had not necessarily taken place only once: 'it may have taken place, for the different races of mankind, after the earth had been more or less extensively desolated, at widely-distant epochs in the course of those many thousands of years which were required to form the alluvial land of Egypt, Babylonia, Lombardy, or Louisiana'.[53] Niebuhr also postulated the existence between the 'completely poetical age' and 'the purely historical age', of a mixed age 'which may be called the mythic-historical'; and, whilst insisting on 'the claims of reason to take nothing as historical which cannot be historical', he was prepared to claim that the poetical story was 'something other, but ... also something better, than pure history, on the field of which we only find again what wearies and troubles us in life'.[54]

A casual reference in a footnote to a completely unrelated article in the *Quarterly Review* in January 1829 disparaged Niebuhr (in Wordsworth's words about Voltaire) as 'a pert, *dull* scoffer', while acknowledging that one of the translators was a 'man of great talents', because of his prefaces to Schleiermacher on St Luke and to some novels from the German.[55] This provoked Hare to a 'Vindication', which contrasted this footnote with the article on Early Roman History (by Thomas Arnold) in No. 63 of the *Review*, which had found no dangerous political principles in the work. (The implication had been that Niebuhr's ideas had contributed to student dissatisfaction in post-war Germany.) Hare said that no philological work had effected so much in the last fifteen years, shedding 'an entirely new light over the whole region of ancient history'. Politically he was clearly on the side of history over against reason 'in the great controversy as to the first principles of government', and thus 'with Burke, and against the *Contrat Social*'. Hare confessed that he did not know what Niebuhr's religious faith was, but he did know 'that it is very possible in Germany, under the present aspect of religious feeling and knowledge, to unite a fervent faith in Christianity, and a hearty love of it, with considerable doubts and scruples about the historical value of certain passages in Scripture'. Thirlwall added a postscript for good measure saying that no one of 'common understanding and decent education' could imagine that there was anything inconsistent with their

---

52    B.G. Niebuhr, *History of Rome*, trans. J.C. Hare and C. Thirlwall (Cambridge, 1828), i, p. v.

53    Ibid. (Cambridge, 1832), ii, pp. 23, 116, 145–6.

54    Ibid., ii, pp. 173, 210.

55    *Quarterly Review*, xxxix, 77 (January 1829): 8–9.

(clerical) profession 'in giving publicity to a historical work containing two or three speculations not sanctioned by the most approved commentators of the first ten chapters of Genesis'.[56] In other words, the issues about the historical credibility of the Genesis accounts of the origins of the world were in the open.

Thirlwall wrote to Bunsen in 1831 that he had not imagined that Bunsen's prediction that he would be attacked in the *Quarterly Review* would be literally fulfilled, and he put it down to the current universality of the millenarian persuasion. He had realised that it was unavoidable that such people would be scandalised by Nierbuhr's divergence from Genesis, but had not expected the *Quarterly* to avoid the task of reviewing the book by such a stupid attack. Neither had the *Edinburgh* done much better by giving the review to a young Scottish lawyer who knew nothing about the subject.[57]

Hare left Cambridge in 1832, and this ended further work on the *History*. It also meant that Hare was away when Thirlwall entered the lists in favour of the relaxation of subscription to the Thirty-Nine Articles by signing the Cambridge Petition to that effect in 1834. But the crisis arose when (to Coleridge's dismay) Thirlwall responded to the pamphlet by Turton, the Regius Professor of Divinity, which argued that to have no religious tests would result in what had happened at Doddridge's Academy at Northampton, with an inevitable slide into Arianism and Unitarianism.[58] Thirlwall argued that the comparison was inapt, because Cambridge colleges were not theological seminaries, and very little time was spent on theology. Moreover, there was little evidence that compulsory chapel had anything other than a detrimental effect and college lectures in Divinity were not concerned with the peculiar principles of religion. William Whewell, under whom Thirlwall worked as an Assistant Tutor issued his own pamphlet rebutting Thirlwall on the same day; and on 26 May the Master of Trinity, Christopher Wordsworth, wrote to Thirlwall inviting him to resign his office. This he did under protest, but not without circulating the correspondence to the resident Fellows making it clear that he did not accept that the Master was within his rights to make such a demand. Rose was regarded by some as the Master's adviser in the matter, since he had preached his University Sermon on 'The Duty of Maintaining the Truth' the week before, but this may have been unfair.[59] Hare thought that Thirlwall's action in publishing his views was unwise, but he also wrote to Whewell saying that the Master's action had been outrageous: 'The high church party

56    J.C. Hare, *Vindication of Niebuhr's History of Rome from the Charges of the Quarterly Review* (Cambridge, 1829), pp. 15, 21, 59, 61.

57    Perowne and Stokes, *Letters of Thirlwall*, pp. 101–2: see *Edinburgh Review*, li, 102 (July 1830): 358ff.

58    T. Turton, *Thoughts on the admission of persons without Regard to their Religious Opinions, to certain Degrees in the Universities of England* (Cambridge, 1834). Coleridge is reported to have said on 1 May 1834, 'The *time* – the *time* – the *occasion* and the *motive* ought to have been argument enough, that even if the measure were right or harmless in itself, not *now*, nor with such as *these* was it to be effected': *Table Talk*, ed. C. Woodring, (Princeton, 1990), ii, p. 284.

59    Perowne and Stokes, *Letters of Thirlwall*, pp. 113–24.

seems all gone stark-mad, and to have been all seized with a fanatical desire of martyrdom at all costs and risks'.[60] Thirlwall resigned his Fellowship in December 1834, having been offered the living of Kirby Underdale by Lord Brougham. Although Lord Melbourne did not offer him the bishopric of Norwich in 1837, because the translation of Schleiermacher's *Essay on St Luke* was regarded as of dubious orthodoxy, in 1840 he offered him the bishopric of St David's, after Archbishop Howley had assured the Prime Minister that the book contained nothing heterodox.[61] Wordsworth never recovered his authority in Trinity and eventually resigned as Master in 1841, to be succeeded by Whewell.[62]

Hare's removal to Herstmonceux also ended his direct influence on theological study at Cambridge. Thereafter he was only an occasional preacher. His best known sermons were two series which he preached at Cambridge, *The Victory of Faith* in 1839 and *The Mission of the Comforter* in 1840. The first series was based on 1 John 5:4, and, by its vigorous defence of the doctrine of justification by faith, could almost be seen as a deliberate corrective to the Tractarian disparagement of the Reformation. But Hare's aim was never solely polemical. For Hare a living faith was necessary so that Faith should not be reduced to a matter of the Understanding only. A theology based solely on 'general propositions about the divine nature and attributes' failed to place man in any immediate personal relation to God; 'whereas to Christ, the Incarnate God, our relations are wholly personal'.[63] The consequence of this notional theology, as Hare called it, was that in the eighteenth century the church lost its hold upon the poor, a point he made to his Cambridge congregation with characteristic sharpness: 'We in this place may dream we are fed, when we get nothing but the husks of knowledge: the poor must have the living Gospel; else they starve'.[64] He attributed the drawing together of the opposite parties in the church to the growth of a stronger living Faith: 'a living Faith seeks unity, which implies diversity, and manifests itself therein: whereas a notional Faith imposes and exacts uniformity, without which it has no ground to stand on'.[65] Because faith required an act of will, it was moral as much as intellectual; so it was wrong to describe it as 'the assent of the mind to certain truths, beyond the reach of Reason, delivered by testimony supported by the evidence of miracles'.[66] Thus he argued that 'the true antithesis is not between Faith and Reason, but between Faith and Sight, or more generally between Faith and Sense'.[67] In all this, the unseen (and unmentioned) antagonist was Locke; and these sermons may be read as a continued critique of the Cambridge approach to philosophy.

---

60    Ibid., p. 125; Distad, *Guessing at Truth*, p. 145; D. Winstanley, *Early Victorian Cambridge* (Cambridge, 1940), pp. 73–8.
61    Perowne and Stokes, *Letters of Thirlwall*, pp. 128–32, 159–61.
62    Winstanley, *Early Victorian Cambridge*, pp. 79–82. Coleridge did not like Christopher Wordsworth either: *Table Talk*, i, p. 91.
63    Hare, *The Victory of Faith*, p. 85.
64    Ibid., p. 86.
65    Ibid., p. 87.
66    Ibid., p. 92.
67    Ibid., p. 93.

Hare's final sermon argued that Christian Faith, in the sense he had described it, was the natural parent of Natural Science; and it culminated in a rhetorical *tour de force*, based on the Epistle to the Hebrews, in which he brought the roll call of faith up to date. Beginning with the first believers who 'sold their possessions and goods, and had all things common', he proceeded through a list of apostles and martyrs to the Waldensians, Wicliff ('the morning-star of the Reformation'), Luther, Ridley and Latimer. He concluded with Clarkson and Wilberforce in their work to overthrow the slave trade and Simeon through whose preaching in Cambridge preachers of Christ had been sent forth into all parts of the country 'and thus contributed, under God's blessing, more than any other man, to that revival of true religion, which has taken place of late years amongst us'.[68]

The second series, *The Mission of the Comforter*, was based on John 16:7–11. It was dedicated to Coleridge (just as the previous year's had been dedicated to Thirlwall) – 'the great religious philosopher, to whom the mind of our generation in England owes more than to any other man'.[69] In the Preface, written in 1846, Hare said that his original intention had been to point out 'how the work of the Comforter, in all its parts is fulfilled by His taking of the things of Christ, and shewing them to us'.[70] Ideally this would have necessitated considering the 'false notions of Christ's personality, which regard Him as the mere Founder of a system, whether morally or philosophical, or religious, and place Him at the head of it, but leave the system to work itself out through the impulse it originally received'.[71] These false notions were dealt with in 267 pages of notes (the Sermons took up 180 pages), particularly the errors of Strauss, who had moved from denying the Son to denying the Father, and from Pantheism ended up in Atheism. Hence it was a primary task to assert 'the divine personality of Christ, ... the redemption and reconciliation He has wrought for mankind, and ... His abiding presence in His Church through the Spirit glorifying Him'; and these primary truths had to be established 'on irrefragable grounds, philological, historical, and philosophical, as well as theological'.[72] Hare's assumption about the basis was as significant as his identification of the task.

Other issues too had contemporary relevance. For example, the study of the theology of earlier ages was to be welcomed, but it was not enough merely to 'repeat by rote what was said in the fourth century, or in the fourteenth'; that would make us more foolish, not more wise.[73] The truths of former ages had to be truly appropriated and assimilated:

They who swallow the theology either of the Fathers, or of the Middle Ages, in the gross, find themselves out of place in a Protestant Church; and while they wish to revive the

---

68    Ibid., pp. 225–32.
69    J.C. Hare, *The Mission of the Comforter*, ed. E.H. Plumptre (London, 1886), p. xii.
70    Ibid., p. vii.
71    Ibid.
72    Ibid., p. viii.
73    Ibid., p. ix.

> Church of the Middle Ages, and confound faith with credulity, they are just fitted for the surrender of their reason and conscience to the arbitrary mandates of the Papacy.[74]

Consequently Hare emphasised again and again 'the inestimable blessings of the Reformation, as evinced in the expansion of theology, no less than in the purification of religion', especially as the Reformers had been attacked 'with unscrupulous ignorance and virulence'.[75] He pointed out that his note on the development of Christian doctrine[76] had been printed before Newman's book on the same subject. Finally, he tried to guide students to what was valuable in German theology. In the 1850 edition he noted that his attempt to point out where that good is to be found, had 'excited some vehement denunciations, as I expected, from those who know nothing about it'; and he separated his Note on the Vindication of Luther into a separate volume.[77]

The first sermon was on the expediency of Christ's departure. Hare suggested that 'we must lose Christ as a man, to regain Him as God'. The death of Christ was not merely 'the consummation of human patience and meekness', but was 'fore-ordained by God from the beginning to be the central act in the history of mankind'.[78] In the second sermon on the conviction of sin, Hare argued that this was not a product of conscience, or the Law, but rather the work of the Spirit through the gift of faith: 'Seeing that we shrank in awe from the contemplation of [God's] Infinitude and Omniscience, or lost ourselves in stargazing thereat, Christ came to us in the form of a Servant, to prove to our unbelieving, carnal minds that what is most godlike in God is not His power'.[79] The sermon on the Conviction of Righteousness was even more compelling. Arguing that human beings were intrinsically selfish and that 'they who call themselves philosophers, tell him that he cannot act from any other motive, that he must seek his own good, that the notion of seeking anything else is a fantastical delusion', he said that this yoke could not be shaken off, unless some higher power made it possible.[80] Civil society compounded this problem by being more concerned to protect from evil than to promote good:

> Even laws, which are the utterance of the moral voice of the State, confine themselves to prohibition and repression. They do not attempt to cultivate the fields of righteousness, but merely to erect a palisade and network against the inroads of crime, driving in new stakes, and weaving new meshes, in proportion as evil devises new snares and new modes of attack.[81]

Neither poetry nor philosophy could produce righteousness; and there was a particular danger to young men at Cambridge 'to regard genius, or what you

---

74   Ibid.
75   Ibid., p. x.
76   Ibid., Note G, pp. 202–26.
77   Ibid., p. xv.
78   Ibid., p. 29.
79   Ibid., p. 67.
80   Ibid., pp. 75–6.
81   Ibid., p. 80.

may deem to be such, as an excuse, if not a warrant, for all manner of moral aberrations'.[82] In the moral order, however, genius carried greater responsibilities: 'The possessors of eminent intellectual gifts are the more bound to employ their gifts diligently and faithfully in the service of the Giver.'[83] Hare lamented that 'even in this University' it had been taught that 'the act of self-sacrifice, whereunto Christ has called them, is a fantastical dream, and a sheer impossibility'.[84] Only the Spirit could convince us of Christ's righteousness: 'We must feel that without Him we can do nothing; that through our sins we have cast ourselves out from the presence of God; and that of ourselves we can no more return into His presence, than we can fly up and bathe in the fountains of light which are ever welling up from the heart of the sun.'[85] Hare's concluding sermons were on the conviction of judgement – a judgement felt most keenly at the foot of the cross – and the threefold conviction of the Comforter.

Hare was uncompromising in preaching the doctrine of justification by faith. William Carus suggested to the young Hort that he read Hare, because *The Mission of the Comforter* was a vindication of Luther from attacks by the Tractarians.[86] However, in the sermons (as distinct from the Notes in the published version) Hare did not attack any school of thought in the church; instead he reserved his fire for what he regarded as the perils of philosophy and speculative materialism. In both series he set out an approach, which emphasised the incarnation as much as the atonement, and on the duty to pursue active righteousness rather than to concentrate on the perils of sin. The thrust of his theology was aptly expressed in his final sermon:

> The judgement against the Prince of this world was indeed completed and consummated by the Sacrifice on the Cross. As the Crucifixion however *was not the whole of the sacrifice offered up by Christ for the sins of the world, but only its closing, perfecting act*, – as the whole of our Saviour's life, from the humiliation of His Incarnation down to the still deeper humiliation, when He, who had humbled Himself that He might enter into life in the shape of an innocent babe, humbled Himself still more that He might pass through the gates of death with the agony and shame of sin, was one continual sacrifice for sin, – so was it one continual warfare against sin, and victory over sin, and judgement against sin.[87]

---

82    Ibid., p. 87.

83    Ibid., p. 88.

84    Ibid., pp. 90–91.

85    Ibid., p. 107.

86    A.F. Hort, *Life and Letters of Fenton John Anthony Hort* (London, 1896), i, p. 46.

87    Hare, *Mission of the Comforter*, pp. 159–60 (emphasis added). It is a passage that might be compared with J.A. Froude's account of Newman preaching on the Passion: 'Then in a low, clear voice, of which the faintest vibration was audible in the farthest corner of St Mary's, he said, "Now, I bid you recollect that He to whom these things were done was Almighty God". It was as if an electric stroke had gone through the church': J.A. Froude, *Short Studies on Great Subjects* (London, 1893), iv, p. 286.

However, the unfortunate affair of Hare's *Life of Sterling* revived the attack on 'the Germano-Coleridgean school' and its supposed influence on Cambridge. Sterling was one of Hare's pupils in the 1820s; like Maurice he moved to Trinity Hall and for a while was involved as a writer in London, principally for *The Athanaeum*, to which Maurice also contributed. Sterling was always in frail health, suffering from tuberculosis. After his marriage in 1830 he went to the West Indies for a year in 1831–32, to find a better climate for his lungs. Here he decided to be ordained, and after meeting him in Bonn in 1833 Hare offered him a curacy at Herstmonceux. He was ordained deacon in 1834, but resigned within six months on health grounds. In view of this it is remarkable that he did not die until September 1844, his later years being spent finding a suitable climate either in Europe or in southern England. Hare and Thomas Carlyle were Sterling's literary executors, and Hare published a collection of Sterling's *Essays and Tales* in 1848, prefaced by a 232-page biography, seemingly to avoid a Life by Mill or Carlyle. However, Carlyle felt that Hare spent too much time on Sterling's religious doubts. In 1851 he published his own *Life of John Sterling*, presenting him not 'as a vanquished *doubter*' but rather 'as a victorious *believer*, and under great difficulties a victorious doer'.[88]

By then the damage was done. William Palmer's review of Sterling's *Essays and Tales* in the *English Review* in December 1848, entitled 'Tendencies towards the Subversion of Faith', picked out for attack both crucial passages in Sterling's letters to Hare and Hare's apparent acquiescence in such unorthodox ideas. Hare's riposte, *'Thou shalt not bear false Witness against thy Neighbour'*, intensified the conflict without abating it. The *English Review* reviewed it in March 1849, and followed it up with an attack on Coleridge's *Confessions of an Inquiring Spirit* in December 1849.

What had Hare written which caused such a fuss? Sterling's letters to Hare on several occasions reflected on the need for more, better-educated clergy, particularly in large towns – which could only happen if the general and theological education provided by the universities were improved.[89] Hare believed that Sterling, deprived of the opportunity for practical ministerial labour, had drifted into too negative a view. Sterling thought that Paley's saying, 'It is a happy world after all', was 'one of the most cruelly heartless of all human utterances' because of the sheer scale of human misery throughout history.[90] The only hope was that, in the Christian understanding, this was due to the corruptions rather than the nature of humanity. So he pondered the possibility of 'breaking the charmed sleep of English Theology by a book on the authority of the Scriptures'.[91] He had read Coleridge's *Confessions of an Inquiring Spirit* in manuscript, and transcribed

---

88   T. Carlyle, *The Life of John Sterling* (London, 1897), p. 6.

89   J. Sterling, *Essays and Tales, with a Memoir of his Life by Julius Charles Hare* (London, 1848), i, pp. lxxix–lxxxii.

90   Ibid., p. lxxxix; the sentence comes from W. Paley, *Natural Theology; or Evidences of the Existence and Attributes of the Deity* (London, 1802), p. 490.

91   Sterling, *Essays and Tales*, i., p. xciv.

them.[92] Now he turned to the German writers, first Schleiermacher's sermons and eventually Strauss's *Leben Jesu* (which he read in German).

As he indicated in the Preface to *The Mission of the Comforter*, Hare believed that Strauss's *Life of Jesus* was 'a book which a person can hardly read without being more or less hurt by it'.[93] Sterling's early acquaintance with Coleridge prepared him to welcome its Hegelian philosophy, rather than being put off, as many English people might have been. So Hare concluded sadly that Sterling had been unable to 'resist the fascination of those pantheistic tendencies, which Philosophy, in her wiser moments, has ever been trying to escape from'.[94] Hare and Sterling disagreed and their correspondence became less frequent. But Sterling believed that his earlier prejudices about Strauss were mistaken, that Strauss did assert 'the ethical greatness and divine wisdom of Jesus', and that Strauss's criticism left the doctrines of the trinity, the incarnation, the atonement and the offices of the Spirit entirely untouched. Moreover he believed that 'men of distinct historical faith' should not confuse Strauss with 'the materialist, empirical infidels, to whom all claim of anything more than brutal for man appears as a fraud or a dream'.[95] It is easy to see how Sterling, who had developed a keen antipathy for utilitarian materialism, could be attracted by the idealist tone of Strauss's thesis, as well as the shortcut it offered through a variety of problems of biblical criticism. For his part Hare felt that Sterling's optimistic view of Strauss had been disproved by Strauss's later two-volume Dogmatics, which broke decisively with traditional ecclesiastical doctrine.[96] For example, he no longer spoke of the virgin birth of Christ, his resurrection and so on as eternal truths, which he had done at the end of the Preface to the *Life of Jesus*.[97] Its general tone may be aptly judged by Strauss's statement that 'He who is unable to determine his own self, seeks to be determined by an authority; he who is not yet mature enought to trust in reason, remains trusting in revelation'.[98] Fortunately most of Hare's readers did not read German, and therefore had not read the later work, but while it was important to Hare, the reference did not help readers to understand Sterling's own position.

In his later letters Sterling abandoned hope of change in the Church of England:

the time is past, when the realization of our old Church institutions and Reformation theology would have satisfied the best minds, a reconstructive revolution in thought being

---

92    Ibid., p. cxxix.

93    Ibid., p. cxxxiii.

94    Ibid., p. cxxxvi.

95    Ibid., pp. cxxxviii–cxxxix.

96    Ibid., p. cxl.

97    Letter to Märklin, 3 November 1839, quoted in H. Harris, *David Friedrich Strauss and his Theology*, (Cambridge, 1973), p. 136.

98    D.F. Strauss, *Die christliche Glaubenslehre in ihrer geschichtlictlichen Entwicklung und im Kampf mit der modernene Wissenschaft dargestellt* (Tübingen, 1840–41), i, p. 355; quoted in Harris, *Strauss*, p. 137. Strauss's *Glaubenslehre* has never been translated into English.

inevitable, which will destroy much still held sacred among us, and will readjust all to the one great modern principle of the self-conscious and Christianly sanctified Reason.[99]

More positively on another occasion he suggested that 'Christian truth is that, and only that, doctrine which commends itself to the minds of all who share in the spirit of Christ', and taking all ages and countries into account 'this essential doctrine will be found to resolve itself into the acknowledgement of Christ as the Ideal Man, and therefore the representative of the Divine Mind towards us'.[100]

Sterling knew that the standard high church response to such views was that, as enunciated by Rose, among others, they represented a dangerous surrender to subjectivity instead of the obedience required by traditional doctrine. Commenting in the *Quarterly Review* for 1840 on an article on Carlyle by William Sewell (described as 'more Puseyite than Pusey'),[101] Sterling commented acidly:

> One can hardly conceive how so quick and sharp an advocate fails to perceive that his doctrine of unlimited obedience and docility serves just as well for a Calvinist, or a Unitarian, nay, for a Brahmin or a Bonze, as for an Oxford high Churchman, and can therefore be of no use to any of them.

Without that assumption of obedience there was no basis for the Truth, and consequently 'the Romanist is sure to reap the final fruits of all these Anglican victories'.[102] Although Sterling was writing before Newman's secession to Rome, Hare's readers in 1848 were keenly aware of what happened subsequently. In fact, Sterling put the alternative between his own 'Coleridgean' views and Rome so sharply, that Hare must have felt that it tested his own belief that a spirit of free enquiry in the Church of England could guarantee a home for everyone sincerely seeking the truth.

By the time Hare's book on Sterling was published, times had changed: Coleridge's *Confessions of an Inquiring Spirit* had been posthumously published in 1840, there had been a furore over Tract 90 and the publication of the tracts had been stopped in 1841, the Jerusalem bishopric had been set up jointly with Prussia in the same year, Pusey had been condemned by the Oxford Heads of Houses for his sermon on the Eucharist in 1843, Newman had become a Roman Catholic in 1845, and George Eliot's translation of Strauss's *Life of Jesus* had been published in 1846. In short the Tractarians' world view was falling about their ears, and those of them left in the Church of England looked to a more traditional theology to save them. William Palmer's essay – well described as a 'cry of agony' by Owen Chadwick[103] – was more of an attack on Hare than Sterling, who, with others, was presented as 'distressing evidence of studies misdirected,

---

99    Sterling, *Essays and Tales*, i, p. cliii.

100   Ibid., pp. clix–clx.

101   *Quarterly Review*, lxvi, 132 (September 1840): 446ff. A sharp picture of Sewell is painted in W. Tuckwell, *Reminiscences of Oxford* (London, 1900), pp. 234–42: the description is on p. 235.

102   Sterling, *Essays and Tales*, pp. clviii–clix.

103   O. Chadwick, *The Victorian Church* (London, 1966), i, p. 541.

talents misapplied, and truth subverted'.[104] The pain of the Tractarians was also indicated by the castigation of Hare and others as supporters of R.D. Hampden, either when appointed Regius Professor at Oxford in 1836 or when made Bishop of Hereford in 1848, and the suggestion that it was because the Oxford Movement had 'lost its hold upon the public mind' that it was now possible for 'men of unsettled principles, and of a speculative disposition' to raise more fundamental questions about the truth of Christianity.[105] The only matter not mentioned was the continuing rage of the Tractarians at the Jerusalem bishopric, which Hare and Maurice, among others, had supported.

Hare's detailed account of Sterling's doubts was made worse for his critics by his position as Archdeacon of Lewes. Palmer implied that he had been 'assailing the Act of Uniformity with all the virulence of a Dissenter'.[106] He repeated the charge in responding to Hare's self-defence in March 1849, saying that it was 'a most painful part of the reviewer's duty to point out offences against Christianity on the part of those who are its appointed teachers', but it was 'indispensably necessary to do so, when we conceive that the foundations of all Christian belief are, even unconsciously, shaken by writers whose names carry any weight with the public'.[107] And he blamed Hare for being a disciple of Coleridge, and for supporting the introduction of German theology into England.

This was why the *English Review* published an article on the second edition of Coleridge's *Confessions* in December 1849. It noted 'the pernicious, *and increasingly pernicious*, results of false maxims on most material points, which his speculative and philosophical mind adopted, and *which a number of his admirers have eagerly caught up and retailed*'.[108] J.H. Green's Introduction to the new edition discussed Coleridge's debt to, and difference from, Lessing. The *English Review* homed in on the debt, and ignored the differences, quoting a long passage, the heart of which was, 'The Christian religion is not true because the Evangelists and apostles taught it, but they taught it because it is true'.[109] The reviewer scornfully rejected this trust in human reason, saying that Coleridge objected 'to any view of Scripture inspiration which gives it authority and control over REASON, which he supposes to be just as divinely inspired as Scripture itself'.[110] He returned to Sterling's views, as described by Hare, and compared them with J.A. Froude's *Nemesis of Faith* and Blanco White's *Autobiography*. All these sceptics 'will not have so uncertain a guide as Holy Scripture joined with the instructions of God's

---

104   *English Review*, x (December 1848): 399.

105   Ibid., 424, 437.

106   Ibid., 441.

107   *English Review*, xi (March 1849): 181.

108   *English Review*, xii (December 1849): 250 (emphasis added).

109   S.T. Coleridge, *Confessions of an Inquiring Spirit*, ed. H.StJ. Hart (London, 1956), p. 20; cf. *English Review*, xii: 252. The quotation from Lessing comes from his 'Editorial Commentary on the "Fragments" of Reimarus', G.E. Lessing, *Philosophical and Theological Writing*, ed. H.B. Nisbet (Cambridge, 2005), p. 63; cf. *Gottwald Ephraim Lessing Werke*, vii (Munich, 1976), p. 458.

110   *English Review*, xii: 256.

ministers, and the traditions of the Catholic church of all ages as a check on the
license of private speculation'. In contrast the faith of the Christian stood on
a 'foundation far elevated above the contests and uncertainties of philosophy
falsely so called':

> He knows that, if he were to doubt the grounds on which Scripture, *i.e.* on which the
> facts and doctrines of Christianity depend, he might just as reasonably doubt every
> event in history, or even question the evidence of his senses. He knows that high
> probability, amounting to moral certainty, and founded on experience, and moral
> reasonings, is all that we can attain to in this life.[111]

The allusion was to the argument of Butler's *Analogy*. Perhaps this also indicates
another difference between Oxford and Cambridge – that conversions to Roman
Catholicism at Cambridge were relatively rare because of the absence of any
significant movement corresponding to Tractarianism, and thus it was not
necessary to adopt such a static view of the inspiration of scripture in order to
defend the Church of England. Both Hare and Sterling had also lived in Italy,
and were thus not tempted to follow the Roman path.

A more balanced account may be found in the pages of the dissenting *Eclectic
Review*. Its review of Sterling's *Essays and Tales*, together with his poems and
letters, was much more extensive, and observed that the 'mere episode' of his
half-year as a curate 'seems to have been exaggerated ... into the culminating and
glorious Act'.[112] After a careful discussion of his letters and poems in relation to
his religious and philosophical thought, the *Eclectic* took issue with only one thing
– Sterling's contrast of his own belief in the possibility of discerning Absolute
Truth with that of Locke; and in defence of 'Lockites' it complained that the
new school confounded belief and knowledge, 'and then, because we insist on
discriminating knowledge from belief, they most unjustly attack us as holding the
theory of materialists void of faith'.[113] But to find such men as Archdeacon Hare
among the dignitaries of the English Church was 'truly refreshing, and may well
make us exclaim – If all were such as he, how easy would cordial co-operation
be, in spite of diversity of opinion!'[114]

However, the *Eclectic* really went to town in exposing the shallowness of the
*English Review* in June 1849, when it reviewed the December 1848 article and
Hare's response. Beginning with the standard justification for establishment that
the Church of England was the church of the nation and the embodiment of
comprehensive charity, the reviewer believed that Hare better represented this
self-understanding than the *English Review*. Whereas 'the principles upheld by
the English Reviewers *avowedly forbid earnest search after the highest truth*, and

---

111 Ibid.: 269–71.

112 *Eclectic Review*, xli (February 1849): 229. There is no list of attributions for
articles in the *Eclectic*, but it has been suggested that this was written by Richard Monckton
Milnes (later Lord Houghton): I. Campbell and A. Chrisianson (eds), *The Collected Letters
of Thomas and Jane Welsh Carlyle* (Durham, North Carolina, 1995), xxiv, pp. 57–8.

113 *Eclectic Review*, xli: 235.

114 Ibid.

thereby stifle truthfulness of every kind' (because for them truth is accepted from without on the basis of authority), Hare's 'point of departure is fixed *within the soul*; in which he finds a direct discernment of what things are pure, lovely, and excellent, and a yearning after God as the fountain of all excellence'. So he 'often sympathises more deeply with those who stand outside the pale of the Church, or even of Christianity, than with many who stand within'.[115] Although Hare had perhaps overreacted to the criticism, the 'lamentable evidence of very low morality' in the *English Review* was set out systematically by listing over four pages its errors and misrepresentations of what Hare actually wrote. After two lengthy quotations from Hare about the *English Review*'s cribbed and cabined party spirit and its ignorance of German theology, the reviewer concluded that it was so long since 'the Evangelical School combated as men who knew and felt truth and God to be more sacred than the Church, that it is a refreshment to us to witness the fervid simplicity of the Archdeacon'; and he concluded that the younger clergy would need 'to decide between dead forms and a living spirit'.[116]

The *Eclectic*'s comment on the comprehensiveness of the Church of England, even though somewhat ironic, summed up what Hare always believed; and in this respect he also influenced F.D. Maurice (1805–72). Although Maurice returned to Cambridge eventually as Knightbridge Professor in 1866, his death six years later meant that he did not significantly influence Cambridge theology in that last period. Nevertheless the rejection of party spirit and strife was an abiding characteristic of Cambridge theology, and perhaps its most obvious difference from Oxford. It should not be confused, as so often, with an identification of both Hare and Maurice as 'broad church' in an overall party scheme of precisely the kind which they both abhorred.[117] Connop Thirlwall rejected the idea that 'broad church' described any group 'held together by a common set of theological tenets'. Rather it was 'a disposition to recognise and appreciate that which is true and good under all varieties of forms, and in persons separated from one another by the most conflicting opinions ... The proper antithesis to Broad is not High or Low but Narrow'.[118]

Maurice was one of Hare's favourite pupils, and the feeling was mutual. Maurice's testimony to the influence of Hare's teaching of Sophocles has already been mentioned. Although Hare never gave his own opinions, from his teaching Maurice discovered 'that the poem *had* a unity in it, and that the poet *was* pursuing an ideal, and that the unity was not created by him, but perceived by him, and that the ideal was not a phantom, but something which must have had a most

---

115  *Eclectic Review*, xli (June 1849): 660–61.

116  Ibid.: 669.

117  See, for example, C.R. Sanders, *Coleridge and the Broad Church Movement* (Durham, North Carolina, 1942), which is an excellent book but perpetuates this notion.

118  J.J.S. Perowne (ed.), *Remains Literary and Theological of Connop Thirlwall* (London, 1878), iii, p. 481. Thirlwall was commenting on an article by R.F. Littledale in the *Contemporary Review*, xxiv (July 1874): 287–320, in which he complained about the under-representation (as he saw it) of high churchmen in the hierarchy.

real effect upon himself, his age, and his country'.[119] Of Hare's lectures on Plato's
*Gorgias* Maurice said:

> They taught me that there is a way out of party opinions; a principle which is not a
> compromise between them, but which is implied in both, and of which each is bearing
> witness. Hare did not tell us this. If he had, he would have done us little good. Plato
> himself does not say it; he makes us feel it; and his interpreter was only useful as he
> led us to his author, and did not put himself between us and him. But Hare's mind was
> clearly penetrated with the conviction, – his after life ... must have been the acting out
> of it. If he had tried to form a party afterwards, we who were his pupils could not have
> become members of it till we forgot all that we had learnt from him.[120]

Thus Hare believed 'that every party triumph is an injury to the whole Church,
and an especial injury to the party which wins the triumph'.[121]

Nevertheless Maurice was not influenced theologically by Hare. As an
undergraduate he did not talk to him on theological subjects; and when they met
again, many years later, his own theological convictions had been formed by a
very different experience from Hare.[122] For example, Hare differed from Maurice
on subscription to the Articles and on baptism, both key issues for the latter.
Although Hare did not agree with Maurice's reasoning in *Subscription No Bondage*
(1835), he recommended him for the permanent chaplaincy at Guy's Hospital
because of the power of thought which it displayed.[123] Similarly Maurice told
Ludlow in December 1849 that he was 'poles away' from Hare on baptism: 'he
wishes to make every one comfortable in the Church; and I want no one to be
comfortable in it, so cross-grained am I.'[124] Although Hare's apologia against the
*English Review* in February 1849 contained a letter from Maurice to him as an
appendix, Maurice agreed with Hare's sister that they differed on the position of
the English Church: 'I am content to be strictly national; he has been nourished
on German food'.[125] In August 1849 Hort told John Ellerton a story about a
stranger who had travelled on a train with a clergyman who had recommended
him to read Maurice's *Kingdom of Christ*; the clergyman was Henry Manning,
and Hort commented that 'he sees, what so few do see, the tremendous chasm of
opinion on *Church* matters that separates Maurice from Hare'.[126]

In 1840 Hare suggested to Daniel Macmillan that Maurice was the person
best able to respond to those who expressed dissatisfaction with current theology,
a point he repeated two years later.[127] Maurice told Hare in August 1842 that he

---

119  Maurice, Introductory Notice to Hare, *Victory of Faith*, p. xxiii, cf. Maurice,
*Life of Maurice*, i, p. 53.
120  *Victory of Faith*, pp. xxvi–xxvii (this is not included in Maurice's biography).
121  Ibid., p. lxxxvii.
122  *Victory of Faith*, p. xxiv, cf. Maurice, *Life of Maurice*, i, p. 55.
123  Maurice, *Life of Maurice*, i, pp. 190–91.
124  Ibid., ii, p. 30.
125  Ibid., i, p. 509.
126  Hort, *Life of Hort*, i, p. 110.
127  Maurice, *Life of Maurice*, i, pp. 283, 288, 329.

would like to write on the 'principle of acknowledging the people ... as reasonable creatures, really desirous to know what is true, and as already having thoughts and feelings upon the subjects in which we are interested'.[128] In resisting Hare's suggestion in 1843 that Maurice be a candidate for Principal of King's, Maurice responded that his business was 'very much with the outlying sheep more than with those in the fold'.[129] This is comparable to what Sterling (who was Maurice's brother-in-law) had written about the needs of the masses, and helps to explain Maurice's later involvement with the Christian Socialist movement of 1848–54. Maurice suggested a series of Cambridge tracts on the subject to parallel the Oxford ones, but typically neither Hare nor Macmillan were enthusiastic, precisely because of the implied opposition to Oxford.[130]

Maurice was not concerned with questions about the inspiration of scripture: he wrote to Georgina Hare in March 1849 during the conflict with the *English Review* that 'I feel more and more the importance of the history, of the history in its simplest, most direct form'; and the only way to read the gospels simply and directly was to consider them as the 'revelation of Him upon earth who is the light that lighteneth us and all men, whether they walk in His sight or dwell in darkness'.[131] Maurice was, however, concerned with the political uses to which church and scriptural teaching were put. When he began *Politics for the People* in May 1848 – his most obvious written appeal to the sheep outside the fold – he asked Charles Kingsley to write an article about the right and wrong use of the Bible, by which he meant 'the notion of turning it into a book for keeping the poor in order'.[132] The result was Kingsley's second 'Letter to the Chartists', in which he confessed that parsons had not told people that the 'true reformer's Guide, the true poor man's book' was the Bible. Instead they had 'used the Bible as if it was a mere special constable's handbook – an opium-dose for keeping beasts of burden patient while they were being overloaded – a mere book to keep the poor in order'.[133] Maurice had first referred to this in a published letter to Samuel Wilberforce defending W.G. Ward at the time of the furore over him at Oxford, when he wrote 'nothing seems to be so important for the interpretation of Scripture and for the establishment of a sound theology as that the revelation of God, and not the notion of rewards and punishments, should be felt to be the end of the Divine dispensation'.[134] Ironically his defence of Ward probably

---

128  Ibid., i, p. 330.

129  Ibid., i, pp. 354, 355, 358.

130  Ibid., i, p. 368.

131  Ibid., i, p. 510.

132  Ibid., i, p. 463.

133  *Politics for the People*, 4 (27 May 1848): 58 (London, 1848; reprinted New York, 1971). Kingsley's pseudonym was 'Parson Lot'. There is no evidence to suggest that Kingsley had read Marx's *Communist Manifesto*, with its reference to 'the opium of the people' at this point.

134  'The New Statute and Mr Ward', *Two Letters to a Non-Resident Member of Convocation*, quoted in Maurice, *Life of Maurice*, i, p. 398.

secured him the Chair of Theology at King's in 1846, which he subsequently lost when he took the criticism of the idea of eternal punishment a stage further in *Theological Essays* in 1853. One of the main reasons he declined to resign (partly on Hare's advice) was that he denied that there was any theological error in what he had written. As he put it to his friend, J.M. Ludlow:

> I must bear what testimony I can for the right of English divines to preach the gospel of God's love to mankind, and to maintain that Lord Shaftesbury and the Bishop of London do not care more for the outcasts of the race than He does. If Humanity and Theology are not to be for ever apart, the regeneration of the working classes is not to be given up by Christians to infidels.[135]

Hare did not think that Maurice had 'fallen into error', and said that he did 'not believe that there is any other living man who has done anything at all approaching to what Maurice has effected, in reconciling the reason and conscience of the thoughtful men of our age to the faith of our Church'.[136]

From 1844 Hare and Maurice were linked by marriage, and when Hare died in 1855 Maurice wrote to Daniel Macmillan that his 'whole life for the last eighteen years had been closely bound up with his'.[137] He wrote a Memoir of Hare to accompany the edition of his collected Charges in 1856, but his truest testimony came in a letter to Kingsley in February 1855: 'The clergy in the Archdeaconry, from the highest Tractarian down to the strongest Evangelical, are now expressing their affection for him, and their belief that he did them a good which they could have got nowhere else. So that life has come out of death, after all.'[138]

---

135  Ibid., ii, p. 176.
136  Ibid., ii, p. 184.
137  Ibid., ii, p. 255.
138  Ibid., ii, p. 256.

# Chapter 5

# Theological Reconstruction: Historical Criticism

He exercised from the first a very powerful influence on me, by the magnetism of the good greatness of his personality and the true-hearted kindness which looked always through his reserve. All through those years he was laying the deep foundations of his vast theological knowledge, chiefly in the vacations, and (during term-time) by night. No man ever loitered so late in the Great Court that he did not see Lightfoot's lamp burning in his study window; though no man either was so regularly present in morning Chapel at seven o'clock that he did not find Lightfoot always there with him. But to us he was not the divine, but the tutor whom we consulted about our questions and troubles, and our admirable lecturer in Herodotus, Euripides, and Aeschylus.[1]

Handley Moule was writing about Lightfoot, as he remembered calling on him, desperately shy, in June 1860 in the rooms which had been Isaac Newton's nearly two centuries before. Westcott likewise had a magnetic hold over his pupils – though it was not universal. When Herbert Ryle (1856–1925) was elected Hulsean Professor, he called on Westcott to ask for advice: 'Westcott was strangely uncommunicative, and no advice was forthcoming – until, just as he was leaving, there came the bewildering words: "Never tell the undergraduates anything".'[2] Hort was not popular as a lecturer with undergraduates, but, according to Armitage Robinson, 'probably no Professor in any subject lectured to so many Bachelors and Masters of Arts. He taught the teachers'.[3]

This was the new generation to whom the torch of Cambridge scholarship had passed by the time Hare died in 1855. Brooke Foss Westcott (1825–1901) was the guiding light. He was Regius Professor of Divinity, 1870–90, and Bishop of Durham, 1890–1901. More than anyone else, Westcott shaped the way in which theology was studied at Cambridge for a century after 1871. The changes made in the Tripos in the early 1970s began a new emphasis; but only with the most recent revision in 1999 was Westcott's pattern finally abandoned.

Westcott was born on 12 January 1825 in Birmingham; his father was a Lecturer in Botany and Vegetable Physiology at Sydenham College Medical School, Birmingham, and his mother was the daughter of a Birmingham

---

1    H.C.G. Moule, *My Cambridge Classical Teachers* (Durham, n.d. [1913]), pp. 13–14.

2    H. Chadwick, *The Vindication of Christianity in Westcott's Thought* (Cambridge, 1961), p. 6.

3    J.A. Robinson, 'The Late Professor Hort', *The Expositor*, 4th series, vii (1893): 70.

manufacturer. His background was thus essentially middle class. He went to King Edward's School, Birmingham, where he was taught by Dr James Prince Lee, later the first Bishop of Manchester. As a boy he went to Chartist meetings to hear Feargus O'Connor, and this was the beginning of his lifelong hatred of injustice. His son wrote that 'he even later disapproved of his father's fishing excursions, because his sympathies were so entirely on the side of the fish'.[4]

From King Edward's, Westcott went up to Trinity College, Cambridge, in 1844. After winning various University medals and prizes, he graduated in 1848; he was elected to a Fellowship at Trinity in 1849, and was ordained in 1851. In January 1852 he moved to Harrow, where he remained as a Master until 1869, when he became a Canon of Peterborough Cathedral. He was elected Regius Professor of Divinity at Cambridge on 1 November 1870, and consecrated as Bishop of Durham on 1 May 1890.

In 1897 Westcott published a collection of his sermons and addresses as Bishop of Durham, under the title *Christian Aspects of Life*. It was dedicated to 'the most dear memory of Joseph Barber Lightfoot, Lord Bishop of Durham, Fenton John Anthony Hort, Lady Margaret's Professor of Divinity at Cambridge, and Edward White Benson, Lord Archbishop of Canterbury, whose friendship has been inspiration and strength throughout my life'. Here is the Cambridge quartet, or two overlapping trios. Although it is usual to regard the Cambridge trio as Westcott, Lightfoot and Hort, there is a sense (and perhaps more than one) in which Benson was the third and Hort was the outsider.[5]

Joseph Barber Lightfoot (1828–89) was born in Liverpool. His father was an accountant from Yorkshire and his mother was from Birmingham, the daughter of Joseph Barber, a landscape artist. Lightfoot was, in Hort's words, 'a sickly child', who was educated by tutors at home until he was thirteen.[6] After some two years at the Liverpool Royal Institution his father died in 1843. The family moved to Birmingham and Lightfoot went to King Edward's School. There he became one of a brilliant group of pupils under Prince Lee. Westcott left King Edward's for Cambridge just before Lightfoot arrived; but Edward White Benson (1829–96), later Archbishop of Canterbury, was a year younger than Lightfoot and they rapidly became firm friends. Both lived a little way out of Birmingham and arranged to meet each day where their two roads converged, so that they could walk to school together.[7]

When Lightfoot went up to Trinity College, Cambridge in 1847, he corresponded regularly with Benson. Towards the end of his second term he told Benson that the object of his greatest admiration was Westcott, and that he was more inclined to become a curate than a schoolmaster. 'It is surprising,' he wrote,

---

4     A. Westcott, *Life and Letters of Brooke Foss Westcott* (London, 1903), i, p. 7.

5     See D.M. Thompson, 'Lightfoot as Victorian Churchman' in J.D.G. Dunn (ed.), 'The Lightfoot Centenary Lectures', *Durham University Journal* (special issue January 1992): 5–11. The same point is made by P. Hinchliff, *God and History: Aspects of British Theology, 1875–1914* (Oxford, 1992), pp. 75–6.

6     *DNB*, xxxiii, p. 232.

7     A.C. Benson, *The Life of Edward White Benson* (London, 1900), i, pp. 27–8.

'how anyone who has health and opportunities can make up his mind to live in ease and idleness on a Fellowship: but,' he added shrewdly, 'it is very easy to talk coolly and dispassionately on such matters when there are no temptations in the way.'[8] Temptations soon fell in Lightfoot's way. At the end of his first year he became a pupil of Westcott and read classics with him. He was top of the Classical Tripos in 1851 winning the first of the two Chancellor's Classical Medals, and he was also thirtieth wrangler. He was elected to a Fellowship at Trinity in 1852, and in 1857, before he was twenty-nine, he became one of the three tutors of the college. In 1861 he was elected Hulsean Professor of Divinity, and in 1875 Lady Margaret's Professor. He became Bishop of Durham in 1879. So the curacy he looked forward to in 1848 never materialised.

How then was Fenton Hort (1828–94) different? One obvious point was his Irish background. His family had lived in Ireland for several generations, even though his great-grandfather Josiah Hort who finished his career as Archbishop of Tuam had in his early years been a dissenter, educated at the same academy as Isaac Watts. His father moved from Dublin to Cheltenham in 1837, and Hort was brought up in a strong evangelical atmosphere.[9] When he went to Rugby in 1841 he was exposed to a different influence, and he wrote in 1865 that in theology 'what I am chiefly is … what Rugby and Arnold made me'.[10] Only when he went up to Trinity College, Cambridge, in 1846 did his path start to run along the same lines as Westcott and Lightfoot; and even then, slowly. Westcott seems to have become his classical tutor in 1850 but Lightfoot is not mentioned in any close sense until 1856, as much because of their common interest in climbing as their cooperation as editors of the *Journal of Classical and Sacred Philology*.[11] After his marriage in 1857 Hort spent fifteen years as vicar of St Ippolyts, near Hitchin, finding some time to help out the infant Girton College in its Hitchin days, before returning to Emmanuel in 1872. Hort was elected Hulsean Professor in 1878 and Lady Margaret's Professor in 1887. He was one of the prime movers behind the establishment of the Dixie Chair of Ecclesiastical History in 1884. Once back in Cambridge he was busy with University committees as well as his lectures – the busyness of a man who never enjoyed completely good health. Perhaps his premature death in 1892 at the age of 64 is not surprising.

Westcott was thus the link between Lightfoot, Benson and Hort as the teacher of all three at Trinity. Westcott and Hort later worked together on the text of the New Testament. Lightfoot sought to involve Westcott and Hort in various schemes for writing on wider theological questions. Westcott, Benson and Lightfoot had holidays together and corresponded on matters concerning the church. By the mid-1850s only Lightfoot was still at Cambridge: Westcott and Benson both married and became schoolmasters – Benson at Rugby and

---

8     Lightfoot to Benson, 8 March 1848: ibid., i, p. 56.

9     A.F. Hort, *Life and Letters of Fenton John Anthony Hort*, i, pp. 1–10.

10     Hort to a friend, 4 November 1865: ibid., ii, 63, cf. Hort to Tait, 12 November 1869, i, pp. 116–17.

11     Hort to Ellerton, 2/7 January 1856; Hort to Blunt, 20 March 1856: ibid., i, pp. 317, 322–3.

Wellington College, and Westcott at Harrow – and Hort also married and became a country clergyman. Lightfoot secured Westcott's election as Regius Professor in 1870 by refusing to stand himself. In 1875, when the Hulsean chair became vacant, by Lightfoot's election as Lady Margaret's Professor, Lightfoot and Westcott both urged Benson to stand. Hort told him he would probably have a majority of the votes, and promised not to stand if Benson did. But Benson decided to stay at Lincoln Cathedral, and not to succumb to the temptations of combining University and cathedral work.[12] By the time Hort was elected to the Hulsean chair in 1878, Benson was Bishop of Truro. The trios had ceased to overlap; scholarship and the church were separating. But not for long. Lightfoot became Bishop of Durham in 1879. Benson's correspondence as Archbishop of Canterbury from 1882 shows the extent to which he still consulted Westcott and Lightfoot; and Westcott became Bishop of Durham in 1890 as a result of pressure from Benson and the Queen upon the Prime Minister, Lord Salisbury. Hort alone remained the academic. Gordon Rupp described him as 'the embodiment of that unfashionable ideal, the Man of Learning'.[13] Hort's portrait in the Lightfoot Room of the old Divinity School, which was directly opposite the Chairman of the Faculty Board as he or she presided over meetings, showed a twinkle in the eye – perhaps almost the memory of so much time spent in committee work – that was much more encouraging than Lightfoot's sideways glance out of his good eye on one's left side. Herbert Ryle spoke of 'the bright glee of [Hort's] merriment', and this certainly comes through in his letters.[14]

The correspondence between Lightfoot, Westcott, Benson, and to a lesser extent, Hort, reveals a shared vision of an Anglican response to contemporary theological scepticism, which required an institutional expression, but which was clearly distinct from that of Evangelicals and Tractarians. Westcott was the guiding light behind that vision, and an understanding of that makes it possible to see the wholeness of Westcott's thought. Westcott, unlike Hort, made no reference to Hare in his diaries, letters or books, though he did refer to Maurice, Arnold and Stanley, and he shared Hare's antipathy to church parties. Lightfoot, on the other hand, acted as the collector in Cambridge for the Hare Memorial Committee, which in 1861 established a Hare Prize for a dissertation in Ancient Greek or Roman political or literary history or the history of Greek or Roman philosophy.[15]

Westcott saw clearly the need to provide an appropriate defence of Christianity. In 1846 he noted with approval Maurice's comment that 'the danger of our

12    Benson to G. Cubitt, 15 June 1875: Copies of Correspondence 1873–77, Benson Papers, Trinity College, Cambridge.

13    G. Rupp, 'Hort and the Cambridge Tradition' in *Just Men* (London, 1977), pp. 164–5.

14    Hort, *Life of Hort*, ii, p. 380.

15    G.R. Treloar, *Lightfoot the Historian* (Tübingen, 1998), p. 57; J.W. Clark, *Endowments of the University of Cambridge* (Cambridge, 1904), pp. 401–2: the terms of the Prize, now governed by Statute E, V, have since been extended to include law and geography.

Church is from atheism, not Romanism' as something he had often affirmed.[16] His familiarity with natural science, and particularly biology, made him aware of the centrality of the question of science in defending religion. That in turn led both to his defence of miracle, and to his organic approach to human development. His belief, derived from Thomas Arnold, that 'the true revelation of the Bible is original righteousness and not original sin', profoundly affected his view of the human condition – again similar to Maurice.[17] Hence the church had to model that new way of living, and this explains his view of both the universities and the cathedrals, and ultimately his Christian socialism.

Westcott's teacher, Prince Lee, had been significantly influenced by Arnold, and it is not surprising, therefore, that Westcott should have imbibed Arnold's influence at one remove. When he went up to Cambridge Tractarianism was reaching its final breaking point. Part of his staple devotional reading was Keble's *Christian Year*, about which he once wrote 'I owe more to that book almost than to any other'.[18] He constantly returned to it for comfort and reassurance.[19] Among his closest friends at Trinity were C.B. Scott (who was placed first equal with him in the Classical Tripos), J. Llewellyn Davies and David Vaughan. The latter two were keen disciples of Maurice, and the four were frequently engaged in theological conversation. Although Westcott never mentioned Hare by name, there were several occasions when he and his friends discussed themes which were closely related to Hare's later writing. On one occasion at tea with Vaughan they talked about 'the present temper of religious things, the character of Luther, and the modern Pantheisms'.[20] That almost reflected some of the themes of Hare's *Mission of the Comforter*, but the date of the preface to the first edition (2 June 1846) makes that impossible. A month or so later he was discussing faith and reason with Vaughan and Scott, where he disagreed with their view that faith was part of reason; in suggesting that the will was distinct from reason, he was drawing a distinction to be found in Hare's *Victory of Faith*.[21] In December 1846 he wrote:

> We are apt here to encourage the idea that promotion and dignity are the chief objects to be sought after. May I ever be reminded that the object of our life is not personal aggrandisement, but the good of one's neighbour, and that all the advantages of education are talents to be employed in this glorious work.[22]

This was almost an echo of Hare's sermon on 'The Conviction of Righteousness'.

---

16  Diary 8 May 1846: Westcott, *Life of Westcott*, i, p. 43. 'The question of our day … is really between God and Atheism, much more than between Protestantism and Romanism': F.D. Maurice, in Westcott, *The Epistle to the Hebrews* (London, 1846), Preface, p. xliv.

17  Diary, 28 November 1848: Westcott, *Life of Westcott*, i, p. 109.

18  Diary, 30 January 1846: ibid., i, p. 41.

19  Westcott to Mary Whittard, 1 February 1846: ibid., i, p. 60.

20  Diary, 18 April 1846: ibid., i, p. 43.

21  Diary, 23 May 1846: ibid., i, p. 43.

22  Diary, 2 December 1846: ibid., i, p. 45.

In the arguments of November–December 1847 about the nomination of R.D. Hampden as Bishop of Hereford, Westcott was very much exercised, because in reading extracts from Hampden's works in *The Times*, which some condemned, he 'found the development of the very system I have been endeavouring to frame for myself'.[23] He wrote to his future wife, 'I believe he holds the truth; if *he* be condemned, *I* cannot see how I shall ever enter the Church'.[24] The Hampden case led him to lament the dangers of church controversy. He also concluded that 'the battle of the Inspiration of Scripture has yet to be fought', and he prayed that he 'might aid the truth in that'.[25]

In March 1848 he read Coleridge's *Confessions*, which he thought 'exceedingly sensible, sometimes eloquent; though they do not nearly enter into many of the real difficulties', because 'he believes antecedently too much for an investigator'.[26] A year later he used Coleridgean language to express himself: 'Wild as my doubts are, I cannot but feel that the N.T. "finds" me; and that with its deepest mysteries – but as *mysteries*, not as *dogmas*.'[27] So he was not surprised by the 'fiery trial of scepticism', and it would be more worrying if doubt were absent. He was delighted to discover in January 1848 that when he took his BA, he did not have to subscribe to the Thirty-Nine Articles, but simply to declare that he was a member of the Church of England, which he felt he could do in good conscience: 'that I am, I fully believe, in all her ancient spirit.'[28] Mary had apparently misunderstood the nature of his objection to the Articles, because not long after his words about doubt being unsurprising he wrote to her, saying

> You quite misunderstand my scruples about Articles; it is that I object to them *altogether*, and not to any particular doctrines: I have at times fancied that it is presumptious in us to attempt to define, and to determine what Scripture has not defined; to limit when Scripture has placed no boundary; to exact what the Apostles did not require; to preach explicitly what they applied practically. The whole tenor of Scripture seems to me opposed to all dogmatism, and full of all application; to furnish us with rules of life, and not food for reason.

Although it might be necessary to prescribe some limits to reasoning, he wished that 'men would pay more attention to acting and less to dogmatising'.[29] This emphasis was a constant throughout Westcott's life, and perhaps more than anything else marked the profound difference from the characteristic Oxford temper of the time.

He was concerned about the gulf between rich and poor, but had no more faith in schemes for social reconstruction than Maurice. In 1849 he wrote to Mary

---

23   Diary, 25 November 1847: ibid., i, p. 52.
24   Letter to Mary Whittard, Advent Sunday (28 November) 1847: ibid., i, p. 94.
25   Ibid., i, p. 95.
26   Diary, 13 March 1848, ibid., i, p. 54.
27   Diary, 20 May 1849, ibid., i, p. 112.
28   Letter to Mary Whittard, 6 January 1848: ibid., i, p. 99.
29   Letter to Mary Whittard, 12 August 1849, ibid., i, pp. 160–61.

I don't believe we can ever much improve, but at any rate let us not deceive ourselves; let us remember that we have to live, if all around us are sleeping; and let us, moreover, remember, which too many of those who teach this doctrine forget, Carlyle among them, that the New Testament will help us to live so, and nothing else. We cannot be 'heroes' unless God's Spirit works with us.[30]

The text of his first sermon was Romans 12:1, 'I beseech you therefore, brethren, by the mercies of God, that ye present your bodies a living sacrifice to God, which is your reasonable service'.[31]

In 1849 the topic for the Norrisian Prize the following year was announced as, 'The plenary inspiration of the four Gospels is not invalidated by the alleged discrepancies which are objected against them', and this was Westcott's opportunity to 'aid the truth in the battle for the inspiration of Scripture'. His essay, submitted on 14 March 1850, was awarded the prize; and it was published in 1851 with the title *The Elements of the Gospel Harmony*. A revised and expanded version was published in 1860, entitled *An Introduction to the Study of the Gospels*, which went through several further editions.[32] The Introduction (on Inspiration) and first three chapters of the first edition had been rewritten, and the notes and appendices were new. The context for his discussion was clearly the Hampden controversy, Coleridge's *Confessions*, and German criticism more generally – though nowhere was there any reference to Hare or Thirlwall, apart possibly from one indirect reference to the latter. What is more striking in any comparison of *The Elements* and *An Introduction* is the extent to which the later work is a toned-down version of the former. The later version was also longer – 406 pages, without appendices, compared with 146.[33]

Westcott's discussion of inspiration began with the philosophical background. The first edition mentioned names in a way in which subsequent editions did not: 'If, on the one side, we have advanced from Hobbes to Hegel, on the other we have passed from Toland to Strauss. Religion and metaphysics are not contemplated from within and not from without, the world has been absorbed in man.'[34] He explained the last point in later editions by adding, 'In spite of partial reactions the idea of the Society, whether in the State or in the Church, has yielded to that of the Individual'; but also added a footnote in 1871 saying that there were signs of a reaction against this.[35] Then he continued with a highly rhetorical passage:

---

30    Letter to Mary Whittard, 22 May 1849: ibid., i, pp. 157. Westcott's scepticism about Carlyle had been expressed eighteen months earlier at the time of the Hampden crisis, when he had written, 'We must soon fall back on a mere moral atheism, or what is still as bad, a "hero-worship"': letter to Mary Whittard 28 November 1847: ibid., i, p. 95.

31    Ibid., i, p. 167.

32    Ibid., i, p. 114.

33    A description of the rearrangement is given in Westcott's letter to Macmillan of 19 July 1855: ibid., i, pp. 231–2.

34    B.F. Westcott, *Elements of the Gospel Harmony* (Cambridge, 1851), p. 3.

35    B.F. Westcott, *An Introduction to the Study of the Gospels* (5th edn, London, 1875), p. 3. He may have felt this as a result of reading Comte, on which see more in Chapter 6.

The opponents of Christian doctrine in the 17th and 18th centuries were generally men of reckless and abandoned impiety, while now they claim its blessings without a Church, affect its morality without a covenant, assume the name of Christ without acknowledging a personal Saviour, and regard Christianity itself as a necessary truth independent of any Gospel-histories, and unsupported by any true redemption. They have abandoned the 'letter' to secure the 'spirit', and, in return for the mysteries of our faith, they offer us a law without types, a theocracy without prophecies, a Christianity without miracles: – a cluster of definite wants with no reality to supply them; for the 'mythic' theory, as if in bitter irony, concedes every craving which the Gospel satisfies, and only accounts for the wide spread of the 'delusion' by the intensity of man's need.[36]

In 1860 the specific historical reference was removed; 'mythic' became 'mythic and critical' without inverted commas, 'delusion' became 'orthodox error', again losing its inverted commas.[37] The original target was clearly Strauss; later it was more generalised. In the second edition Westcott inserted a new section after this suggesting that views of inspiration changed at the end of the first period of the Reformation, as a result of which the followers of the Reformers 'invested the Bible as a whole with all the attributes of mechanical infallibility which the Romanists had claimed for the Church'.[38] But in both versions he emphasised what he called a 'dynamical' understanding of inspiration.[39] In the *Introduction* he used this idea to imply development. 'The divine teaching, though one, is not uniform. Truth is indeed immutable, but humanity is progressive; and thus the form in which truth is presented must be examined in relation to the age in which the revelation was made.'[40] Hence there was an inevitable human element in the expression of truth.

Westcott then applied this argument to the gospels. 'The history of Jesus for the Christian is concrete doctrine, as doctrine is abstract history.' The Christian needed to find in the story of Jesus 'a perfect pattern for his own guidance, and the realization of the Apostolic teaching'; but he also needed 'to feel that the Evangelists felt truly the inner meaning of the events they record, and truly told their outward details'.[41] This represented a strong commitment to historical accuracy. Yet the fundamental error of heathen philosophers lay in seeking 'a system of absolute truth, independent of the specific laws of human life'. 'They had no gospel for the simple and poor, for the mechanic or the slave.' 'In the pursuit of wisdom they disparaged [their] common duties, and deferred the business of social life and the explanation of the popular faith till they should have resolved the riddle of self-knowledge.' This was a reference to Plato's *Gorgias* and *Phaedrus*. 'Christ, on the contrary, finally uniting in one person God and man, fixt the idea

---

36   Westcott, *Elements*, pp. 3–4.
37   Westcott, *Introduction*, pp. 3–4.
38   Westcott, *Introduction*, p. 5.
39   Westcott, *Elements*, p. 8; *Introduction*, p. 14.
40   Westcott, *Introduction*, p. 16.
41   Westcott, *Elements*, p. 10; cf. *Introduction*, p. 17.

of spiritual life in the harmonious combination of faith and works, and left his disciples in the world, though not of it.'[42]

Throughout Westcott was aiming at a view of inspiration which was based on more than an individual argument. 'It is in the perfection and oneness of their "social" teaching, so to speak, that the strongest internal proof of the plenary Inspiration of the Gospels is to be found.'[43] Thus in developing his argument about the working of Providence, which he regarded as more properly a social than an individual doctrine, he intriguingly cited statistics as modern confirmation that 'we are taught to recognise the working of providence, not only in the outer world of nature, but also in the inner world of action; as the control of the general result is reconciled with individual freedom'.[44] And he was prepared to argue that such an understanding of the working of providence was no more problematic than seeing how the feuds of party could be part of the divine scheme for the government of the world, or how the convulsions of the earth, which had covered it with scars and ruins, could be needed to 'fashion the fair diversity of woods and waters'.[45] This is a good illustration of Westcott's perennial optimism and his readiness to use the discoveries of science positively. The same material is often cited by modern sceptics as decisive proof of the non-existence or the non-necessity of God.

Confident in the social basis of inspiration, Westcott was therefore able to relativise other problems. 'The common objections urged against any doctrine of a plenary Inspiration of the Scriptures, which are drawn from an uncertain canon, an unsettled text, and a doubtful interpretation, need cause us but little anxiety. Their whole force depends on a misconception of the relation of an inspired Bible to the Church and the individual.'[46] Such objections could be dealt with by the ordinary rules of scholarship.

> The Church, indeed, must avail itself of the ordinary laws of criticism, when it has fixed by its own power the principles on which the canon must be formed; the Christian must follow the common rules of language when he has been awakened to the true meaning of Scripture; yet both have also the promise of God's Spirit to aid them in their work.[47]

Westcott's confidence in what could be achieved by minute verbal scholarship seemed to be almost unbounded.

Westcott next turned to writing a history of the canon, which was published in 1855 and dedicated to Prince Lee. Essentially this was written to combat the

---

42   Westcott, *Elements*, p. 11; cf. *Introduction*, p. 18. The sentence about the simple and poor is only found in the *Introduction*, and 'their' was omitted in the later edition. It is interesting that Westcott used Hare's spelling of 'fixt' in the *Elements*, but not the *Introduction*; he did this is one or two other places as well, but without any reference to Hare.

43   Westcott, *Elements*, p. 15; cf. *Introduction*, p. 25. The inverted commas around 'social' are removed in the later edition.

44   Westcott, *Elements*, p. 19; cf. *Introduction*, p. 28.

45   Westcott, *Introduction*, pp. 31–2.

46   Westcott, *Elements*, p. 21. There is no direct parallel to this in the *Introduction*.

47   Ibid., p. 22.

arguments of the Tübingen School about the origins of the New Testament. The Tübingen scholars, epitomised by F.C. Baur (1792–1860) and his pupils, A. Schwegler (1819–57) and E. Zeller (1814–1908), argued that the existing New Testament books reflected the early conflict between Jewish and Gentile forms of Christianity, a conflict which was only resolved by the end of the second century and which later writing, particularly that of the letters of Ignatius (which were regarded as forgeries) had attempted to conceal. Westcott acknowledged the merits of the Tübingen scholars in drawing attention to the distinctive characteristics of the New Testament writings, but argued, rather as he had in *The Elements of the Gospel Harmony*, that diversity was evidence of authenticity. In fact, the significance of his book lay not only in the treatment of that particular controversy, but also in the provision of a more complete survey of the history of the canon than had anything written hitherto. He also drew attention to the need for better editions of the Apostolic Fathers than were then available; and this was the substance of Lightfoot's later work.

The essence of Westcott's argument appeared in the Introduction, the subtext of which was a saying of Bishop Butler, 'The truth of our Religion, like the truth of common matters, is to be judged by all the evidence taken together'.[48] For Westcott the Bible could no longer be regarded as 'an acknowledged exception to the rules of literary criticism'. But the recognition of the relationship of the various books to the particular circumstances of their origins had enabled them to be seen as 'organically united with the lives of the Apostles'; thus 'they are felt to be a *product* as well as a *source* of spiritual life'.[49] The history of the formation of the canon was the story of the building of the Catholic Church. Such a task required an awareness of context, and particularly of the difference between the characteristics of an earlier age and our own. Thus 'any one whose ideas of communication are suggested by the railway and the printing-press' needed to realise how difficult it was for the early Christian churches to communicate with one another. Copying of manuscripts was expensive and the fall of Jerusalem destroyed the natural meeting point for Christians. It was not therefore surprising that the churches growing up around separate centres should enjoy 'the freedom of individual development'. Yet Westcott concluded confidently that 'the common Creed is not a compromise of principles, but a combination of the essential types of Christian truth which were preserved in different Churches'.[50] From the end of the second century the history of the canon was simple; the crucial period was the time before then. The limitations of evidence meant that there was room for the suggestion of plausible but false hypotheses: the strength of negative criticism lay 'in ignoring the existence of a Christian society from the Apostolic age, strong in discipline, clear in faith, and jealous of innovation'. Hence 'the written Rule of Christendom must rest finally on the general confession of the Church, and not on the independent opinion of its members'.[51] After an exhaustive consideration

---

48    B.F. Westcott, *A General Survey of the History of the Canon of the New Testament* (6th edn, Cambridge, 1889), p. 1.

49    Ibid., p. 2.

50    Ibid., pp. 3–4.

51    Ibid., p. 12.

of all the canonical and apocryphal texts in existence, Westcott continued the story
to the Reformation, concluding that:

> [the] whole history is itself a striking lesson in the character and conduct of the
> Providential government of the Church. The recognition of the Apostolic writings
> as authoritative and complete was partial and progressive, like the formalizing of
> doctrine, and the settling of ecclesiastical order. But each successive step was virtually
> implied in that which preceded; and the principle by which they were all directed was
> acknowledged from the first.[52]

It was therefore impossible to identify any period as marking the date when the
canon was determined. 'When it first appears, it is presented not as a novelty but
as an ancient tradition.'[53]

Westcott's third book, *Characteristics of the Gospel Miracles*, contained
University sermons preached at Cambridge in Epiphany 1859. Ironically, this was
a year before *Essays and Reviews* brought the whole question of biblical criticism
back into the public mind. But Westcott said in his Preface that there was now
less need than ten years earlier 'to insist on the divine authority of the Gospels as
a complete record of the work of the Saviour'. The intervening period had been
fruitful for biblical criticism, and 'in fostering this study Cambridge has taken a
foremost place' – probably a reference to the presence and work of Lightfoot.[54]
He reiterated his conviction

> that a study of the sacred texts which rests on the laws of the most rigorous scholarship,
> and is carried out with the most candid appreciation of the various elements combined
> in the Apostolic age, will lead to the only convincing answer to the objections against
> the essential doctrines of Christianity, which are at present most current.[55]

'The miracles,' said Westcott, 'are all faint reflections of the glory of the
Incarnation ... In this sense the miracles are themselves an Epiphany.'[56] The
commentaries he quoted in these sermons were mainly those of the Fathers,
though there were references to Dean Trench and to Strauss. Westcott recognised
that 'we *cannot* view miracles as the first Christians viewed them, for we live in
another world'. But in the midst of progress, the moral significance of the Gospel
miracles remained unaltered'; and the message of hope was that we should be
raised 'from a blind idolatry of physical laws' to a sense of a 'nobler Presence' or
'higher Power'. God's creative energy was not exhausted: 'we are not bound up
in a system which is eternal and unchangeable'.[57] This was a strike against a kind
of scientific determinism; but it also explains why some thought that Westcott
took refuge in a form of mysticism.

---

52    Ibid., p. 500.
53    Ibid., p. 501.
54    B.F. Westcott, *Characteristics of the Gospel Miracles* (Cambridge, 1859), p. x.
55    Ibid., pp. x–xi.
56    Ibid., p. 3.
57    Ibid., pp. 30–31.

Lightfoot's contribution to historical criticism also began with a Norrisian Prize Essay. It was seen most substantially in his Commentaries, and at a more popular level in his attack on *Supernatural Religion*, where he defended Westcott. The successful Norrisian Essay for 1853 was for many years thought to be lost. But in the 1980s Geoffrey Treloar identified an undated manuscript in the Lightfoot Papers in the Dean and Chapter Library of Durham Cathedral as almost certainly the draft of the Essay.[58] Since it was never published, absolute certainty is impossible, but there seems to be no reasonable doubt.

The subject set was 'The Gospels could not have originated in any or all those forms of religious opinion which prevailed among the Jews at the time of our Saviour's incarnation'; and Lightfoot saw this as derived from Strauss's argument in his *Life of Jesus* that the gospels contain stories about Jesus arising from the consciousness of their authors.[59] He began with a stanza from Tennyson's *In Memoriam*:

Let knowledge grow from more to more,
  But more of reverence in us dwell,
  That mind and soul, according well,
May make one music as before,
But vaster.[60]

Lightfoot proposed that 'the study of past history should come to the rescue of a wavering faith' – which might almost be a motto for his career. Like Westcott, he distinguished between the attacks of the eighteenth century, which he regarded as an irreligious age, prepared to scoff as much at scientific discoveries as at religious truth, and those of the modern period. Now, although the historical basis of Christianity was attacked, the pre-eminence of its moral code was conceded, and the main case depended on the scientific spirit of the age. Thus the old objection to miracles was replaced by a more general argument that the supernatural was contrary to the conclusions of modern science, and two alternatives were proposed: the rationalist, which removed the supernatural elements from the gospel narrative, and the 'mythical theorist', who 'was disposed to find in the biblical records merely a collection of legends, the spontaneous product of national feelings and expectations'.[61] However, it was crucial to the latter group to demonstrate that the documents did not come from eye-witnesses, which was why the authority of the apostolic writings was attacked. 'The mythical interpreter is controlled by regard to conformity with the spirit and modes of the people and age.'[62] Lightfoot did not discuss the difficulties surrounding the growth of such

---

58    G.B. Treloar and B.N. Kaye, 'J.B. Lightfoot On Strauss and Christian Origins: An Unpublished Manuscript', *Durham University Journal*, lxxix, 2 (June 1987): 165–200.

59    Ibid., 165–6. The reference is assumed to be from D.F. Strauss, *The Life of Jesus Critically Examined*, ed. P.C. Hodgson (London, 1973), pp. 86–7.

60    A. Tennyson, *In Memoriam A.H.H.*, Prologue, stanzas 7–8, in A. Tennyson, *Poetical Works* (Oxford 1953), p. 230.

61    Treloar and Kaye, 'Lightfoot on Strauss and Christian Origins', p. 176.

62    Ibid., pp. 176–7, quoting Strauss, *Life of Jesus*, §12.

myths; instead he proposed only 'to show how inadequate is the cause assigned – the state of national feeling and belief – for the formation of the collection of facts and doctrines presented to us in the Gospels'.[63]

In essence Lightfoot's argument was that a close examination of the first-century Palestinian context, with particular attention to the Jews of Palestine (the Sadducees, Pharisees and Essenes) and the Dispersion (Philo and the Jews of Alexandria) made this hypothesis extremely unlikely. None of the contemporary expectations of the Messiah corresponded with what was found in the gospels. In discussing early Christianity, with particular attention to the 'Judaizing Christians' he acknowledged Baur's point about the conflicts in the early church. He also referred to the differences between the synoptic gospels and John, opting for the argument that the Synoptists provided the facts, while John provided the ideas – but both were complementary. Indeed if the gospels were written for catechetical instruction, he suggested, 'we can understand why their authors should have been led to record facts rather than ideas, history rather than doctrine'.[64]

Lightfoot's conclusion was that, in the light of all the evidence, it was most improbable that the gospel stories could have been simply invented:

> It has been asked – and no adequate reply has yet been given – how it is that these writers, who had such a mighty influence in moulding the thought of after ages, who have left a deeper and a more lasting impress on society, than Plato or Zoroaster, should have chosen the strange – not to say dishonest – means of palming off their writings under feigned names; that doing so they should never for a moment have been suspected, but have obtained an immediate circulation for their falsehoods – above all that they should not have left behind them the faintest traces of their existence, though they were as immeasurably in advance of the genius of their age; such are some of the most obvious results of the difficulties which beset the results of the 'new criticism', irrespectively of the weakness of their proofs and positive arguments on the opposite side – so great are the demands which it makes upon our credulity.[65]

Clearly Lightfoot's position was not simply defensive. In unpublished lecture notes for the Lent Term 1855 he stated:

> the timidity, which shrinks from the application of modern science or criticism to the interpretation of the Holy Scriptures evinces a very unworthy view of its character ... It is against the wrong application of such principles ... that we must protest ... From the full light of science and criticism we have nothing to fear.[66]

---

63    Ibid., p. 176.

64    Ibid., p. 196.

65    Ibid., p. 200.

66    J.B. Lightfoot, 'Greek New Testament Lectures, Lent Term 1855' in Kaye and Treloar, 'J.B. Lightfoot and New Testament Interpretation: An Unpublished Manuscript of 1855': 174; quoted by M. Hengel, 'Bishop Lightfoot and the Tübingen School on the Gospel of John and the Second Century', and J.D.G. Dunn, 'Lightfoot in Retrospect', Lightfoot Centenary Lectures, *Durham University Journal* (January 1992): 39–40 and 72.

And he quoted again the stanza from *In Memoriam* that he had used in the Norrisian Essay. He developed a similar argument, with special reference to Paul's epistles, in his University Sermons as Select Preacher in May 1858. A contextual approach to the Pauline letters enabled readers to appreciate 'the demands of natural reason and the claims of inspiration', as well as showing that they were the product of genuine religious experience. Thus 'philology broadly conceived actually served religious interests'.[67]

A second area in which reconstruction was necessary related to the text of the New Testament. Here the main contributors were Westcott and Hort. A diary entry in 1846 was the first hint of Westcott's interest in the idea: 'what a glorious employment for one's leisure hours it would be to prepare a new edition of the New Testament'.[68] Many might not share that view of leisure, and its eventual fulfilment involved much hard work. Hort's interest in the textual problems of the New Testament derived from an article in the *Edinburgh Review* for July 1851 by J.W. Blakesley, Fellow of Trinity from 1831 to 1845 and later Dean of Lincoln. This was a review of new editions of the New Testament text by Lachmann, Tischendorf and Alford. In a letter to Ellerton in December 1851, Hort said how recent his interest in textual matters was. Westcott had advised him to get Bagster's *Critical Greek Testament*, which he had appreciated, but Tischendorf had been a great acquisition: 'Think of that vile *Textus Receptus* leaning entirely on later MSS.'[69] The first hint of the proposal that Hort and Westcott should prepare a critical edition of the Greek text of the New Testament came in a letter from Hort to John Ellerton in April 1853: he hoped it might be ready in two or three years' time![70] Westcott and Hort began work on the text in the spring of 1853.[71]

There are references to the work being under way in letters to Hort in 1859, 1864, 1868, 1878 and 1879, and the text of the gospels was published in 1871. The complete New Testament was eventually published on 5 May 1881, a few days before the publication of the Revised Version. The Introduction, explaining the principles of textual criticism used and mainly written by Hort, appeared a few months later.[72] As a statement of the principles of textual criticism this remains a classic, although Westcott's thirteen principles in Smith's *Dictionary of the Bible*

---

67    Treloar, *Lightfoot the Historian*, pp. 311–12.

68    Diary, 8 February 1846: Westcott, *Life of Westcott*, i, p. 42.

69    Hort to C.R. Gregory, 26 April 1885, Theological Correspondence of F.J.A. Hort, Cambridge University Library Add Mss 6597, f. 723; 'The Greek Text of the New Testament', *Edinburgh Review*, xciv (July 1851), 1–46; Hort to Ellerton, 29/30 December 1851: Hort, *Life of Hort*, i, p. 211.

70    Letter to Ellerton, 19 April 1853: Hort, *Life of Hort*, i, p. 250; ii, 7; cf. Hort to Westcott 19 April 1853, CUL Add Mss 6597, fol. 25.

71    There is a brief account of the project in S.C. Neill, *The Interpretation of the New Testament, 1861–1961* (London, 1964) pp. 69–76, although either the proof-reading or the original text seems to be subject to the kind of errors in transmission, which he describes, e.g. the starting date is given as 1863.

72    Westcott, *Life of Westcott*, i, pp. 237, 285, 296, 399–404.

of 1863 are a valuable summary.[73] Despite the proximity of the publication dates of the Greek Text and the Revised Version, the two should not be confused. The Greek text used for the Revised Version differed considerably from the Westcott and Hort text. Although both of them were on the Revision Committee (which had privately printed copies of the Westcott-Hort text), decisions in the Committee were based on a two-thirds majority of the whole, and the Cambridge scholars did not necessarily win. Nevertheless Hort said that Lightfoot's pleading at the first meeting of the Revisers against perfunctory or inadequate revision determined the whole enterprise.[74]

The third area of work was the production of a new style of biblical commentary, in which Lightfoot and Westcott were the key players. In 1859 Lightfoot described to Westcott a plan for a complete edition of the Epistles, beginning with 'a thin volume … of introductory matter', followed by each epistle in chronological order with the Greek and English text side by side, a commentary beneath and those subjects, which could not be dealt with in a note, being handled in separate dissertations.[75] More or less at the same time Alexander Macmillan suggested to Westcott a Cambridge commentary on the New Testament, which Lightfoot and Hort enthusiastically agreed to, especially as the possibility of William Smith's larger commentary on the whole Bible was receding. Lightfoot therefore dropped his own scheme, but in the event the result was the same, because he was allotted most of the Epistles. Westcott was to take the Johannine writings, and Hort the synoptic gospels, Acts, James, 1 and 2 Peter and Jude.[76] Martin Hengel observed that 'Lightfoot took on those texts in which he could most successfully develop his philological and historical genius specifically over against the Tübingen faction'.[77]

However, the first to appear was *Galatians* in 1865, rather than *1 Thessalonians*. In the Preface Lightfoot explained why. Despite the current attention to the Old Testament (as a result of *Essays and Reviews*), the issues in Galatians were intrinsically more important because 'they touch the vital parts of Christianity':

> If the primitive Gospel was, as some have represented it, merely one of many phases of Judaism, if those cherished beliefs which have been the life and light of many generations were afterthoughts, progressive accretions, having no foundation in the

73 W. Smith, *Dictionary of the Bible* (London, 1863), ii, pp. 528–31, cf. W. Smith, *A Concise Dictionary of the Bible* (London, 1865), pp. 616–17; Westcott, *Life of Westcott*, i, pp. 203–4; G.A. Patrick, *The Miners' Bishop* (2nd edn, Peterborough, 2004), p. 22.

74 *DNB*, xxxiii, p. 234.

75 Letter to Westcott, 4 December 1859, quoted in Treloar, *Lightfoot the Historian*, p. 312.

76 Westcott to Lightfoot, 7 December 1859; Westcott to Macmillan: 7 December 1859: Westcott, *Life of Westcott*, i, pp. 205–7; Hort to Lightfoot, 29 April 1860: Hort, *Life of Hort*, i, pp. 417–18; Treloar, *Lightfoot the Historian*, pp. 312–13.

77 M. Hengel, 'Lightfoot and the Tübingen School', p. 36.

Person and Teaching of Christ, then indeed St Paul's preaching was vain and our faith is vain also.[78]

Whilst he was confident that the views of the Tübingen school would not prevail, mere denunciation might be unjust and was certainly unavailing: 'Moreover for our own sakes we should try and discover the element of truth which underlies even the greatest exaggerations of able men, and correct our impressions thereby.'[79]

Hort recognised Lightfoot's historical strength, but was critical of his doctrinal comments:

> One misses the real attempt to fathom St Paul's own mind, and to compare it with the facts of life which one finds in Jowett. On the other hand, he is surely always admirable on historical ground, and especially in interpreting passages which afford indirect historical evidence, as also in all matters of grammar and language and such like essential externalities.[80]

Hort's later verdict was that what he offered was 'not a refutation of the Tübingen scholars, but a rival interpretation and a rival picture'.[81] Thus the Congregational scholar, A.M. Fairbairn, regarded Hort as

> more the pure scholar and critic than either of the other two ... too conscious of the possibilities of error and the limitations of knowledge to reach the clear-cut and assured conclusions of Lightfoot; too much alive to the complexities of thought and the inadequacies of human speech to be as prolific and facile a writer as Westcott.[82]

Whilst acknowledging that all three appreciated theology as a problem in literature rather than in history, Fairbairn thought that Lightfoot had little interest in the history of doctrine and not much real comprehension of its inner meaning: 'He does not so much construe history as compel us to find room in any future attempt at reconstruction for documents he has proved to be authentic and for the facts they describe.'[83]

*Galatians* was followed by *Philippians* in 1868, and *Colossians and Philemon* in 1875. Lightfoot had already published an edition of Clement of Rome in 1869, which was subsequently revised, and then he turned his attention to Ignatius and Polycarp. A three-volume edition appeared in 1885, which he reckoned might have appeared three or four years earlier, had he not been appointed Bishop of

---

78    J.B. Lightfoot, *St Paul's Epistle to the Galatians* (3rd edn, London, 1869), p. xi.

79    Ibid.

80    Hort to Ellerton, 21 February 1867: Hort, *Life of Hort*, ii, p. 79.

81    *DNB*, xxxiii, p. 238; compare R. Morgan, 'Non Angli set Angeli: Some Anglican Reactions to German Gospel Criticism', in S.W. Sykes and J.D. Holmes, *New Studies in Theology 1* (London, 1980), pp. 5–8.

82    A.M. Fairbairn, 'Some Recent English Theologians', *Contemporary Review*, lxxi (March 1897): 345.

83    Ibid.: 346–7.

Durham in 1879.[84] Parts of Commentaries on the other Pauline epistles were posthumously published, based on lectures given at Cambridge.[85] They covered 1 and 2 Thessalonians, 1 Corinthians 1–7, Romans 1–7, and Ephesians 1.

All Lightfoot's Commentaries were characterised by their thoroughness, and particularly their knowledge of other commentators. Kingsley Barrett noted that in discussing the patristic interpretation of the dispute between Peter and Paul at Antioch (Gal. 2:11) he cited thirty-seven patristic commentaries, adding that 'he seldom quotes modern sources'.[86] He also had an instinctive feeling for a Greek phrase or sentence, but was most lucid in his historical analysis. (Barrett disagreed with Hort's criticism of his lack of theology.[87]) One of the most significant contemporary appreciations of Lightfoot came from Harnack: 'His editions and commentaries ... and his critical articles are of lasting worth, and even where one cannot agree with his conclusions, one can never pass over his arguments.' Harnack felt that there was no conservative scholar in Germany who was Lightfoot's equal and continued, 'His respect for his opponent, which marked him out – I cannot recall a single derogatory comment in any of Lightfoot's writing: the strongest form on which he commented on a quite untenable argument was to express amazement – brought him the utmost respect of all parties'. He added that 'he never defended a tradition for tradition's sake; but how often he rescued the tradition, which previously had not been defended adequately, and therefore risked losing its credibility!'[88]

Hort's commentaries never appeared, though some of his work on James and I Peter was published after his death. Westcott published *The Gospel according to St John* in 1880 (his commentary on the Greek text was published posthumously), *The Epistles of St John* in 1886, and *The Epistle to the Hebrews* in 1889, both of the latter being on the Greek text after the manner of Lightfoot's. Westcott provided what is regarded as the classic defence of John's authorship of the fourth gospel; it

---

84    J.B. Lightfoot, *The Apostolic Fathers, Part II* (London, 1885), i, pp. x–xi.

85    J.B. Lightfoot, *Notes on Epistles of St Paul from Unpublished Commentaries* (London, 1895).

86    C.K. Barrett, 'Joseph Barber Lightfoot', *Durham University Journal*, lxiv, 3 (June 1972): 197–8.

87    C.K. Barrett, 'J.B. Lightfoot as Biblical Commentator', Lightfoot Centenary Lectures, *Durham University Journal* (January 1992): 59. Barrett instanced Lightfoot, *Galatians*, pp. 142ff., and said that he could not find where Lightfoot had indicated that he was more concerned with history than theology. However, the comparison of 2 Corinthians, Galatians and Romans in the Introduction (pp. 44–56) suggests that, while Galatians marks a more developed doctrine of justification by faith than 2 Corinthians, the more 'comprehensive and systematic treatise' is found in Romans, where Paul's personal authority was not under direct attack (p. 49). Barrett also did not agree with Hort's later remark that Lightfoot's doctrinal comments belonged to 'the mere Protestant version of St Paul's thoughts' (Hort, *Life of Hort*, ii, p. 79).

88    A.V. Harnack, 'Review of Edwin Hatch, *Essays in Biblical Greek*', in *Theologische Literaturzeitung*, 15, no. 12 (14 June 1890), cols 297–301. (The copy of this in the Cambridge Divinity Faculty Library originally belonged to Hort.)

followed therefore that he must have been the author of the epistles.[89] In relation to *Hebrews* he discussed all the evidence about authorship and concluded that it was not Pauline but that this did not mean that it lacked apostolic authority: 'The [Alexandrines] were wrong in affirming Pauline authorship as the condition of canonical authority. The [Western Fathers] were wrong in denying the canonical authority of a book of which St Paul was not the author.'[90] However conservative (relatively speaking) Westcott might have been about questions of authorship, he showed the same scholarly depth as Lightfoot. Kingsley Barrett noted his extensive word studies, and also the range of patristic commentaries used.[91] The commentaries of Lightfoot and Westcott certainly succeeded in their aim of outclassing those of Jowett and Stanley.

Harnack may have been right in saying that Lightfoot never indulged in derogatory comments, but he did use the English technique of irony. This is nowhere better seen than in his series of articles in the *Contemporary Review*, published at irregular intervals from December 1874 on the then anonymous book, *Supernatural Religion*.[92] It has to be said that the articles make heavy going, lightened only by periodic irony or sarcasm. The reason traditionally given for the time Lightfoot spent on this enterprise was the need to combat various aspersions cast on Westcott's *History of the Canon*; but Geoffrey Treloar has pointed out that a more significant reason was probably Lightfoot's fear that the success of the book (it went through four editions in the first year) indicated the extent to which the battle against negative biblical criticism still had to be won. Moreover, the articles coincided with work that Lightfoot was doing on the Apostolic Fathers anyway, and in a sense they were a 'popular' version of the three-decker volume, which came out in 1885.[93] *Supernatural Religion* began with a traditional attack on miracle and the supernatural, seeking particularly to discredit those clergy who were downgrading their significance. It noted with appreciation John Stuart Mill's *Three Essays on Religion*, published at the beginning of 1874. What was new in a work of that type was the extensive discussion in Parts II–V – the overwhelming majority of the book – of the Fathers and the New Testament literature. Its apparently detailed scholarly apparatus worried Lightfoot, because there had not really been a book like that in English before. So Lightfoot early on in his first article responded in kind:

> I have been assuming however that the work entitled 'Supernatural Religion', which lies before me, is the same work which the reviewers have applauded under this name. But, when I remember that the St Mark of Papias cannot possibly be our St Mark, I feel bound to throw upon this assumption the full light of modern critical principles; and, so tested, it proves to be not only hasty and unwarrantable, but altogether absurd.

---

89    B.F. Westcott, *The Gospel according to St John* (London 1890), pp. v–xxxii; *The Epistles of St John* (Cambridge 1886), p. xxx.

90    Westcott, *Hebrews*, p. lxxi.

91    C.K. Barrett, *Westcott as Commentator* (Cambridge, 1958), pp. 16–21.

92    The subtitle was 'An Inquiry into the Reality of Divine Revelation' and the author was a retired Indian merchant, W.R. Cassels: O. Chadwick, *The Victorian Church, Part II* (London 1970), p. 71.

93    Treloar, *Lightfoot the Historian*, pp. 341–53.

It is only necessary to compare the statements of highly intellectual reviewers with the work itself; and every unprejudiced mind must be convinced that 'the evidence is fatal to the claims' involved in this identification. Out of five reviews or notices of the work which I have read, only one seems to refer to our 'Supernatural Religion'. The other four are plainly dealing with some apocryphal work, bearing the same name and often using the same language, but in its main characteristics quite different from and much more authentic than the volumes before me.[94]

This was an apt burlesque of the tone of the book; and there was much more. Cassels provided a detailed rebuttal in his Preface to the sixth edition in 1879, but H.E. Savage, later Dean of Lichfield, alleged that before the series of articles was complete 'the book was already a glut in the second-hand book market'.[95] Lightfoot received many letters of thanks. The British religious, and non-religious, public seemed to retain its ability to be either shocked or delighted to see clergy on the defensive. But the issues were now being routinely debated, and even if people could not follow the scholarship the genie was out of the bottle; and in the end the consequences were *not* disastrous.

How then should the achievements of the trio in biblical criticism be assessed? They can be very simply stated. First, Westcott and Hort produced a new critical Greek Text of the New Testament; in effect they launched a process of continual revision in the light of new manuscript discoveries (which continued after their deaths), which has not only overthrown the 'Received Text',[96] but even in the Roman Catholic Church removed the normative character of the Vulgate. Secondly, they decisively challenged the Tübingen dating of the New Testament books, and finally laid to rest the eighteenth-century suggestion that they were forgeries. Thirdly, they secured the acceptance of critical methods in biblical study in a way which went beyond the generalities of Coleridge or Hare. In effect they redefined the terms of the debate about inspiration and authority, bringing the significance of the church back into the equation in a more dynamic way than that of either the older high churchmen or the Tractarians. It is not surprising that for half a century or more after their deaths they were seen as heroes of the late nineteenth-century Church of England.

With the passage of time a more dispassionate view has emerged. Kingsley Barrett said that Westcott lacked 'a *systematic* theory of inspiration and of the authority of Scripture; and this lack is not entirely compensated by his profound reverence for Scripture, and the exceptionally acute theological apprehension of the

94   J.B. Lightfoot, 'Supernatural Religion', *Contemporary Review*, xxv (December 1874): 4. The articles were collected into a single volume: J.B. Lightfoot, *Essays on the Work entitled Supernatural Religion* (London 1889).

95   [W.R. Cassels], *Supernatural Religion*, 6th edn (London 1879), pp. 4–52; G.R. Eden and F.C. Macdonald, *Lightfoot of Durham* (Cambridge, 1933), p. 10.

96   The name 'Received Text' derives from the second Elzevir (Leyden) edition of the Greek New Testament (1624) in which the reader is informed that this is 'the text received by all': B.F. Westcott and F.J.A. Hort, Introduction to *The New Testament in the original Greek* (Cambridge, 1882), p. 12. This Introduction was substantially written by Hort.

meaning of the text under discussion'.[97] Henry Chadwick quoted Henry Sidgwick's comment on Maurice and Westcott that 'the difference is that Westcott is orthodox in his conclusions, and only paradoxical in his arguments, whereas Maurice was to some extent paradoxical in both'.[98] And he elucidated the point thus:

> To many who already believed in God Westcott spoke words of gold. He was interpreting an experience in which they shared ... But to materialists, pantheists, and atheists, and to anyone who did not intuitively understand his passionate sense of the mystery of life and of the inconclusiveness of our space-time existence, Westcott's words could never be effective or impressive in the same way.[99]

Peter Hinchliff suggested that the Cambridge trio or quartet 'seem sometimes to have taken refuge in the facts of history, to evade the difficult theological problems' and noted that Westcott avoided the question of 'whether the miracles actually happened'.[100] Finally, Robert Morgan suggested that Lightfoot 'inaugurated the century-long tradition of defending the doctrine of the incarnation by maintaing the essential historicity of the gospels. This was only one stream in Anglican theology, and it was in the long run a failure.' More importantly, the establishment of the authenticity of the Ignatian epistles and the discrediting of Baur's chronology of second-century Christianity did not in itself establish the historicity of the gospels.[101] What response can be made to these criticisms?

By comparison with Hare and Thirlwall, Westcott's Norrisian Prize Essay, even in its revised form,was remarkably conservative. In the *Elements* the first sentence of chapter 1 read, 'It has been well remarked by Paley that our habit of viewing the whole Bible as one book – one in form rather than in substance – leads us to undervalue the individual testimony of its component parts'.[102] Westcott argued strongly against the idea that there was an 'original gospel' or even that the writers of the gospels consulted one another, by which presumably he meant used one another. In this respect, although he did not mention or refer to Marsh, he was presumably distancing himself from his hypothesis. Instead he declared himself in favour of oral histories as the origin – which was more like Thirlwall, except that he did not cite him or Schleiermacher either.[103] In later editions he summarised his conclusion

---

97   Barrett, *Westcott as Commentator*, p. 12.

98   A. Sidgwick and E.M. Sidgwick, *Henry Sidgwick: A Memoir* (London, 1906), p. 394.

99   Chadwick, *Vindication of Christianity*, pp. 8–9.

100  Hinchliff, *God and History*, p. 95.

101  Morgan, 'Non Angli sed Angeli', pp. 4–5, 8.

102  Westcott, *Elements*, p. 26. The reference is to W. Paley, *Evidences of Christianity*, bk. I, ch. 8 and bk. II, ch. 9: 'being from our infancy accustomed to regard the New Testament as one book, we see in it only one testimony ... Yet in this conception of the subject we are certainly mistaken; for the very discrepancies among the several documents which form our volume, prove ... that in their original composition they were separate, and most of them independent productions', ed. T.R. Birks (new edn, London, n.d.), p. 99. It was dropped from the *Introduction*.

103  Westcott, *Elements*, pp. 38, 92–3.

thus: 'Individuality is a sign of independence. The more closely any one compares parallel passages of the gospels the more certainly he will feel that their likenesses are to be referred to the use of a common source and not to the immediate influence of one Gospel upon another.'[104] In other words, 'individuality and independence, when presented in such a form as to exhibit complementary spiritual aspects of the same facts, are signs of Inspiration'; in effect, the argument against Christianity from the discrepancies in the gospels was turned on its head (as Paley had done), to be used as proof: 'Nothing less than the constant presence of the Holy Spirit … could preserve perfect truthfulness with remarkable variations.'[105]

Westcott and Lightfoot were convinced that criticism would ultimately prove the truth of scripture. This conviction illuminates the exchange between the three of them in 1860, when for a moment or two Hort seemed to be too unsound on the synoptic gospels for the joint commentary proposed by Macmillan. In December 1859 Westcott had originally suggested to Lightfoot that Benson might do the synoptic gospels for Macmillan.[106] He explained to Macmillan that he would welcome Hort as a fellow contributor because he sympathised with his principles, even though in detail he and Lightfoot might differ from him. He explained the difference thus, 'I confess … to a most profound and ever-growing belief in words, and I should rejoice if all who might share in any such Commentary as is proposed could bring to the work an absolute faith in language, and so in Scripture'.[107] When the Smith scheme collapsed and Hort became available, the three met at Harrow. Clearly Lightfoot expressed some doubts, the precise nature of which can only be guessed at from Hort's side of the correspondence, because he responded by return of post. Hort said that his first feeling was that it might be better for him to withdraw at once: 'if your idea is, to have an uniform commentary, which shall demonstrate that the final results of accurate and honest criticism do not disturb "orthodox" assumptions, you are quite right not to admit a coadjutor who cannot feel certain of having equal good luck.'[108] But he then went on to consider whether they were really at variance:

> If you make a decided conviction of the absolute infallibility of the N.T. practically a *sine qua non* for co-operation, I fear I could not join you, even if you were willing to forget your fears about the origin of the Gospels. I am most anxious to find the N.T. infallible, and have a strong sense of the Divine purpose guiding all its parts; but I cannot see how the exact limits of such guidance can be ascertained except by unbiassed *a posteriori* criticism.[109]

Hort presumed that Westcott and Lightfoot would say that apparent errors discovered by criticism were the result of imperfect knowledge; whilst Hort felt that this was possible for many, he did not think it probable for all, and if there

---

104  Westcott, *Introduction*, p. 337.
105  Ibid., p. 338.
106  Westcott to Lightfoot, 7 December 1859: Westcott, *Life of Westcott*, i, p. 206.
107  Westcott to Macmillan, 7 December 1859: ibid., p. 207.
108  Hort to Lightfoot, 1 May 1860: Hort, *Life of Hort*, i, pp. 418–19.
109  Ibid., i, p. 420.

were natural explanations of such errors they ought to be admitted. Such a position, developed in a commentary, was bound to offend both the orthodox, and Jowett and his friends. Westcott wrote a letter at the same time, and to him Hort explained that, while he recognised a special providence which controlled the formation of the canonical books, he was not prepared to make *a priori* assumptions about infallibility; but he also added (in a rather Mauricean way) that, although he would be sorry to admit occasional errors, it would not shake his conviction 'of the providential ordering of human elements in the Bible'.[110] Apparently Hort's responses satisfied Lightfoot and Westcott, though the latter wrote that the more he learned, the more he felt that fresh doubts came from his own ignorance, and he found the presumption in favour of the absolute truth of Holy Scripture (he rejected the word 'infallibility') overwhelming.[111]

It is interesting that the issue between them related to the question of a common source for the synoptic gospels. Hort agreed with Westcott that the common foundation was an oral or traditional narrative, but disagreed about why it was localised. In his subsequent response to Westcott, he agreed that it was 'most essential to study each Synoptist by himself as a single whole'. But he added that 'such a study soon leads one to the fact of their having all largely used at least one common source, and that fact becomes an *additional* element in their criticism. Their independent treatment is most striking; but it is not identical with the independence of three absolutely original writers'.[112]

In the light of the line taken by Westcott in the *Elements*, and not retracted in the *Introduction*, it is not surprising that he was sensitive to disagreement. This detailed example reinforces Kingsley Barrett's point that at times it seemed as though Westcott 'diminished the miracle of Scripture by neglecting its human element'. 'The historical narrative of the Bible, and this includes the story of Jesus, comes to us through the medium of human tradition, with all the uncertainties of human tradition.'[113] Westcott and Lightfoot were reluctant to face the uncertainties.

The question of miracle is rather different. Certainly Westcott and the others were anxious to examine what could be established by historical research; and they had a confidence in facts, which seems problematic today. But Westcott and his companions recognised that the chances of being able to establish the historicity of miracles on the basis of historical evidence were very limited; and that most people adopted an *a priori* position in relation to the possibility of miracles, rather than an *a posteriori* one, whether they believed in them or not. Furthermore Westcott thought that the contemporary obsession with historicity was beside the point theologically; for in New Testament times the ability to work miracles did not in itself carry any theological implications about the identity of the miracle worker.

The important question therefore was the boundary between faith and credulity; and hence the significance of the miracles was crucial. Westcott said

---

110  Hort to Westcott, 2 May 1860: ibid., i, pp. 421–2.
111  Westcott to Hort, 5 May 1860: Westcott, *Life of Westcott*, i, p. 207.
112  Hort to Lightfoot, 1 May 1860; Hort to Westcott, 4 May 1860: Hort, *Life of Hort*, i, pp. 419, 423.
113  Barrett, *Westcott as Commentator*, pp. 24, 25, cf. pp. 14–15.

that 'a Gospel without miracles would be … like a Church without sacraments. The outward pledge of the spiritual gift would be wanting'.[114] Similarly, in commenting on the healings and the raisings from the dead, he wrote, 'Step by step He led His disciples by works of increasing glory to realize the mystery of His Resurrection, and to anticipate their own'.[115] The image of steps recurred later when he remarked 'Step by step we have been led to regard the entire range of the Divine working, as far as it affects man, in acts of creation, of redemption, of judgment'. Although there were other ways of looking at the miracles, that way 'sets forward most clearly their permanent significance'.[116]

In the summer of 1865 Westcott, Lightfoot and Benson visited the monasteries of La Grande Chartreuse and La Salette, where there had been various visions of the Virgin Mary. The three were moved by their experience, and Westcott wrote an article for *Macmillan's Magazine*. Lightfoot intervened to prevent publication, fearing that Westcott would be exposed to charges of Mariolatry.[117] Benson supported publication, but he noted to Westcott that Lightfoot was 'not cautious – he is concentrated caution'![118] Westcott had a few copies privately printed, and at least one survives. The emphasis of the article was not on Mary, but on faith.[119] Westcott noted Lecky's observation that belief in miracles had died out in the civilised world, but said that so far from the belief having died out 'it would be nearer the truth to say, that in the average mass of men it was never more powerful, or more eager for present satisfaction'.[120] He explicitly denied any interest in the truth or falsehood of the vision of Mary: 'the apparition may have been illusory, but the faith which it has quickened is most real and unquestionable.'[121] Thus Westcott was quite open about his interest in faith rather than historicity, the point of Professor Hinchliff's criticism. After describing a number of testimonies from pilgrims, Westcott remarked that 'an age of faith was restored before our sight in its ancient guise', and quoted the comment of a young man to whom they had talked, 'Sans croire, comment l'expliquer?'[122] He concluded that 'the vitality of a

---

114  Westcott, *Miracles*, p. 43.

115  Ibid., p. 62.

116  Ibid., pp. 91–2.

117  Westcott, *Life of Westcott*, i, pp. 254–5.

118  Benson to Westcott, 30 Oct 1865, Benson Papers, Trinity College, Cambridge, Copies of Correspondence, 1853–68, fol. 193; this passage is omitted from the text published in Benson, *Life of Benson*, i, pp. 237–8.

119  The episode is referred to in A.M. Allchin, *The Joy of all Creation* (London, 1984), p. 114, but the text does not suggest that Allchin had read the original article, and there is no cross-reference to Benson, so he does not seem to have realised that the trip was made by all three.

120  B.F. Westcott, 'La Salette in 1865', privately printed, pp. 1–2: Westcott Papers, Westcott House, Cambridge (on permanent loan from Selwyn College).

121  Ibid., p. 6.

122  Ibid., p. 13; part of this paragraph is quoted in Westcott, *Life of Westcott*, i, p. 254. Benson wrote with characteristic irony that 'Here there are Fathers simple, pure and pious – a devout and humble race of believers – in fact they will believe anything!' Benson to his wife, 20 August 1865: Benson, *Life*, i, p. 235.

religion may be measured by the intensity of the belief in the immediate working of a divine power which it produces' and that 'when the belief in the miraculous ... as an element in common life, is destroyed, religion is destroyed at the same time, so far as religion includes the ideas of worship and prayer'.[123] Thus the vitality of Mariolatry suggested that it was 'at least the shadow of some truth', and perhaps indicated something neglected in their own teaching. His final hope was that 'the solution would set before us that aspect of truth to which the great masses in our cities would most gladly turn'.[124] Benson's only critical comment on the article was that he should clarify what the neglected aspect of truth was – 'the need of grasping more personally the Person of Jesus'.[125]

Westcott's concern with miracle culminated in his *Gospel of the Resurrection*, which was published in 1866, though it was written in 1864 before the visit to La Salette. In the Preface to the first edition Westcott wrote that there seemed to be a growing impression 'that such a fact as the Resurrection cannot be brought into harmony with what we see of the life of the world or what we feel of the laws of individual thought'.[126] The opponents of Christianity assumed that a miracle must be explained away, while its defenders failed to notice the lines of culture and thought which converged towards the central lessons of the Gospel. Indeed, he suggested, 'it is not too much to assert that the fact of the Resurrection (as the typical miracle of the Gospel) becomes more natural as we take a more comprehensive view of history, and more harmonious with reason as we interrogate our instincts more closely'.[127] The links drawn between nature and history, and between reason and instincts, were characteristic.

For Westcott the events recorded in the gospels 'while they are most truly historical are not merely history. Their significance is not in the past only or even chiefly.'[128] Thus the authority of testimony was supplemented by the human instinct to look for a sign of the reality of fellowship with the unseen. He considered what could be taken for granted and what had to be proved.

> If, for example, a miracle is inherently incredible, it is idle to reason about a fact which in the end must be explained away. If on the other hand we hold that miracles are, in certain cases, as credible as ordinary events generally, it is necessary that we should shew how this belief is reconcileable with the ideas which we entertain of an Infinite GOD and of the constancy of natural laws.[129]

The resurrection 'like all historical facts' differed from the facts of physics 'as being incapable of direct and present verification', and it differed 'from all other

---

123  Westcott, 'La Salette', p. 14.

124  Ibid., p. 16.

125  Benson to Westcott, 30 Oct 1865: Benson, *Life of Benson*, i. pp. 237–8.

126  B.F. Westcott, *The Gospel of the Resurrection* (5th edn, London, 1884), p. xix.

127  Ibid., p. xx. This argument is strikingly like that advanced by both Charles Gore and William Temple thirty or fifty years later; and it is perhaps significant that Westcott taught Gore at Harrow.

128  Ibid., p. 12.

129  Ibid., p. 14.

facts of history because it is necessarily unique'. But that did not mean it was incapable of verification: 'Its verification lies in its abiding harmony with all the progressive developments of man and with each discovery which casts light upon his destiny.'[130]

Westcott was absolutely clear that 'the essence of Christianity lies in a miracle; and if it can be shewn that a miracle is either impossible or incredible, all further inquiry into the details of its history is superfluous in a religious point of view'.[131] He believed that a miracle could not 'be declared impossible by anyone who believes in a Personal GOD'.[132] On the contrary he suggested that 'under particular circumstances which may happen if GOD reveals himself to men, miracles are as probable as ordinary phenomena under common circumstances'.[133] Further, 'to affirm that miracles are unnatural is to constitute general laws of observation into a fate superior to GOD, or to deny His personal action'.[134] Nor did it make sense to affirm that God acted on the hearts of human beings if God's personal action in the physical world was denied. Consequently 'the moral element in miracles is both essential and predominant'.[135] But whilst the development of science might make people less aware of the indeterminate elements in the world, if it also led to a neglect of the moral element of life, they were driven back to an entirely physical view of the world. In such a situation not only miracles but every expression of will was eliminated from the world, and 'all life falls under the power of absolute materialism, a conclusion which is at variance with the fundamental idea of religion'.[136] Again determinism was rejected.

Peter Hinchliff was therefore right to say that Westcott did not investigate the historicity of miracles; but this did not necessarily make Westcott any less good a historian or a theologian. Indeed most biblical scholars since Westcott have remained firmly on the fence on this matter. They have been prepared to talk about almost anything in relation to the biblical miracles rather than whether they actually happened; and for one very simple reason, which Westcott recognised. There is no way of producing any historical evidence on the matter, which is more significant than the general philosophical question of antecedent probability. What Westcott did was to consider the significance of the affirmation that the resurrection happened, not whether it did. Westcott's book on miracles was reprinted in the Allenson's Sixpenny Series (one of the first religious paperbacks) in 1913. Winnington-Ingram, Bishop of London, commented in the Preface, 'When I once asked Bishop Westcott what sort of answer he made to objectors

130 Ibid., p. 17.
131 Ibid., pp. 34–5.
132 Ibid., p. 36.
133 Ibid.
134 Ibid., p. 38.
135 Ibid., p. 44.
136 Ibid., p. 48.

to the Gospel, his face lighted up and he said, "I just preach it as the good news of the world and then leave it".[137]

Lightfoot's commitment to history is commemorated by his endowment in 1870 of the Lightfoot Scholarships in History, especially Ecclesiastical History. Ecclesiastical History was chosen not only because of his connection with the Theological faculty, but also because he regarded it 'when properly treated, as the most important and instructive branch of historical study'.[138] The benefaction is said to mark his gratitude for Westcott's return to Cambridge as Regius Professor, and thereby emphasises their shared historical commitment. However, Lightfoot's comment in his response to *Supernatural Religion*, that 'it is not easy to imagine the havoc which would ensue, if the critical principles of the Tübingen school and their admirers were let loose in the classical literature of Greece and Rome', indicated his awareness of the limited degree of certainty to be obtained by historical study.[139]

A more fundamental criticism about the concern for historicity is made by Robert Morgan. Westcott and Lightfoot may have been right about the dating of the gospels vis-à-vis Tübingen; but getting the history right (so far as one can) does not prove the doctrine of the incarnation. A similar point at a more mundane level arises from Graham Patrick's comment on the distinction made by Westcott in relation to the different Greek words for 'love' in John 21:15ff.[140] He notes that 'modern commentators generally do not press these when used as verbs'.[141] This may be true, but the critical historical question is, Did Jesus actually say this? Westcott, of course, assumed that John was an eye-witness and that he was the author.

Both Westcott and Lightfoot almost seemed to distrust clarity in opinions. Scott Holland told the story of the pupil who said to Westcott, 'You have made that perfectly clear to me'. 'Oh,' replied Westcott, 'I hope not! I hope not!'[142] Eden recalled that Lightfoot 'begged me not to be too sure of very clear-cut definitions'.[143] The explanation probably lies in their understanding of mystery. As early as 1848 Westcott had written that 'it is never possible to be too secure or too clear in our views'. This was because of 'the close connexion between reason and faith': 'To believe firmly we must know distinctly; many of the objects of our

---

137   B.F. Westcott, *Characteristics of the Gospel Miracles* (first cheap edn, London, 1913), p. 5. The Sixpenny Series offered a wide range of views, with books by H.P. Liddon, James Martineau, J.H. Newman, F.W. Robertson, Charles Spurgeon and many more.

138   Clark, *Endowments*, p. 329.

139   J.B. Lightfoot, '*Supernatural Religion*: III The Ignatian Epistles', *Contemporary Review*, xxv (February 1875): 354.

140   Westcott, *Gospel of John*, pp. 302–3.

141   Patrick, *The Miners' Bishop*, p. 38.

142   H.S. Holland, *Brooke Foss Westcott, Bishop of Durham* (London, 1910), p. 11.

143   Quoted by Treloar, *Lightfoot the Historian*, p. 372 from R. Wilson, 'Lightfoot, Savage and Eden – Sidelights on a Great Episcopate', *Theology*, lv, 386 (August 1952): 294–9. Since the context of this remark was whether the absolute language of the Prayer Book service on baptismal regeneration implied an *ex opere operato* view of sacramental grace, one might have some sympathy with Lightfoot's warning.

faith may be mysteries, but we must at least know they are such, and we must feel their immensity.'[144] Both of them understood this essentially in terms of the incarnation. Lightfoot spoke in an early sermon of Christ as the link between God and man: 'By Him we have knowledge of the Father. Through Him we have access to the Father. In Him we are united with the Father. Thus this central doctrine of Christianity is the very soul of Christian practice also.'[145]

Whatever limitations the trio may be seen to have had, they did ensure that critical scholarship was accepted in Cambridge as a matter of course. The next generation included Harold Browne (Norrisian Professor 1854–64), who wrote on 'Inspiration' in *Aids to Faith* (a response to *Essays and Reviews*), and J.J.S. Perowne who succeeded Lightfoot as Hulsean Professor (1875–87). Perowne reviewed Pusey's Lectures on Daniel in 1866, disagreeing with Pusey that the Old Testament canon was closed from the time of Nehemiah and arguing that Daniel came from the Maccabean period. He lamented 'that one holding the chair of Hebrew in one of our great universities should have lent the weight and authority of his name to criticism and interpretations which are as mischievous as they are untenable'. The study of Hebrew in England was stifled

> when the most certain results of modern investigation are thrust aside unless they happen to favour some preconceived theory, when imagination is substituted for grammar, rabbinical fancies valued more than sober canons of exegesis, and the wildest licence of interpretation or of criticism indulged in to save a text or to support a doctrine.[146]

Although the efforts of the trio were concentrated on the New Testament, the recognition that the battle was still not won over the Old spurred Herbert Ryle to stand for the Hulsean Chair after Hort in 1887.

---

144 Letter to Mary Whittard, 27 August 1848: Westcott, *Life of Westcott*, i, p. 139.

145 Lightfoot, ms sermon 22 April 1860, 'Life hidden with Christ in God', quoted in Treloar, *Lightfoot the Historian*, p. 57.

146 J.J.S. Perowne, 'Dr Pusey on Daniel the Prophet', *Contemporary Review*, i (January 1866): 122.

# Chapter 6

# Theological Reconstruction: Atonement, Incarnation and Church

> One other name remains ... the greatest, from the scholar's point of view, of all our names, one who, with an outlook quite as wide as that of the very best of the Germans, unites a commanding scholarship, a keen and subtle penetration, and an exactness in the handling of details, superior to anything which their theologians have to show; but he sits apart, like Achilles in his tent, and whether it be from fastidiousness, or whether it be from weakness of health ... which forbids him to face the effort of composition, he lets the precious days pass by and will not go down into the battle. We must not complain, because he has already given us so much; but it is only the tenth part of what he might give us.[1]

William Sanday's description of Hort in 1889 was a remarkable tribute from the Lady Margaret Professor of Divinity at Oxford. Eight years later, when reviewing Hort's biography, he called him 'our greatest theologian of the century', and explained that by the greatest theologian he did not mean the one who had influenced most minds, written most powerfully or published the most books. Rather he meant

> the one whose insight into truth was at once the largest and the most penetrating; ... who was possessed of the most extended knowledge and who combined with that knowledge the surest method; ... who while not behind the foremost in depth of religious feeling united with this a higher and juster claim to the epithet 'scientific' than any of his fellows.[2]

The result was, Sanday claimed, that Hort saw further than other English theologians, and on the whole more soundly.

But the reference to 'Achilles in his tent' was also a rebuke, like that which many make on those whose publications fall below the expected level. Benson made the same point to Hort more politely in 1882. Hort had written to Benson to congratulate him on his appointment as Archbishop, but said

> The convulsions of our English Church itself, grievous as they are, seem to be as nothing beside the danger of its calm and unobtrusive alienation in thought and spirit from

---

1    W. Sanday, 'The Future of English Theology', *The Contemporary Review*, lvi (July 1889): 47.

2    W. Sanday, 'The Life and Letters of F.J.A. Hort', *American Journal of Theology*, i (January 1897): 98.

the great silent multitude of Englishmen, and again of alienation from fact and love of fact; – mutual alienations both.

To which Benson replied, 'I do not believe that the two alienations you speak of are *naturally* progressing on us. They may surely yet be arrested. But what if those who have insight only prophesy in closets – when they ought to be speaking from the house-tops?'[3]

The main difference between Hort and his colleagues, Westcott and Lightfoot, was his theological perspective and concerns. This is what Sanday meant by saying that he saw further than others. It may have something to do with the fact that Hort was an Apostle and the others were not, which linked him to Maurice and gave him an interest in Hare. Although Hort is remembered as a textual critic, he did not begin that way and did not really intend to end that way. After his death Dr Kirkpatrick recalled a conversation in which Hort had spoken sadly of the proportion of his life spent on textual questions and said, 'It was not for its own sake that textual criticism interested him, but for the sake of the greater problems which lay beyond it'; and his son commented that, whilst truth of all kinds was precious in his eyes, 'the attainment of truth in matters of historical or linguistic fact was to him always not an end but a means'.[4] Thus he responded sadly to Sanday's accusation about his silence:

> It is only by accident, so to speak, that I have had to occupy myself with texts, literary and historical criticism, or even exegesis of Scripture. What from earliest manhood I have most cared for, and what I have at all times most longed to have the faculty and the opportunity to speak about, is what one might call fundamental doctrine, alike on its speculative and on its historical side, and especially the relations of the Gospel to the Jewish and Gentile 'Preparations', and its permanent relations to all human knowledge and action.[5]

Some said he protested too much, and did relish the accuracy of scholarship. Armitage Robinson remembered how 'book after book came down from his shelves in the course of conversation; fact after fact was verified'; but despite his minuteness in investigation he always escaped the charge of pedantry. And, although he usually had all the necessary references, he would rarely provide an inquirer with a ready-made opinion.[6]

---

3    Hort to Benson, 13 January 1883 (emphasis original): A.F. Hort, *The Life and Letters of Fenton John Anthony Hort* (London, 1896), ii, pp. 290–91; A.C. Benson, *The Life of Edward White Benson* (London, 1900), i, pp. 560–62. After a further exchange Benson said he wanted *talk* from Hort, not words, adding that his was 'the most historical and real letter' he had had.

4    Hort, *Life and Letters*, ii, pp. 483, 53–4.

5    Ibid., ii, p. 406.

6    J.A Robinson, 'The late Professor Hort', *The Expositor*, 4th series, vii (1893): 63–4, 68–9; Hort, *Life and Letters*, ii, p. 369; T.F. Taylor, *J. Armitage Robinson* (Cambridge, 1991), p. 17.

The assessment of Hort's significance is affected by his relatively small published output. Most of his works were published after his death, in varying stages of completeness, even though he had been working on them for twenty or thirty years. In the preface to one of the last fragments to be published, Hort's commentary on the first three chapters of Revelation, William Sanday wrote that it was 'scholarship in undress – utterly in undress, but perhaps on that account all the more impressive'.[7] His letters when published in 1896 seemed very much more exciting than some of his published work, rather like those of F.D. Maurice whom he very much admired. The very brevity of reference leaves much to the imagination, like Dietrich Bonhoeffer's letters from prison. Hort's own comment on Coleridge was that 'the casual remarks written in the margin of his books, and published after his death, give the deepest insight into his convictions'; but he also warned that 'it is doubly necessary not to lay too much stress on casual thoughts which, bubbling to the surface at the moment, are at once set down on paper'.[8] The primary impression is of a man much readier to entertain new ideas than Westcott or Lightfoot, even if ultimately he seemed to end up on the safe side.

Sanday's comments in 1889 were a response to Mrs Humphrey Ward's article in *The Nineteenth Century* noting the failure of English churchmen at the recent Church Congress session on Old Testament criticism to grapple with the questions posed in Germany.[9] He hoped that patient critical work in the English style would render some of the German speculations untenable. Had he seen correspondence between Hort, Westcott and Benson in early 1890 in the aftermath of *Lux Mundi*, he would have been less encouraged. In March Benson wrote to Westcott after hearing from the Bishop of Oxford how strongly feeling was running against Gore's essay on 'The Holy Spirit and Inspiration'. Benson thought that sooner or later the question of how far a myth could be inspired would have to be faced. Could inspiration use a myth, like a poem or a fable? And he told Westcott about a 'fairly well-read churchwoman' who agreed to lead a Bible Reading Society, and used Westcott's Commentary on St John.

> She then found (with one exception) *all* these churchwomen most dubious as to the reality of the narrative, clear (I think) that it was not written by St John, very uncertain as to whether we really *knew* anything of the life of Christ, absolutely convinced against the Personality of the Holy Ghost.

He concluded that he was persuaded that this was not untypical. 'And all our time and most of our thoughts taken up with these dreadful lights and ablutions!'[10]

Westcott responded that the picture Benson had painted was sad, and also true. But what was needed was a living faith: 'When we are quite sure that God

7     F.J.A. Hort, *The Apocalypse of St John* (London, 1908), p. ii.

8     F.J.A. Hort, 'Coleridge' in *Cambridge Essays 1856* (London, 1856), pp. 341–2.

9     M. Ward, 'The New Reformation', *The Nineteenth Century*, xiv (March 1889): 454–80.

10    Benson to Westcott, 2 March 1890 (emphasis original): Benson, *Life of Benson*, ii, p. 299.

is speaking now ... we shall not grow wild in discussing how He once spoke.' He had deliberately not read *Lux Mundi*, but was quite sure that 'our Christian faith ought not to be perilled on any predetermined view of what the history and character of the documents contained in the O.T. must be. What we are bound to hold is that the O.T. ... is the Divine record of the discipline of Israel'. He did not suppose that anyone could believe that Genesis 1–3 gave a literal history, and he added 'Poetry is, I think, a thousand times more true than History'.[11] It is not surprising, therefore, that when Hort wrote to Westcott in May, after his appointment as Bishop of Durham, asking him to say in public what he had said to the Clergy Training School about the Old Testament question, Westcott replied saying that he had not got time at present, and Gore was perfectly able to take care of himself. Westcott's fear was that the reaction would go too far. He added that the critical details were 'purely neutral and indeterminate': 'David is not a chronological, but a spiritual person in relation, e.g. to Ps cx.'[12] The distance from Old Testament critical questions could scarcely be better illustrated. Nor can one imagine Westcott's comments helping the women in Benson's Bible Reading Society.

Hort did pursue his own theological agenda, which was different from the German one. His answers to certain questions may no longer suffice, not least because of the significant manuscript discoveries in the twentieth century. But the questions were addressed. Behind the long list of gnostic authors begininng with A and B in the *Dictionary of Christian Antiquities* there is a concern about the origin and nature of gnostic beliefs. And in his *Two Dissertations* he tackled fundamental theological questions behind the meaning of John 1:18 and the emergence of the Constantinopolitan Creed. Buried in the Preface is an interesting little sentence:

> Continental criticism is unfortunately silent, with a single exception, on most of the questions which I have had to raise: and it has been disappointing to find how little help was to be contained, even on conspicuous points, from the studies in the history of doctrine which have been carried on for the last two or three generations.[13]

He also continued to work at an appropriate understanding of the doctrines of sin and redemption, highlighted by the Reformation, and his work on the Epistle of James and the Epistles to the Romans and Galatians, though incomplete, illustrated the way in which he related those doctrines to the New Testament text.

The significance of Old Testament questions was as much moral as chronological. Charles Darwin's *Autobiography* is a convenient illustration. When it was originally published in 1887, the Darwin family were divided on the question

---

11    Westcott to Benson, 4 March 1890: A. Westcott, *Life and Letters of Brooke Foss Westcott* (London, 1903), ii, pp. 68–9.

12    Hort to Westcott, 10 May 1890: Hort, *Life and Letters*, ii, p. 416; Westcott to Hort, 12 May 1890: Westcott, *Life of Westcott*, ii, p. 147.

13    F.J.A. Hort, *Two Dissertations* (London, 1876), pp. viii–ix.

of whether the passage on Charles's religious beliefs should be included. It was not, but the family feeling on the matter did not die down until the complete edition was published in 1958. As an undergraduate Darwin had been delighted by the logic of Paley's *Evidences* and his *Natural Theology*. But although on the *Beagle* (1836–39) he was quite orthodox, he wrote that he

> had gradually come, by this time, to see that the Old Testament from its manifestly false history of the world, with the Tower of Babel, the rainbow as a sign etc., etc., and from its attributing to God the feelings of a revengeful tyrant, was no more to be trusted than the sacred books of the Hindoos, or the beliefs of any barbarian.

The fixed laws of nature made miracles increasingly incredible; and although he was reluctant to give up belief he came eventually to the point of wondering how anyone should wish Christianity to be true, 'for if so the plain language of the text seems to show that the men who do not believe, and this would include my Father, Brother and almost all my best friends will be everlastingly punished. And this is a damnable doctrine'. Thus 'the old argument of design in nature, as given by Paley, which formerly seemed to me so conclusive, fails now that the law of natural selection has been discovered'.[14]

The urgency of the right methods of defending the truth of Christianity was brought home to the trio by the personal crisis of Henry Sidgwick (1838–1900). Not only was Sidgwick a personal friend of Westcott and Lightfoot; he was also Benson's brother-in-law. He dropped the idea of ordination soon after the publication of *Essays and Reviews* in 1860, saying in a letter to *The Times* on 20 February 1861 that what was wanted was 'not a condemnation, but a refutation'.[15] His crisis of faith was protracted, lasting for much of the 1860s. In 1862 he read Comte, and in reaction became 'willing enough to believe in a man who came and brought humanity into communion with the Divine Spirit, but Sin! Punishment! Mediation!'[16] He decided to learn Hebrew in order to ascertain 'with regard to Biblical Criticism, that it is impossible to demonstrate from themselves the non-infallibility of the Hebrew writings'.[17] Spending time in Göttingen in the summer of 1864, he met Ewald, who urged on him 'the importance of studying Hebrew in a country where no one was able properly to answer Colenso'.[18] After being briefly attracted by Maurice and then by Seeley's *Ecce Homo* (1865) he moved to a position of agnosticism, as much as anything because he could not accept even the Apostles' Creed, because of the miracle of the Virgin Birth (though Lightfoot had said the creed was not binding on laymen). He decided to resign his Fellowship.[19] Sidgwick's crisis of faith finally persuaded Lightfoot to support the

---

14   N. Barlow (ed.), *The Autobiography of Charles Darwin, 1805–1882* (London, 1958), pp. 59, 85–7.

15   A. Sidgwick and E.M. Sidgwick (eds), *Henry Sidgwick: A Memoir* (London, 1906), p. 64.

16   Ibid., p. 81.

17   Ibid., p. 89.

18   Ibid., p. 117.

19   Ibid., p. 198.

abolition of religious tests for Fellowships. Benson told Lightfoot (in a letter which his son marked as 'not for publication') that he distrusted the whole principle of subscription to the Thirty-Nine Articles anyway; for him the Apostles' and Nicene Creeds were sufficient, but Sidgwick confessed that he had given up talking to Benson about religious matters because it was too upsetting.[20]

It is not therefore surprising to discover the significance of discussions about the atonement and the doctrine of everlasting punishment in the second half of the nineteenth century. From his time as an undergraduate Westcott had been sceptical about the sufficiency of an atonement-centred Christianity. He once attended a meeting of the teachers at the Jesus Lane Sunday School, when the subject was the simplest method of communicating the doctrine of the atonement to children. He felt that there was 'no earnestness, no life, no spirit in the whole', and he did not go again.[21] Moreover, although Westcott emphasised that Christianity, like Judaism, was a revelation within the events of history, and not just a collection of wise sayings, he thought it inappropriate to apply time to the internal life of the deity. Many years later in 1882 he reminded Llewellyn Davies that 'in very old days I could never hold that time entered as an element into the absolute relation of things'. He had always found it 'equally easy to see how a thing "causes" another when it follows it as when it precedes. The whole is one in the divine order'. He thought that 'nearly all our difficulties come from making our present selves the measure of all things, as if "five senses" could exhaust the universe'.[22] Not surprisingly he had difficulties with transactional understandings of the atonement, which required the incarnation to be a response to the Fall, rather than the culmination of God's purpose of self-revelation in the world. There are echoes of Maurice and McLeod Campbell here.

Before, and during, his involvement with the text of the Greek New Testament Hort had an overarching concern with Christian doctrine, and particularly with the deficiencies of what might be termed the popular evangelical theology. His evangelical upbringing meant that when he went up to Cambridge he first sought out the teaching of Simeon's successor, Dr Carus; but his encounter as an undergraduate with J.C. Hare, especially *Guesses at Truth*, and Coleridge changed his mind.[23] He rejected the Tractarian alternative to evangelicalism, noting Hare's vindication of Luther from Tractarian attack in 1846, and was instead drawn towards F.D. Maurice, whose book *The Kingdom of Christ* he began to read in January 1848.[24] Hort's interest in Maurice's Christian socialism is well known, and he was one of the founders of the Cambridge Working Men's College in 1855;[25]

20    Benson to Lightfoot, 17 June 1863: Benson Papers, Copies of Correspondence, 1853–68, fols 154–5; Benson, *Life of Benson*, i, p. 251.
21    Westcott, *Life of Westcott*, i, p. 50.
22    Westcott to Llewellyn Davies, 10 July 1882: ibid., i, p. 439.
23    Hort to his father, 29 April 1847: Hort, *Life of Hort*, i, pp. 41–2, 54–5.
24    Hort to his father, 4 November 1846; Hort to Ellerton, 19 January 1848: ibid., i, pp. 46, 64–7.
25    Hort to Blunt, 18/26 November 1855; Hort to Ellerton, 2/7 January 1856: ibid., i, pp. 300, 315, 317–18.

but it was Maurice's theology that attracted him. He once wrote of a service he attended in Westminster Abbey with 'very poor music and a dreary sermon on the fear of God'. Fear generally, they were told, was the cause of most good things, such as prudence in marriage; one main instance was fear when they heard a great noise in the night, from which they might understand what was meant by the fear of God. He had heard a grand sermon from Maurice at Lincoln's Inn on Deborah, Jael and the Judges immediately before, which perhaps heightened his sense of disappointment; but the negative approach of the Westminster Abbey sermon illustrated the difficulties he had with orthodoxy.[26] The reference to prudence in marriage illuminates a sentence in his son's address at the Modern Churchmen's Conference in Birmingham in 1927, when he said that 'another cause for his early break with Evangelicalism was the distrust of the reason which at that time prevailed in that school'.[27] The rationalism of evangelical theology worried him, as it had done Coleridge.

In November 1849 Hort wrote his oft-quoted letter to Maurice asking whether he believed in everlasting punishment. The striking thing about this letter from a twenty-one year old undergraduate even a century and a half after it was written is the succinct discussion of the problem. He declined to rest on isolated texts, though he found St Paul's words, 'As in Adam all die, so in Christ shall all be made alive' very compelling. Further he was worried by Paley's argument that the line of distinction between the lowest place in heaven and the highest in hell was not very great, and saw the force of the universalist objection that finite sins did not deserve an infinite punishment. He was particularly anxious about arguments that suggested that the goodness, mercy and justice of God bore only a fleeting resemblance to human conceptions of the same qualities. Thus he worried about the idea of substituted punishment, which though distinct from the atonement, pervaded many interpretations of it. In turn that led him to the personality of the devil, and the problems of the Manichaean controversy and the relation of spirit and flesh. All in all it was a bold letter to write to someone whom he had never met.[28] Maurice's answer was interesting because as a Unitarian he had been brought up to believe in universal restitution: he now found that inadequate because it seemed to make good nature the highest attribute of deity. Instead he regarded the starting point of the Gospel as the absolute Love of God, and the death of Christ as showing that God's love had no limits. He was also reluctant to pass judgement on anyone, and certainly not to make any judgements about anyone's eternal destiny.[29]

26 Hort to Ellerton, 26 June 1851: ibid., i, pp. 197–8; cf. F.D. Maurice, *The Patriarchs and Lawgivers of the Old Testament* (5th edn, London, 1878), pp. 320–35.

27 A.F. Hort, 'Fenton John Anthony Hort', *The Modern Churchman*, xvii (October 1927): 491.

28 Hort to Maurice, 16 November 1849: Hort, *Life of Hort*, i, pp. 116–23.

29 Maurice to Hort, 23 November 1849: F. Maurice, *Life of Frederick Denison Maurice* (London, 1884), ii, pp. 15–23; cf. J.O.F. Murray, *The Goodness and the Severity of God* (London, 1924), pp. 179–208 (Murray was a pupil of Hort's).

Hort therefore took a keen interest in the events surrounding Maurice's dismissal from King's College, London in 1853 because of his statements in *Theological Essays* which cast doubt on whether 'eternal' and 'everlasting' should be regarded as synonyms. It figured in his correspondence for several months, and shows how Hort saw the issues at stake. For example, he wrote to John Ellerton in October 1853 that he expected a considerable number of high churchmen to stand by Maurice, a sentiment he repeated to Gerald Blunt a few days later.[30] By the end of the year, however, he was telling Westcott that he was 'astonished at the small number of even thoughtful men at Cambridge who were able to recognise the distinction between time and eternity'.[31] The reason for Hort's hopes in the high churchmen was that he held Maurice to have said nothing which was not already implied in the *Confessions* of St Augustine, and also that, as he wrote to Ellerton in March 1854, the power of repentance is not limited to this life. He had already suggested this in his letter to Maurice in 1849, but now he wrote with characteristic trenchancy that 'the modern denial of [this view] has ... had more to do with the despiritualizing of theology than almost any[thing] that could be named'.[32] He cited Pearson's dismissal of the views of all the Fathers on this question as an illustration of the way in which he flung antiquity boldly aside because it clashed with modern dogma.

Hort's concern with the doctrine of the atonement continued through the years. John McLeod Campbell had been expelled from the Church of Scotland in 1831 for holding unorthodox views on the subject. Hort read his book on *The Nature of the Atonement*, published in 1856, while it was in the press – Campbell visited Cambridge in the Michaelmas Term 1855, and Hort wrote of it that 'it expresses my own ideas better than any book I ever saw', though he also commented that 'unluckily he knows nothing except Protestant theology'.[33] In his essay on Coleridge he affirmed that Coleridge had not denied the doctrines of original sin and the atonement as had been asserted ever since the attack on the Coleridgean school launched in the 1840s, but he did not develop the reasons for his affirmation at any length.[34]

In 1856 Benjamin Jowett's commentary on Romans included an essay on the atonement in which, as his biographer put it, 'the moral objections to the popular Evangelical doctrine were stated with a passionate vehemence, that broke through the habitual serenity of the style'.[35] Lightfoot reviewed it, together with Stanley's commentary on Corinthians, in the *Journal of Classical and Sacred Philology* for March 1856. He damned the critical scholarship of both Jowett and Stanley,

30     Hort to Ellerton, 31 October 1853; Hort to Blunt, 4 November 1853: Hort, *Life of Hort*, i, pp. 260–63.

31     Hort to Westcott, 31 December 1853/3 January 1854: ibid., i, p. 266.

32     Hort to Ellerton, 19 March/2 April 1854: ibid., i, p. 275.

33     Hort to Blunt, 18/26 November 1855; Hort to Ellerton, 2/7 January 1856; Hort to Blunt, 20 March 1856: ibid., i, pp. 316, 319, 322.

34     Hort, 'Coleridge', pp. 343–4.

35     E. Abbott and L. Campbell, *Life and Letters of Benjamin Jowett* (London, 1897), i, pp. 233–4.

whilst acknowledging that Jowett's metaphysical and doctrinal discussion was the more important part. But he criticised Jowett's 'habit of viewing great questions in their contradictory aspects without attemptiong to reconcile them, and of finding difficulties without resolving them'. He also criticised the unhistorical tone, suggesting that the historian 'strives to detect hidden resemblances' and 'traces the thread of connexion between different ages', whilst Jowett sought out 'the contrasts in different nations and ages' and violently dissevered one epoch from another.[36] The reactions of Benson and Hort to this article were interestingly different. Benson wrote to Lightfoot that it was the best thing that he had done yet and pointed the way to sound study of the New Testament: Hort wrote to Blunt that it was 'a most excellent review of Stanley and Jowett "as critics" by Lightfoot, but he purposely avoids the theology'.[37]

The problem continued to worry him. In 1859 there was an exchange of letters with Westcott over the term 'ideal Christian' which Westcott had used to suggest that it was the work of all life to realise this idea. Hort thought that the truth of death to sin was a fundamental fact, secured by Christ's death on the cross, but that this eternal and invisible truth required a temporal and outward embodiment, which 'can be only by baptism'.[38] The influence of Maurice is clear. Again, when Llewellyn Davies published his sermons on *The Work of Christ* in 1860, Westcott was hesitant about the use of ideas of human justice, and wrote to Hort that there was something

> unspeakably sad in controversy on such a subject as the Atonement … Have we the slightest hope to gain an intelligible theory of the fact? Is it not enough to say that the death of our Blessed Lord was necessary for our redemption? and that we are saved by it? Is it not absurd to expect that we can conceive how it is necessary – since the necessity is divine?[39]

Hort was not impressed: 'Certainly such a mere statement of results seems to me very preferable to the popular attempts at explanation, but it still seems to me a mere product of despairing (but not unbelieving) speculation opposed to the actual revelations made to us in the Bible.' To say that the necessity was Divine was not sufficient reason for not being able to apprehend its nature 'as I do not admit your (?) axiom that man cannot know God as He is'. He acknowledged that human notions of justice were inadequate, but thought that many of the current problems arose from taking what he called jural justice rather than moral justice as a standard. The *facts* recorded in scripture showed that it was not unjust that the innocent should suffer and that such suffering should benefit the guilty; but this was very different from making a human *explanation* or *interpretation* of

---

36     J.B. Lightfoot, 'Recent Editions of St Paul's Epistles', *Journal of Classical and Sacred Philology*, iii, (March 1856): 118.

37     Benson to Lightfoot, 6 April 1856: Benson, *Life of Benson*, i, p. 127; Hort to Blunt, 20 March 1856: Hort, *Life of Hort*, i, p. 322.

38     Westcott to Hort, 6 April 1859: Westcott, *Life of Westcott*, i, pp. 234–5; Hort to Westcott, 7 April 1859: Hort, *Life of Hort*, i, pp. 407–8.

39     Westcott to Hort, 6 August 1860: Westcott, *Life of Westcott*, i, pp. 239–40.

the facts (such as the 'plan of salvation') a criterion of justice. But this was not for Hort the main point: 'surely the essence of the Atonement must consist in the forgiveness itself, and not in the abolition of such suffering.'[40] That exchange captures the difference between Hort and Westcott in their approach to doctrine. Westcott was inclined to say that everything was a mystery: Hort did not deny the mystery, but thought that the incarnational nature of divine truth made it possible to say more.

When Harold Browne, as Bishop of Ely, asked Hort to become his examining chaplain in 1871, he characteristically hesitated before agreeing, pointing out the extent to which he had been influenced by Maurice. In particular Hort sought assurance that the bishop understood his position on the atonement; and once again the question of substitution was at the heart of the matter. He wrote 'the uniqueness of the great Sacrifice seems to me not to consist in its being a substitute which makes all other sacrifices useless and unmeaning, but in its giving them the power and meaning which of themselves they could not have'.[41] The bishop replied that he did not believe that there was any fundamental difference between them on the doctrine, and Hort was appointed.

The final illustration of Hort's concern on these subjects comes in 1886 when an Oxford undergraduate, H. Brinton, asked his help over the Thirty-Nine Articles. Those which particularly concerned him were Articles IX on original sin, X on free will, XVII on predestination and election, XVIII on obtaining salvation only by the name of Christ, and XXII on purgatory. Hort's reply provoked a further question on Article XIII on good works before justification. Even to enumerate the articles is to give a sense of the problems the undergraduate had, though his letter does not survive. Hort's answers illustrated both his knowledge of the Reformation background, and the extent to which he wished to go beyond it. On original sin he wished to deny that the flesh was evil in itself; on election he criticised the individualist emphasis in the way the Reformers interpreted the doctrine. He thought that Article XVIII on salvation only in the name of Christ was not happily expressed, and could 'easily be understood as setting forth a doctrine which the authors may very possibly have had in their own minds, and which appears to me utterly untenable'.[42] The reason for this appeared when he referred to Article XXII on purgatory: although he rejected the Roman doctrine, he did not believe 'that God's purposes of love can ever cease towards us in any stage of our existence, or that they can accomplish themselves by our purification and perfection without painful processes'.[43] In other words, Hort's belief that human purification would continue after death was based on the conviction that in the end God's purpose for the whole of humanity would be achieved: the notion of everlasting punishment was therefore unacceptable, just as were too hasty judgements on those who died without confessing the name of Christ.

---

40    Hort to Westcott, 14/16 April 1860: Hort, *Life of Hort*, i, pp. 427–8. The question mark is in the published text.
41    Hort to Browne, 12 November 1871: ibid., ii, p. 158.
42    Hort to Mr H. Brinton, January 1886: ibid., ii, p. 334.
43    Ibid., ii, p. 336.

One reason for this was, as Hort put it in a follow-up letter, that faith itself was not 'an intellectual assent to propositions, but an attitude of heart and mind ... present in a more or less rudimentary state in every upward effort and aspiration of men'.[44]

There is a striking similarity between that understanding of faith and Peter Hinchliff's comment on Jowett in 1855 that he 'no longer thought of faith as believing a set number of "things"'.[45] But how similar was Hort's view to that of the supporters of liberal theology in the mid-nineteenth century, epitomised by Jowett? The conclusion of Jowett's essay on 'Justification by Faith' read as follows:

> Human minds are different, and the same mind varies at different times; and even the best of men have but a feeble sense of the unseen world. We cannot venture further to dim that consciousness by confining it to one expression of belief; and therefore while speaking of faith as the instrument of justification, because faith best indicates the apprehensive dependent character of our Christian life, we are bound also to deny that the truth of Christ is contained in any one statement, of the Christian life linked to any one quality.[46]

It is impossible to imagine Hort saying that, and it is therefore crucial to see the distinction between what Jowett was getting at and what Hort understood by faith. To achieve this is to understand one of the fundamental differences between Oxford and Cambridge theology in the nineteenth century. It also illuminates the different aims of the Jowett/Stanley commentaries on the Epistles and those of Lightfoot.

Hort was not very impressed by the liberal group of Oxford theologians, later to be involved in the publication of *Essays and Reviews* in 1860. When H.B. Wilson's Bampton Lectures of 1851 on *The Communion of Saints* were published, Hort wrote to Ellerton that they were 'perfectly horrible'. More interestingly he went on to say that, although people would quote them as instances of Germanising, the real roots were Locke and Zwingli. In effect they denied that there was any communion between the living and the dead and affirmed that the communion of saints meant good action in different Christians. This was 'dreadfully and calmly philosophically destructive', indicating a hatred of doctrines and a contempt for historical Christianity.[47] When Jowett's commentary was published in 1855, Hort wrote to Westcott that the essay on 'Natural Religion' seemed to lead to a conclusion of 'blank scepticism'.[48] Hort's view of Lightfoot's *Galatians* was discussed in the previous chapter, but the avoidance of doctrinal questions meant that 'Jowett's notes and essays, with all their perversities, are still an indispensable

44    Hort to Brinton, 31 January 1886: ibid., ii, p. 337.
45    P. Hinchliff, *Benjamin Jowett and the Christian Religion* (Oxford, 1987), p. 61.
46    B. Jowett, *The Epistles of St Paul to the Thessalonians, Galatians, Romans* (London, 1855), ii, p. 467.
47    Hort to Ellerton, 29/30 December 1851: Hort, *Life of Hort*, i, p. 210.
48    Hort to Westcott, 2 October 1855: ibid., i, p. 313.

supplement'.[49] Jowett's virtue, in Hort's eyes, was that he tackled the central questions; his weakness was in the answers he gave.

This explains Hort's attitude to *Essays and Reviews*. When Rowland Williams in 1858 invited him to contribute (possibly because of his essay on Coleridge in the Cambridge series), he declined partly because he said he had his hands full with the text of the New Testament (and he was now in a parish rather than in Cambridge), but mainly because he felt that there was a wide difference of principles and opinions between him and the contributors. His explanation of this, though a little long, was very revealing:

> I can go all lengths with them in maintaining absolute freedom of criticism, science, and speculation; in appealing to experience as a test of mere *a priori* dogma; and upholding the supremacy of spirit over letter in all possible applications. Further I agree with them in condemning many leading specific doctrines of the popular theology as, to say the least, containing much superstition and immorality of a very pernicious kind. But I fear that in our own positive theology we should diverge widely. I have a deeply-rooted agreement with High Churchmen as to the Church, Ministry, Sacraments, and above all, Creeds, though by no means acquiescing in their unhistorical and unphilosophical treatment of theology, or their fears and antipathies generally. The positive doctrines even of the Evangelicals seem to me perverted rather than untrue. There are, I fear, still more serious differences between us on the subject of authority, and especially the authority of the Bible; and this alone would make my position among you sufficiently false in respect to the great questions which you will be chiefly anxious to discuss.[50]

Hort also thought that such a publication would bring on a crisis, which would be counter-productive.

In the event Hort's judgement was proved right. In August 1860 Westcott wrote to Hort, saying that it was necessary to show that there was 'a mean between *Essays and Reviews* and Traditionalism'. Hort refused to join in any volume 'which could plausibly be regarded as simply an orthodox protest against the Essays and Reviews'. He thought that the essayists '*believe* very much more of truth than their (so-called) orthodox opponents, and to be incomparably greater lovers of truth'.[51] Westcott came back with a modified proposal in December, which would strike 'the true mean between the inexorable logic of the Westminster and the sceptical dogmatism of orthodoxy'. Hort, although more sympathetic to the new proposal, was not keen on the idea of 'a true mean', since there was no mean between reason and authority.[52] He obviously persuaded Westcott, because in February

---

49    Hort to Ellerton, 7 May 1865: ibid., ii, p. 35.

50    Hort to his wife, 11 January 1889: ibid., i, pp. 399–400.

51    Westcott to Hort, 6 August 1860 (emphasis original): Westcott, *Life of Westcott*, i, p. 213; Hort to Westcott, 14/16 August 1860: Hort, *Life of Hort*, i, p. 428.

52    Westcott to Hort, 13 December 1860: Westcott, *Life of Westcott*, i, p. 214; Hort to Westcott, 14 December 1860: Hort, *Life of Hort*, i, p. 437. The *Westminster Review* had carried the hostile review by Frederic Harrison which suggested that if the Essayists were honest, they would leave the Church; 'the sceptical dogmatism of orthodoxy' may be a reference to H.L. Mansel's Bampton Lectures on *Reason and Revelation*.

1861 Westcott wrote to a friend that he thought 'the assailants of the Essayists, from the Bishops downwards, as likely to do far more harm to the Church and the Truth than the Essayists' and that the result would be an appeal to authority rather than reason.[53] Since Lightfoot refused to take part, the proposed volume from the trio never appeared.[54]

When Hort wrote to Ellerton about *Essays and Reviews* in April 1860 he made a very revealing comment about Jowett. 'His blindness to a providential ordering of the accidents of history is very vexatious. It is curious to see how completely he is leavened with J.H. Newman.'[55] Hort once referred to a saying of Maurice that Newman 'was governed by an infinite scepticism counteracted by an infinite devoutness'.[56] That is the leaven of Newman, which Hort saw in Jowett; and it reflects the statement from Jowett's commentary about the best of men having but a feeble sense of the unseen world. The acknowledgement of human variation[57] and the reluctance to allow human language to give any impression of God; the refusal to make any one expression of belief definitive: all this denied what Hort held most dear. Hence, while he was happy to accept the critical principles of Jowett's essay on 'The Interpretation of Scripture', he was most unhappy about his reticence on doctrinal questions.

A decade later when Newman's *Apologia* was published, Hort wrote to Westcott that 'the total absence of any specific influence of Greek theology upon the Oxford movement' was a 'very striking fact', notwithstanding the extensive reading in the Fathers possessed by its more learned chiefs; and he thought that influence was a leading cause of the largeness of mind in the greater English divines from 1550 to 1650.[58] After Newman's move to Rome in 1845, he wrote to Ellerton saying that he had been struck by 'the unquestioning assumption that there is one absolutely and exclusively Divine system in all things, especially one Church so entirely right that all other bodies must be entirely wrong'. This reflected 'the complete permanence of his Calvinistic religion, changing nothing but its form when it passed most naturally into Romanism'.[59] And when Newman died, he made what must be one of his most crushing remarks. After admitting the reverence he had always felt for Newman and the fact that he had always prized the letter Newman wrote to him after the publication of his *Two Dissertations* in 1876, he wrote to his wife, 'Yet I suppose there is no distinguished theologian in any church, or of any school, whom I should find it so hard to think of as having

53    Hort to Westcott, 14/16 August 1860: Hort, *Life of Hort*, i, p. 428; Westcott to Hort, Westcott, *Life of Westcott*, i, p. 215.

54    Westcott to Wickenden, 25 February 1861: Westcott, *Life of Westcott*, i, pp. 215–16.

55    Hort to Ellerton, 20 April 1860: Hort, *Life of Hort*, i, p. 417.

56    Hort to his wife, 24 August 1890: ibid., ii, pp. 423–4.

57    Cf. J.H. Newman: 'In a higher world it is otherwise; but here below to live is to change, and to be perfect is to have changed often', *An Essay on the Development of Christian Doctrine* (London, 1845), p. 39.

58    Hort to Westcott, 23 July 1865: Hort, *Life of Hort*, ii, p. 38.

59    Hort to his father and mother, 12 April 1846: ibid., ii, pp. 18, 35–6.

contributed anything to the support or advance of Christian truth'. He went on to say that 'but for his indestructible sense of God's reality and presence, he *must* have early become a thorough-going unbeliever'; instead 'he delighted to use his never-failing subtlety in finding reasons or excuse for any belief which he wished to accept'.[60] It is significant that when he wrote a letter to a lady contemplating joining the Church of Rome in 1862, he should not only have marshalled both historical and theological arguments against the Roman claims, but also commented that papal infallibility instead of being a blessing for the assurance it gave would actually be a curse. The reason was that 'in God's real teaching of us, asking and receiving, seeking and finding, are inextricably combined. No truth is vital and fruitful to us at which we have not laboured ourselves'.[61]

Nevertheless Westcott, Lightfoot, Hort and Benson all regarded the church as of central importance in Christian faith. Westcott's invocation of the community against what he regarded as too individualistic an approach to inspiration was discussed in the previous chapter. He also made a very close connection between the apologetic task and the Christian community. Rather like Maurice, he affirmed the objective nature of this divine society: 'The unity of the Christian Society, to which potentially all men belong, depends not on any personal feeling but on a common relation in which men as belonging to the society stand to GOD.'[62] The church's relation to the resurrection is illustrated by a note to the second edition in 1867:

> The Epistle to the Ephesians and the writings of St John contain in a divine commentary on the Resurrection, of which Christian history is the gradual and partial fulfilment, the complete solution of the greatest problems to which the thoughts of men are now being turned, the Solidarity of Humanity and the relation of our World to the whole Kosmos.[63]

He devoted the summer of 1867 to reading Auguste Comte, attracted by the importance he attached to society, but disagreeing over his view of religion. This theme was developed in his essay on 'Aspects of Positivism in relation to Christianity', which was published in the *Contemporary Review* for 1867, and included as an appendix from the third edition onwards. In the Preface to his Westminster Abbey Sermons, *Social Aspects of Christianity* (1887), Westcott described his debt to Comte's *Politique Positive* and Maurice's *Social Morality* (1869): of the former he wrote, 'I found in it a powerful expression of many salient features of that which I had long held to be the true social embodiment of the Gospel, of a social ideal which the faith in Christ is alone, I believe, able to realise'.[64] This not only indicates why Westcott believed that faith in Christ was

---

60   Hort to his wife, 24 August 1890 (emphasis original): ibid., ii, pp. 423–4.

61   Hort to a lady, October 1862: ibid., i, p. 467.

62   B.F. Westcott, *The Gospel of the Resurrection* 5th edn, London, 1884), p. 210. Maurice would not have said 'potentially'.

63   Ibid., p. xxv (notice to 3rd edn).

64   B.F. Westcott, *Social Aspects of Christianity* (London, 1887), p. xii.

the realisation of a social idea; it also indicates the roots and nature of Westcott's beliefs about the 'social gospel'.

The interest in community explains the importance Westcott attached to cathedrals. While an undergraduate he had been attracted by the idea of a monastic life.[65] The diaries and correspondence of Westcott, Lightfoot and Benson suggest that one of the features of the visit to France in 1865 that impressed the trio was the encounter with monastic life. As Westcott and Benson were both married, this was not an option for them; Lightfoot had Trinity, although this was not the most obvious model for an ascetic existence. Westcott's first idea was what he called a 'Coenobium' – community life – and he discussed ways of implementing it with Benson. He envisaged an association of families 'with hall and schools and chapel, with a common income, though not common property, and an organised government'.[66] His son had vivid memories of the Coenobium: 'whenever we children showed signs of greediness or other selfishness, we were assured that such things would be unheard of in the Coenobium. There the greedy would have no second portions of desirable puddings.'[67] Westcott wrote an article on the idea in the *Contemporary Review* for 1870. If the interdependence of human beings was of particular importance and the individual life is but part of a vaster life, he suggested that 'some social manifestation of the energies of our faith' was required: 'Christianity is, indeed, in virtue of the facts on which it rests, social, or rather human, before it is individual.'[68]

The concern for community was also reflected in a concern about the damaging effects of church controversy. Westcott's consistent antipathy to party feeling has already been mentioned more than once. Lightfoot and Benson were of the same opinion. There is an interesting exchange in their correspondence during Lightfoot's first year at Cambridge in 1847–48, which illustrates the attitudes of both men. Benson had asked Lightfoot whether he kept the Canonical Hours in a letter asking for the prayers for None after the last response. Lightfoot replied that he kept them pretty regularly but that 'the College hours are very inconvenient for it'. He also said that he was not at all settled in his church views, but he was certain that he 'could not entertain such uncharitable views as those held by the extreme (so-called) high Church party'. He had in mind the controversy over Hampden's appointment as Bishop of Hereford, remarking that 'if St John had said "hate one another" his precept could scarcely have been better fulfilled'. Although 'it would be unfair to charge this uncharitableness all on the one party, and to overlook the same fault in the other', he felt that 'in the one it seems to be

65    Diary, 1 January 1846: Westcott, *Life of Westcott*, i, p. 40.

66    B.F. Westcott, 'On a Form of Confraternity suited to the Present Work of the English Church', *Contemporary Review*, xiv (April 1870): 111–12; quoted (without reference) in Westcott, *Life of Westcott*, i, p. 264.

67    Westcott, *Life*, i, pp. 264–5. He thought that it really was coming and that they, with the Bensons and Horts and a few other families would find themselves in a community; he even identified Peterborough as a location for it.

68    *Contemporary Review*, xiv (1870): 114.

inseparable from the system, and there must be something wrong in that belief which excites such feelings in men otherwise good and exemplary'.

A few weeks later, however, Lightfoot told Benson 'we ought to feel grateful to the writers of the Oxford Tracts for their efforts against the absurdities of the Evangelical system, particularly the exaltation of preaching to the detriment of praying'. If forced to choose between Tractarianism and evangelicalism, he would have no hesitation about his choice. This alarmed Benson, who pointed out that the next or next-but-one generation of those born into high church principles were likely to follow the pattern of Methodism, which had begun with so many lovely and pleasant things, but had degenerated in their grandchildren 'into the same stern rigidity of demeanour, while within seven other spirits came, with "envy, hatred and malice, and all uncharitableness," with far too many of that happy company'. Lightfoot assured Benson that he was still far from 'the extreme and violent sentiments of some of the Tracts', but was inclined towards the position of someone like Hook (Vicar of Leeds). The reasons he gave for this shift were significant. First, he had become suspicious of the doctrines held by Hampden and his party, and felt 'that there can be as much want of Charity in the very condemnation of uncharitableness, as there is in the so-styled bigotry of the other party'. Secondly, he admired the spirit which animated high churchmen generally, involving a sacrifice of self and selfish desires to principles. So he regarded high churchmen as 'the great regenerating element among us, the only one, I think, which will be able to withstand the assaults of Romanism and Protestant Dissent'. Lastly, he emphasised that many high church opinions were true. So-called 'Puseyism', or church principles, were not a recent invention, but they were 'the faith held by the confessors and martyrs of old, yea and by our own reformers too, whom they so much extol (and justly too) and by Taylor, that pattern of a Bishop, and Hooker, and by many others we could mention'.[69] Now these are the letters of an undergraduate. In reading them one can almost feel the continuous encounter with new ideas and new experiences. But they give important clues to attitudes which remained constant in Lightfoot's later career.

High churchmen in the 1860s were disconcerted by Lightfoot's essay on 'The Christian Ministry' in his *Commentary on Philippians* for two reasons. First, he argued that the episcopate emerged from the presbyterate and that apostolic succession did not consist in identity of office – 'the episcopate was formed not out of the apostolic order by localisation, but out of the presbyteral by elevation'. Secondly, he argued that the Christian ministry was not in origin sacerdotal, and that the minister's function was representative without being vicarial. 'His acts are not his own but the acts of the congregation.' Hence in an emergency, laymen could assume functions otherwise restricted to the ordained minister.[70] Westcott

---

69    Benson to Lightfoot, 29 October 1847; Lightfoot to Benson, 8 March 1848; Lightfoot to Benson 29 April 1848; Benson to Lightfoot, 3 May 1848; Lightfoot to Benson, 19 July 1848: Benson, *Life of Benson*, i, pp. 50, 55–56, 59–60, 61, 64–5.

70    J.B. Lightfoot, *Saint Paul's Epistle to the Philippians* (4th edn, London, 1879), pp. 196, 227, 244–5, 267–8.

welcomed the book,[71] but it is hard to find references to it in the lives of other contemporaries. Pusey was preoccupied with his *Eirenicon* and the approach of the Vatican Council. Nonconformists loved it, whilst not always recognising that Lightfoot had established that episcopacy became universal relatively early, even if not at the beginning, and that he regarded it as a legitimate development rather than a corruption, indeed as an apostolic institution through St John. During Benson's visit to Lightfoot at Bournemouth during his illness in the winter of 1888–89, he discussed 'the foolish deductions drawn by Dissenters from his essay on the Christian Ministry'. Lightfoot declined to offer any explanations for what he had written, and said that if the argument was that what came first was right, one might as well say that everything emerged from the diaconate. 'Of course,' he added, 'everything was imperfect when it was beginning.'[72]

In April 1872 Westcott and Lightfoot encouraged the foundation of the Cambridge University Church Society, which was formed, in Professor Stanton's words, 'with the object of promoting a better understanding of one another, and fuller cooperation among young Churchmen of various shades of opinion'.[73] Westcott gave the opening address under the title 'Striving Together'. In it he said that he regarded 'combination in diversity' as in a peculiar sense the work of England, the English Church, the English Universities and Cambridge especially. The inheritance of the English Church did not begin with the Reformation, but went back to Alban and Augustine; however, solutions to the problems of the present would not be met by referring to the example of the primitive church or the sixteenth century, but by drawing on the whole tradition. 'From one generation to another our Church has brought out of her treasures things new and old.'[74] Truth is one because it is infinite, and no limits for inquiry can be defined beforehand. Westcott described the intellectual spirit of Cambridge as 'grave, sober, patient, self-questioning. There is amongst us a certain reserve, a lingering caution, perhaps an unfitness for action. But out of these qualities springs something of an unbroken sympathy underlying our differences'.[75]

Lightfoot preached the inaugural sermon in St Michael's Church on 23 April 1872 on the text 'All are yours; and ye are Christ's'. The new association was to unite a wide comprehension of men and ideas with concentration of purpose and unity of spirit. Those who joined this association would try 'to overcome the strifes and antipathies which separate not only Christian from Christian but also Churchman from Churchman'; they would 'avoid harshness and exaggeration in stating the principles to which they cling themselves', whilst understanding and absorbing whatever was good and true in the exaggerated statements of others. In this way they would combine the energies which were then dissipated, and thus

---

71    Westcott to Lightfoot, 1 August 1868: Westcott, *Life of Westcott*, i, p. 294.

72    Benson, *Life of Benson*, ii, p. 228.

73    Westcott, *Life of Westcott*, i, p. 383.

74    It may be significant that the same Gospel image was used by Gore in the Preface to *Lux Mundi* (p. viii).

75    B.F. Westcott, *An Address to the University Church Society* (Cambridge, [1873]), pp. 7, 9–10, 11, 12, 13.

'unite in the common service of Christ all the forces of religious zeal which at present spend themselves in neutralising each other'. The same approach would be carried into intellectual and social life outside the church:

> The gulf between faith and science, between religion and society, which others contemplate as widening day by day, will have no existence for you. Each fresh accession of knowledge, each progressive development of social life, will come to you with the force of a special message from God in Christ.[76]

It is surely not a coincidence that Lightfoot illustrated his text with a discussion of the problems of division within the Corinthian Church. Paul did not intend, he suggested, that everyone should approach the Gospel in the same way: 'Man is finite; truth is infinite ... A moment's reflection will show, that uniformity is impoverishment, and that diversity is absolutely necessary if there is to be anything like fulness in the final result. And where diversity is recognised, there is comprehension.'[77] This was because unity in the church depended primarily on unity in Christ; and the Christological basis of truth was why science no less than theology was the inheritance of the Christian.[78]

Should Lightfoot's churchmanship therefore be described as broad? When he was appointed to Durham in 1879, H.P. Liddon, who was Lightfoot's colleague as a canon of St Paul's, wrote to C.L. Wood (later Lord Halifax) that 'Lightfoot's [appointment] will not help Church principles except in *this* way, that he will be *just* to everybody; and justice towards High Churchmen will have all the charm of novelty in the Diocese of Durham ... He is essentially "broad", with generous and – pious – instincts to boot'. Liddon hoped that 'the possession of the Episcopal office may lead a very honest mind to ask itself the question, "What are the principles upon which the Episcopate is to be justified, at all seriously, before God and man?" ... But, for the present, we must read his Essay on "The Christian Ministry" in his book on the Philippians, and limit our expectations accordingly'.[79] Lightfoot himself said at the Church Congress of 1880 that 'the introduction of the term "Broad" has thrown everything into confusion'.[80] If to be 'high' is to be narrow rather than catholic, then Lightfoot was broad, but he was not broad in the same sense as Stanley or Jowett. In his *Primary Charge* in 1882 he said that the great boast of the Church of England was her comprehensiveness. A.P. Stanley and E.B. Pusey had both recently died. 'Each has taught us valuable lessons. The Church would have been seriously impoverished by the exclusion of either.'[81] It is not surprising that Queen Victoria should have written to Archbishop Benson

76  J.B. Lightfoot, *Sermons preached on special occasions* (London, 1891), pp. 2–3.
77  Ibid., pp. 8–9.
78  Ibid., pp. 12–13, 16–17, 18–19.
79  J.O. Johnston, *Life and Letters of Henry Parry Liddon* (London, 1904), pp. 265–6 (emphasis original).
80  D.J. Vaughan (ed.), *Official Report of the Church Congress held at Leicester, 1880* (London, 1881), p. 232.
81  J.B. Lightfoot, *Primary Charge: Two Addresses delivered to the Clergy of the Diocese of Durham in December 1882* (London, n.d.), pp. 91–2.

after his death emphasising the importance of choosing bishops not to satisfy any party in the church or in politics but for their real worth. 'We want people who can be firm and conciliating, else the Church cannot be maintained. We want large broad views – or the difficulties will become insurmountable.'[82]

Hort's understanding of the church may be viewed in the same way. Graham Patrick stated that Hort was a lifelong high churchman, recalling the influence of the Tractarian movement upon him, his agreement with high churchmen in his letter declining to contribute to *Essays and Reviews*, and his introduction of a high church hymnbook into his churches when he was a parish priest.[83] But it is doubtful whether the Tractarians would have recognised Hort as a completely kindred spirit. Hort's sense of the church began with Arnold and Coleridge rather than the *Tracts for the Times*. Indeed he wrote to Westcott in 1852 that he had never read the *Tracts*, but he admired Newman's clarity – 'rather like a very pure knife-edge of ice. I believe he has a really warm heart, but he has put it to school in a truly diabolic way.' However, in a later letter he said that he all but worshipped Newman; it was his sayings and doings he condemned.[84]

In his approach to the sacraments Hort always echoed the language of Maurice. He encountered Maurice's view of baptism when he read *The Kingdom of Christ* as an undergraduate, and admired 'the truth, beauty, wisdom, scripturality, and above all unity' of it, which probably explains why in commenting on Manning's possible secession in 1848 he remarked that it was 'a most fearful thing to quit the church of one's baptism'.[85] At the end of his life, when writing of Holy Communion to Ellerton he said that 'the corporate communion was not merely a universal characteristic of the Eucharist, but its very essence'. 'Before all things,' he continued, 'it is the feast of a brotherhood united in a Divine Head, setting forth as the fundamental law of their existence the law of sacrifice, towards each other and towards Him, which had been made a reality by His supreme Sacrifice.' He felt that this dimension (which had more in common with the twentieth-century 'Parish and People' movement than Tractarianism) was 'entirely obscured in the Roman and Anglican rites alike'.[86] Each of the letters he wrote to his children on their confirmation is interesting, but in that which he wrote from Rome in 1888 to his youngest son, Fred, he repeated this emphasis. When Fred received the bread and wine he would be entering into communion with the whole church and Christ its head; and his parents in the English Church in Rome would be joining in the same communion: 'it is the great pledge that time and distance do not keep apart those whom God has made to be one.'[87] The tentative conclusions about the development of the church which mark Hort's book on *The Christian Ecclesia*

---

82    The Queen to Benson, 3 January 1890: Benson, *Life of Benson*, ii, p. 293.

83    G.A. Patrick, *F.J.A. Hort: Eminent Victorian* (Sheffield, 1988), p. 97.

84    Hort to Westcott, 14 September 1852 and October 8/13 1852: Hort, *Life of Hort*, i, pp. 228–9, 231.

85    Hort to Ellerton, 19 January 1848; Hort to Blunt, 26 April 1848: ibid., i, pp. 67, 71.

86    Hort to Ellerton, 21 March 1886: ibid., ii, p. 343.

87    Hort to his youngest son, 28 March 1888: ibid., ii, p. 392.

(lectures given in 1888–89 and published in 1897), although they worried those in the Tractarian tradition, are not surprising in view of his other writings.[88] He wrote to Edwin Hatch in 1886 that in dealing with churches with different organisations, what was needed was practical tolerance; and 'Anglican prejudice and exclusive theory' needed tender handling if their power was to be sapped. Hort saw the Church of England as 'the mediator of Christendom rather than its *via media*'.[89]

All three of the Cambridge trio understood the church as that which manifested the incarnation. For them the incarnation was the central event of history. When Westcott set out his revised proposal for a set of essays by way of response to *Essays and Reviews* in December 1860, the topics he proposed were: the development of the doctrine of Messiah, including the selection of one people out of many; miracles and history; and the development of Christian doctrine out of the apostolic teaching. 'In other words,' he said, 'I should like to have the Incarnation as a centre, and on either side the preparation for it, and the apprehension of it in history.'[90] Hort wanted the first part 'to include *all* the preparation for the Gospel, heathen as well as Jewish, the "prerogative" position of Israel being of course clearly maintained'.[91]

In his *Gospel of the Resurrection* Westcott explored the significance of the person and work of Christ.

> In proportion therefore as the exposition of Christian Doctrine becomes more complicated, it becomes more necessary to strive to keep ever present to our minds the thought of Christ Himself, Incarnate, Crucified, Raised, Ascended, in whose Person and Work all doctrine is implicitly contained. And the study of the Bible and the study of the Church history are the chief means through which the Holy Spirit opens out our understanding of our personal faith.[92]

Again the centrality of the incarnation is clear.

------

88   F.J.A. Hort, *The Christian Ecclesia* (London, 1897), pp. 1–21.
89   Hort to Hatch, 22 September 1886: ibid., ii, pp. 357–8.
90   Westcott to Hort, 6 August 1860: Westcott, *Life of Westcott*, i, p. 214.
91   Hort to Westcott, 14 December 1860 (emphasis original): Hort, *Life of Hort*, i, p. 438.
92   Westcott, *Gospel of the Resurrection*, p. xiv. There is an illuminating exchange with Benson in January 1865, where Benson could not see why Westcott regarded the Ascension as the '*complement* of the Resurrection of Jesus Christ, and merely its natural consequence', rather than seeing the Resurrection as 'the first necessary step towards the Session – the Introit to the Liturgy'. Westcott replied that the Resurrection could not be understood as a historic fact without such a completion; but 'the Ascension belongs to a new order of existence, of which at present we have and can have no idea in itself'. Thus 'however much I may wish to maintain that the Resurrection and the Ascension are both facts, yet I am forced to admit that they are facts wholly different in kind, and for us the historical life of the Lord closes with the last scene on Olivet': Benson to Westcott, 4 January 1865: Benson, *Life of Benson*, i, p. 231; Westcott to Benson, 7 January 1865: Westcott, *Life of Westcott*, i, pp. 286–7.

Lightfoot's paper to the Croydon Church Congress of 1873 on how to increase interest in theological thought contained the same emphasis on the incarnation that characterised Westcott. He pointed out that the age was distracted by fundamental questions such as the existence of God, the value of prayer, and the question of a future life; and this made it difficult to stimulate interest in the doctrines of the incarnation and atonement. However, a sense of history put such questions into perspective, and acted as a warning against uncritical commitment to the intellectual current of the age. Nevertheless the theologian had to engage with contemporary concerns, rather than repeating the theological forms of three or six centuries ago; and Lightfoot suggested four. The utilitarianism of the age made it necessary to demonstrate that theology did actually have an effect on life. Secondly, it was necessary to take account of Christian contact with Hinduism, Buddhism and Islam; and here he suggested that the Alexandrian emphasis on the logos would be fruitful. Thirdly, it was necessary to use the same means for a sympathetic approach to scientific research. Fourthly, theology had to be related to modern social questions. Here in outline was the theological programme of *Lux Mundi* sixteen years before that book was published.

Hort's own reponse to *Essays and Reviews* came in his Hulsean Lectures of 1871, *The Way, the Truth and the Life*, posthumously published in 1893. Their still unfinished state reflected the difficulty Hort had in being satisfied with his own work. More interesting is their aspiration to give an account of Christian truth, which would take problems seriously without collapsing into either scepticism on the one hand or dogmatism on the other. The scope of his undertaking, drawing on Coleridge and Maurice, was not dissimilar from that attempted in a very different way and at much greater length by Hegel in Germany: they all responded to the problems posed by the Enlightenment and Kant. Hort did not find the role of apologist which John Hulse's will required a congenial one. He noted in his Preface that 'Christian truth never appears so vulnerable as after the reading of treatises written expressly in its defence'.[93] But he noted other more serious difficulties: first, that the desire to offer rational grounds of assurance led to a suppression of the personal factor in what was convincing – so he set out to speak only as a learner to learners, since 'to have become disabled for unlearning is to have become disabled for learning'.[94] (There is here a shadow of his earlier reluctance to presume the infallibility of scripture.) Secondly, he recognised and intended that the lectures should suggest more questions than they answered. 'Beliefs worth calling beliefs must be purchased with the sweat of the brow.'[95] Hort had no time for easy beliefs, easy disbeliefs or an easy acquiescence in suspense between belief and disbelief:

It is from the credulity of Christians that the Christian faith suffers most in days of debate; and it is well when any who might have helpfully maintained its cause among their neighbours, had they not been disabled by too facile acquiescence, are impelled

93    F.J.A. Hort, *The Way, the Truth and the Life* (London, 1893), p. xxix.
94    Ibid., p. xxxiv.
95    Ibid.

to plunge into the deep anew. There is not indeed and cannot be any security that they will emerge on the Christian side: in human minds truth does not always win the present victory, even when it is faithfully pursued. But whatever be the present result to themselves or to others through them, it is not possible that they or that any should fall out of the keeping of Him who appointed the trial: and to the Church any partial loss that may arise is outweighed by the gain from those whose faith has come to rest on a firmer foundation.[96]

His third point (and the Preface was unfinished) was that the problem of Christian evidences was simplified by omitting either the credentials or the contents: but that temptation had to be resisted and the complexity of the task had to be acknowledged.

As the Johannine text suggested, the four lectures took the form of an exposition of the Way, the Truth and the Life, while the fourth lecture picked up the next words of the text, 'No man cometh to the Father but by me'. The significance of that lecture, which is the most incomplete, is indicated by the discussion of Article XIII noted earlier. What is striking about them, since they are impossible to summarise, is the range of material covered, from an understanding of the historical development of Christianity, via a philosphical consideration of different understandings of truth, to a consideration of the significance of life in itself and life in Christ. Once more the attempt to understand the providence of God (a typical evangelical theme) was prominent. Hort had expressed some of the complexities here in a letter to Gerald Blunt about the call to take holy orders in 1854:

We must not think of ourselves as cut off from the complicated mass of events and influences around us, or forget that the same God, who holds them all in His hand, does also call us to His work, and inspire us with the desire and the strength to accomplish it. We do not honour the Spirit, but subject Him to our own private fancies, when we refuse to recognize a call in His ordering of events. I do not mean that outward events or things independent of ourselves entirely constitute our circumstances; our own inward history, our present inclinations, even our felt capacities, are all, I think, part of our circumstances, but in these we need more care to avoid self-delusion, and it is not often that we are justified in consulting them alone.[97]

It was typical therefore that Hort responded to the challenge posed by Darwin's *Origin of Species*. He had taken the Natural Sciences Tripos and got a First in its first year; and his interest in botany, especially Alpine flowers, was legendary. When the *Origin* was published, he wrote to Westcott that he was inclined to think it unanswerable in spite of difficulties; he also immediately pinpointed the moral

---

96   Ibid., p. xxxvi. There is just a hint of Kierkegaard in that passage, though it is unlikely that Hort would have been aware of this; but it is a useful corrective to the view sometimes expressed that Hort found his conclusions too easily, and was somewhat complacent. A better way of understanding it is that he had an underlying assurance, which is rather different.

97   Hort to Blunt, 31 May 1854: Hort, *Life of Hort*, i, p. 281.

implications as the most significant. Within a few months he had decided that the scientific questions were more complicated than Darwin supposed, but still felt that Westcott was clutching at straws in resisting it.[98] When he returned to Cambridge in 1872 as a Fellow of Emmanuel, he wrote to Maurice (in probably the last letter he ever wrote to him) that whereas before (at the time he had stood for the Knightbridge chair in 1866 which Maurice got) he had hoped 'to testify for theology from the non-theological camp', he now hoped 'to bear witness for things not technically theological from the theological camp'.[99] Once back in Cambridge he belonged to a kind of senior version of the Apostles, which included Westcott, Lightfoot, Henry Sidgwick, and J. Clerk Maxwell, Cavendish Professor of Experimental Physics (1871–79). Hort was a particularly close friend of Maxwell, and admired his scientific brilliance, deep earnestness and whimsical humour. When he died in 1879 Hort wrote of the way in which scientific discovery had enlarged for Maxwell the province of reasonable belief.

> Thus in later years it was a favourite thought of his that the relation of parts to wholes pervades the invisible no less than the visible world, and that beneath the individuality which accompanies our personal life there lies hidden a deeper community of being as well as of feeling and action.[100]

That comment illustrates Hort's underlying Platonism in approaching reality: it also explains why he may be read as being sympathetic to the philosophical idealism which grew in the later part of the century. In his Platonism Hort showed himself to be the typical Cambridge man.

---

98   Hort to Westcott, 10 March 1860; Hort to Macmillan, 10 March 1860, 16 March 1860; Hort to Westcott, 15 October 1860: ibid., i, pp. 414–15; 430–34.
99   Hort to Maurice, 10/21 February 1872: ibid., ii, pp. 169–70.
100   Ibid., ii, p. 231; cf. L. Campbell and W. Garnett, *The Life of James Clerk Maxwell* (London, 1882), p. 419.

# Chapter 7

# Some Nonconformist Voices

> It may ... hopefully, if not confidently, be expected, that at no distant future, by proceeding along a course upon which they have already entered, the Universities of Oxford and Cambridge may become, not the schools where three or four thousand of the sons of those who have been vulgarly and invidiously called the better classes may receive the stamp of education without its substance, but gold fields where thirty or forty thousand of the sons of the nation, without respect of class, or sect, or condition ... will find the results and the rewards of their labours. When these universities shall thus become the unrestricted marts of both general and special knowledge, I am sure we shall all agree that our students should become free and ready purchasers therein.[1]

In these words, Neville Goodman (who had gained a First in Natural Sciences at Peterhouse in 1865) challenged the Congregational Union Assembly in October 1869 to consider how dissenters could take advantage of the opening of Oxbridge degrees. His estimate of the total numbers has scarcely been reached over a century later, but the change has been enormous.

The story so far has been essentially an Anglican one. Occasional references have been made to the controversies over the admission of dissenters to Cambridge. Technically this was the admission of dissenters to degrees, since only a declaration of membership of the Church of England was necessary before graduation. Thus both Coleridge and Maurice were undergraduates at Cambridge while they were Unitarians, but did not graduate. The change came in 1856, and from 1871 College Fellowships and most University offices (except certain Divinity chairs) were opened to nonconformists. Degrees in Divinity, however, remained closed to any but Anglicans until 1913.

Nonconformists did not hesitate to take advantage of the freedom allowed by the 1856 Act.[2] The first nonconformist graduate after 1856, William Henry Farthing Johnson, whose father ran a school in Cambridge, became a member of St Andrew's Street Baptist Church in 1845 and was elected a deacon in 1857.[3] The St Andrew's Street Church had originated in a secession from the Great

---

1     N. Goodman, 'How we may best avail ourselves of the Universities of Oxford and Cambridge for the education of our ministers', *Congregational Year Book* (*CYB*) (1870): 95.

2     See D.M. Thompson, 'Nonconformists at Cambridge before the First World War' in D.W. Bebbington and T. Larson, *Modern Christianity and Cultural Aspirations* (London, 2003), pp. 176–200.

3     St Andrew's Street Church Book, 1832–96, pp. 85, 125; K.A. Parsons (ed.), *St Andrew's Street Baptist Church 250th Anniversary* (Cambridge, 1971), p. 43; Thompson, 'Nonconformists at Cambridge', p. 179.

Meeting, and the first church was built on that site in 1764 and rebuilt in 1836. In the 1870s during a long ministerial vacancy undergraduates tended to desert St Andrew's Street in favour of Emmanuel Congregational Church on Trumpington Street opposite Pembroke College. This was the successor to the Great Meeting, which in 1874 moved to a substantial new building with a new name. Increasingly it drew a University membership, even though the majority of members were still from the town. St Andrew's Street was rebuilt again in 1903.[4] Whilst an undergraduate, T.R. Glover, son of the Baptist minister Dr Richard Glover of Bristol, was persuaded to take a Sunday morning men's class at the Castle End Mission, which meant that he was too late for the service at St Andrew's Street; and he was also attracted to Emmanuel Congregational Church by the preaching of W.S. Houghton and P.T. Forsyth. However, on his return from Canada in 1901 he became a member at St Andrew's Street, and was involved in the establishment of the Robert Hall Society for students in the spring of 1902.[5]

The Presbyterian Church of England began to hold services in the Guildhall in 1879 and built St Columba's Church in Downing Street in 1891, again with the intention of drawing on the membership of the University. Two of its most formidable members, the twins Agnes Lewis and Margaret Gibson, were not only significant scholars in their own right, eventually possessing several honorary doctorates between them, but by their researches in the Holy Land brought various biblical and related manuscripts back to Cambridge. In the 1890s they entranced the church with an offer of land, which it could scarcely refuse, to build its theological college in Cambridge. Westminster College was opened in 1899, and its staff soon achieved distinction. Charles Anderson Scott was the first nonconformist to be given a Cambridge DD when the Divinity degrees were finally opened to non-Anglicans. John Oman was a theologian of the first rank in the early twentieth century. In 1907 Cheshunt College, by then predominantly Congregational but originally founded by the Countess of Huntingdon to train ministers for her Connexion, moved to Cambridge and the well-known minister of Westminster Chapel, Campbell Morgan, was appointed Principal – though he continued to preach regularly in London on Sundays.

Wesleyan and Primitive Methodism were the principal Methodist denominations in Cambridge. The main Wesleyan church in the mid-nineteenth century was in Hobson Street (built in 1849), and the main Primitive Methodist church was in St Peter's Street (rebuilt 1864). In 1913 Wesley Methodist Church was built on Christ's Pieces to replace Hobson Street, and a year later the St Peter's Street church was turned around by the acquisition of more land to become Castle Street Church.[6] But the sign of Methodism's awareness of the new world after 1856 was the establishment of the Leys School in 1875. The idea was initially floated by Henry French of Taunton, partly as a consequence

4     C.F. Stell, *Nonconformist Chapels and Meeting-Houses in Eastern England* (London, 2002), p. 29; Parsons, *St Andrew's Street Baptist Church*, pp. 6, 25.

5     H.G. Wood, *Terrot Reaveley Glover* (Cambridge, 1953), pp. 18–19, 65.

6     F. Tice, *The History of Methodism in Cambridge* (London, 1966), pp. 28–33, 54–6; Stell, *Nonconformist Chapels*, p. 31.

of the Report of the Endowed Schools Commission, chaired by Lord Taunton. The Conference was divided on the relative merits of Oxford and Cambridge, with French favouring Oxford. But a leading Wesleyan Methodist layman in Cambridge, Robert Sayle, founder of the department store which bears his name, offered the Connexion a site on Trumpington Road for £14,000, on condition that it was used for Methodist educational purposes. The Conference of 1874 in Camborne took the decision to go to Cambridge, and appointed Dr William Moulton as Headmaster. Moulton already knew Westcott and Hort because he was one of the members of the New Testament Revision Committee, and he moved from Richmond theological college to take up his new appointment.[7] It had originally been intended to establish a theological college on the same site; that did not happen, but the Wesleyan Conference began to raise money for such a project in 1911. A legacy of £20,000 in 1920 assisted this and Maldwyn Hughes was designated the first Principal; in 1921 the first students arrived in Cambridge, and were accommodated in Cheshunt College, while Wesley House was built on Jesus Lane between 1922 and 1925.[8]

In the last quarter of the nineteenth century nonconformists gradually made an impact on the study of theology in Cambridge. The main work was done in biblical studies, associated with a variety of figures. They included the Free Church of Scotland minister William Robertson Smith, an Old Testament scholar who became Lord Almoner's Reader in Arabic in 1883, James Rendel Harris (who began as a Congregationalist and became a Quaker) and the Presbyterian Lewis and Gibson twins. However, it is appropriate to begin with the contrast between two ministers of Emmanuel Congregational Church, James Ward (1843–1925) and Peter Taylor Forsyth (1848–1921), which gives a taste of the kind of theology nonconformist undergraduates could hear from the pulpit.

The Great Meeting had been located in Downing Place, originally Hog Hill: the first meeting-house was built in 1687, and a new building was erected in 1790, which was used until 1874.[9] The idea of a new 'representative church' in Cambridge was first floated in 1861 as a potential candidate to benefit from the Congregational Bicentenary Building Fund, to mark the 200th anniversary of the Great Ejectment. It was not pursued at that stage but it resurfaced in 1867, when it was discussed informally at the Congregational Union autumn meetings in Manchester, though, because of the 'Cotton Famine', the commercial state of the north of England made immediate assistance impossible. The land in Trumpington Street occupied by the Half-Moon Inn was purchased in September 1869, but it was another five years before the new church was completed. Neville Goodman's address in October 1869, at the autumn meeting of the Congregational Union in Wolverhampton, referrred to at the beginning of the chapter, gave added

---

7    Tice, *Methodism in Cambridge*, pp. 79–83; W.F. Moulton, *William F. Moulton: A Memoir* (London, 1899), pp. 112–19.

8    Tice, *Methodism in Cambridge*, pp. 91–5.

9    Stell, *Nonconformist Chapels*, p. 31. The old building was bought by the University, and was the concert room of the Music School until the building of the new Concert Hall in West Road, when it became part of the Computer Laboratory.

publicity to the cause. When Goodman had graduated in 1865, he was ineligible at that stage for a Fellowship at Peterhouse, and devoted himself to natural history and entomology, particularly in South America.[10] In his address he emphasised the value of Mathematics and Classics in instilling habits of precise thinking, adding that Cambridge's scientific training would enable ministers to meet contemporary challenges to Christian faith by concentrating on the positive evidence for Christianity rather than ignorant attacks on science.[11] But he suggested that it would be better to encourage benefactions to enable nonconformist students to study at the existing colleges, than to set up a theological college. The plans for a new church were also advertised widely.[12] A national appeal was made to Congregationalism to support this new venture in a key university town, and subscriptions came from all parts of the country.[13]

The ministry was opportunely vacant and in October 1870 James Ward was invited to preach for a month; the congregation subsequently called him as minister, and he began work in January 1871. Ward was educated at the Royal Liverpool Institute (like Lightfoot) and after working in an architect's office had been a student at Spring Hill College, Birmingham, from 1863 to 1869. He was awarded the Dr Williams's Scholarship, which enabled him to study abroad, and went to Germany, first to Berlin and then to Göttingen. This was a formative experience for him: he had initially been attracted by the philosophy of Hegel, as taught by Dorner and Trendelenburg, and then decisively by Hermann Lotze. Already dissatisfied with traditional evangelical doctrine, he returned to discover several of his college friends in theological difficulties. His initial sermons in Cambridge on the text 'God is Love' shocked one or two of the congregation but also moved several so deeply that they remembered them for the rest of their lives. Neville Keynes, for example, who was a trustee though never a member of Emmanuel, remained a lifelong friend, though by the First World War he too was drifting away from any active religious faith.[14]

William Bond, a Trinity Street grocer and deacon of the church, had been one of those most anxious to draw Ward to Cambridge: his home became a meeting place for nonconformist undergraduates. The two got on well together, but he was only one voice in the congregation. Ward wrote that it was

> a very peculiar one – many of the people are just those you meet with in any country-town, narrow, ignorant and old-fashioned … others have come into contact with the

10   J.A. Venn, *Alumni Cantabrigienses*, Part II, iii, p. 85. Goodman's son, Roger Neville Goodman was a founder member of the Cambridge Nonconformist Union. He was educated at the Perse School and St John's College, gained a First in Natural Sciences in 1883 and an MD in 1892: Venn, *Alumni*, Part II, iii, p. 85.

11   *CYB* (1870): 99.

12   See *CYB*, (1873): 424–6; (1874): 414. By this stage, Matthew Robertson was the minister.

13   B.L. Manning, *This Latter House* (Cambridge, 1924), pp. 4–5.

14   O.W. Campbell, 'Memoir' in J. Ward, *Essays in Philosophy* (Cambridge, 1927), pp. 11–38. Olwen Campbell was Ward's younger daughter. Keynes became Secretary of the Local Examinations Syndicate in 1890, and University Registrary in 1910.

thinking of the time, know what is stirring in the minds of men and have brushed against University people ... then we have all the Scotch in Cambridge with us, and there are a good many of them, travelling tailors for the most part ... Some poor people, a few disaffected Baptists and a sprinkling of students completes the medley ... How am I to cement such a mixture?[15]

Ward's own personal doubts were compounded by questions asked about his orthodoxy by potential contributors to the new chapel, and despite Bond's firm support eventually Ward offered his resignation in March 1872. The congregation, with six dissentients, refused to accept it, but after a fortnight's reflection Ward indicated that his decision was final.[16] When invited to the Jubilee Celebration of Emmanuel Church in 1924, he thanked the church for its invitation but said that the year or so of his ministry had been 'the darkest and saddest of a long and eventful life', and that, while the building was a monument to Henry Allen (*sic*) and William Bond, to him it was 'the tombstone of a buried life to me'.[17]

While at the Great Meeting Ward had felt that being in Cambridge reminded him of 'the golden opportunities I have lost'.[18] So he immediately applied for admission as a non-collegiate student, and in 1873 gained a scholarship in Moral Sciences at Trinity. He obtained First Class honours in the Moral Sciences Tripos in 1874 and won a Trinity Fellowship in 1875 against keen competition. In April 1881 Sidgwick ensured that he was elected to a College Lectureship; and then in 1896 Sidgwick gave £200 p.a. until 1900 to assist in the establishment of a new Chair in Mental Philosophy and Logic, to which Ward was elected in 1897. He died in 1925 and was succeeded by G.E. Moore.[19]

James Ward's story illustrates that the problem of loss of faith, which concerned Anglicans, affected nonconformists too. His problems were the classic ones: the verbal inspiration of scripture, the philosophical difficulties of the concept of eternal life, and the relationship between mind and matter. He believed 'that a life which realises the broad lines of Christ's and a society pervaded by the spirit of Christianity are generally the ideals of men individually and collectively'. He looked forward to a development and purification of Christian doctrines, but believed that Christianity was the absolute religion until it could be shown that there were moral or ethical principles higher than those flowing from the Christian representation of God and man.[20] Were it not for the Thirty-Nine Articles he could have become a broad church Anglican.[21] Eventually under Sidgwick's influence he

---

15   Quoted in ibid., pp. 39–40.

16   Ibid., pp. 40–47.

17   Ibid., p. 52. 'Allen' must have been Henry Allon, minister of Union Chapel, Islington and Chairman of the Congregational Union in 1864. He engaged James Cubitt, architect of Emmanuel, to rebuild Union Chapel in 1875.

18   Ibid., p. 41.

19   Ibid., pp. 47, 53–4, 73, 82–3; J.R. Tanner, *Historical Register of the University of Cambridge* (Cambridge, 1917), pp. 107, 710.

20   Ward, *Essays in Philosophy*, p. 35.

21   Ibid., p. 43.

became an agnostic, but still cherished to the end of his days a wistful nostalgia for the teaching of Jesus.

Ward was elected to the Apostles in 1876, and wrote for them a paper entitled, 'Can Faith remove Mountains?' By faith Ward meant 'not the intellectual acceptance of a creed but that personal trust and confidence in an Unseen Being to which the religious in all ages have attributed their power to "overcome the world"'.[22] In his view there were no grounds for accepting the scientific dogmatism which claimed that religious faith was absurd. If therefore there was nothing in modern knowledge incompatible with religious development, an evolutionary perspective meant that God-consciousness might be a plausible development of self-consciousness.[23] Neville Keynes noted in his diary for 27 March 1881:

> Ward read a most excellent paper on 'Faith as a creative power'. Science certainly cannot *disprove* Theism. Reasoning on the analogies of Evolution, it may be that through basking in the sun, eyes have been developed, so that by means of Faith a clear and satisfying God-consciousness may be capable of being evolved.[24]

Ward continued to be attracted by this possibility for the rest of his life.

In his very last essay, 'The Christian Ideas of Faith and Eternal Life', read to the Cambridge Theological Society in 1924 and published in the *Hibbert Journal* for 1925, he returned to similar themes. Faith was not cognitive, but primarily conative, and also volitional.[25] Eternal life in the fourth gospel and the Pauline and Johannine epistles was asserted as a present possession more than as a future hope: 'In short we miss the meaning of "eternal" in the New Testament, if we associate it with time at all, and especially if we interpret it as referring simply to a future life everlasting.'[26] Religion culminated 'in the Christian's faith in an indwelling presence as the source of a new life of peace and power', which went beyond mere sensory experience.[27] Ward traced the decay of the simplest form of the new life, which Jesus taught, symbolised by the development of creeds, a priesthood and a political alliance with the secular power. The result was an intensified concern on the part of people for 'the *safety* of their own souls' uncharacteristic of true Christian faith.

> It was neither the hope of heaven nor the fear of hell that led them to love their heavenly Father. Love does not, nay cannot, spring from prudential motives, let them be what

---

22   W.B. Lubenow, *The Cambridge Apostles, 1820–1914* (Cambridge, 1998), p. 431; Ward, *Essays in Philosophy*, p. 101.

23   Ward, *Essays in Philosophy*, pp. 108–10.

24   J.N. Keynes, Diary 27 March 1881: Cambridge University Library, Add Mss 7832(1).

25   Ward, *Essays in Philosophy*, p. 349.

26   Ibid., p. 352. He made special reference to John Oman's *Grace and Personality* (Cambridge, 1917).

27   Ibid., p. 355.

they may. Moreover, faith and love here go together, and no one can trust God and not love him or love him and not trust him[28]

But there remained a need for 'more earnest courage and more intellectual honesty' than was generally apparent among religious leaders. He quoted Harnack's definition of Christianity as 'Eternal life in the midst of time, by the strength and under the eyes of God', and said that a Christlike life had never 'failed to attract the unsophisticated and open-minded'.[29] Yet he deliberately refrained from saying anything positive concerning a future life, because we had no experience of it. That meant that we had to confine 'our practical interests to this present world in which alone we are able to work'. But this should not lead to misgivings: 'To regard this life, then, not as intrinsically valuable in itself, but as merely a means to some final perfection ever beyond and yet ceaselessly to be pursued, would, it seems to me, reduce eternal life for God and man alike to nothing better than an endless mirage.'[30] Here there is a glimpse of what Ward might have said in his sermons at the Great Meeting on 'God is love', which was so compelling and yet so alarming. There is also a similarity between several of Ward's emphases and some of the characteristics of the theology of P.T. Forsyth, who was minister at Emmanuel from 1894 to 1901, before becoming Principal of Hackney College, London until his death in 1921.

Emmanuel called Forsyth partly at the initiative of A.W.W. Dale, Fellow of Trinity Hall and son of the Congregational minister R.W. Dale of Birmingham. Forsyth, who was almost a contemporary of Ward, was born in Aberdeen and went to school and university there. Like Ward he went to Germany, spending a term at Göttingen in 1872, studying with Albrecht Ritschl. Then he went to New College, London, but left without completing the course. Nevertheless he was called to Eastwood, Shipley (1876–79), St Thomas's Square, Hackney (1879–85), Cheetham Hill, Manchester (1885–88) and Clarendon Park, Leicester (1888–94). By the time he came to Cambridge he had shifted theologically from what was initially perceived to be a very liberal position, though the perception probably illustrates the looseness of the term 'liberal' as much as anything else. His mature theological works were written after he became Principal of Hackney College in 1901, notably *The Person and Place of Jesus Christ* (1909), *The Cruciality of the Cross* (1909), *The Principle of Authority* (1913) and *Lectures on the Church and the Sacraments* (1917); but the seeds of all his later thought are to be found in his writings of the 1890s during the Cambridge period. If the paper on 'Revelation and the Person of Christ' written just before he came to Cambridge and contributed to *Faith and Criticism* (1893) is included as well, then a series of alternative approaches to the theological issues discussed by the Cambridge trio is readily to hand. The works in question are 'The Holy Father', a sermon preached to the Congregational Union assembly in Leicester in 1896; *The Charter of the Church*, a series of lectures given in Cambridge, also in 1896; 'The Divine

---

28    Ibid., pp. 362, 363.
29    Ibid., pp. 364–5.
30    Ibid., p. 366.

Self-Emptying', a sermon preached in 1895, but not published until 1901; and 'The Evangelical Principle of Authority', a sermon preached at the Second International Congregational Council meetings in Boston, Massachusetts, in 1899. Only the sacraments were not formally dealt with in these works. Unlike Moulton, who already knew Westcott and Hort when he came to Cambridge, there is no evidence of significant contact between Forsyth and members of the Cambridge Theology Faculty during his time in Cambridge; and this was long before the time when nonconformist ministers might be invited to preach in Anglican pulpits. What is also striking in reading Forsyth, by comparison with Hare, Westcott or Hort, is the absence of reference to classical thought: Plato and Aristotle are never mentioned. Readers tend either to love Forsyth or to hate him; the commonest criticism is that the ideas come tumbling out so fast that it is difficult to keep up with them.[31] Although one fellow minister criticised Forsyth's style as 'fireworks in a fog',[32] the main problem is his extensive use of antithesis and paradox, complicated by the fact that, in the words of one reviewer, Forsyth 'never says a thing one way if it can be said four ways'.[33]

Neville Keynes first mentioned Forsyth in his diary entry for 24 January 1892: 'his matter was excellent, but his delivery too rapid ... Personally we liked him very much.' On 29 October 1893 he referred to a 'fine sermon from Forsyth of Leicester', and then on 4 March 1894 to Forsyth's acceptance of the invitation to Cambridge. More interestingly he noted on 21 October that 'Maynard seems quite to appreciate Forsyth's preaching'.[34] Keynes felt that Forsyth took a 'very severe line in his preaching', but he continued to preach remarkably well; and in October 1895 he noted that the first two sermons he preached on Nonconformity drew crowded congregations.[35] These entries may be compared with those in T.R. Glover's diary for the same period. He had supper with the Keyneses within a month of arriving in Cambridge in 1888, because of a mutual friend.[36] Glover's comment on 21 October 1894 was 'Mr Forsyth at last on Acts xii 19 Rhoda opened not the door for gladness. A splendid sermon on the obstructed power of a great

---

31    J. Denney in *The Expository Times* (February 1913): 213, quoted by W.L. Bradley, *P.T. Forsyth: the Man and his Work* (London, 1952), p. 262.

32    D.J.G. Stephenson, letter to the *British Weekly* (31 January 1907): 22, quoted by C. Gunton, 'The Real as the Redemptive: Forsyth on Authority and Freedom' in T. Hart (ed.), *Justice the True and Only Mercy* (Edinburgh, 1995), p. 189. The comment about fog is something which Forsyth had in common with Westcott: Henry Liddon is said to have attributed a dense fog in London to 'Dr Westcott having opened his study window in Westminster': G.W.E. Russell, *Dr Liddon* (London, 1905), p. 174, quoted by H. Chadwick, *The Vindication of Christianity in Westcott's Thought* (Cambridge, 1961), p. 4.

33    *Expository Times* (August 1917): 497–8, quoted by Bradley, *P.T. Forsyth*, p. 262.

34    Keynes, Diary 24 January 1892: CUL Add Mss 7842; 29 October 1893, Add Mss 7843; 4 March 1894 and 21 October 1894, Add Mss 7844.

35    Keynes, Diary, 23 June 1895, 20 October 1895, 27 October 1895, Add Mss 7845.

36    T.R. Glover, Diary, 8 and 21 October 1888, St John's College Archives.

enthusiasm, full of many serious points.'[37] On the evening of 4 November he wrote 'Mr Forsyth on the Sacrament – a striking sermon though I don't follow it all' and a week later, after a sermon on Romans 8, 'He is out of one's reach a great deal. But it is stimulating and good'.[38] On 23 February 1896 he wrote, 'Dr Forsyth a great sermon on Mt 9.20 The woman who touched the hem. An act of superstition in wh[ich] Christ saw and accepted the latent faith. The value of seeing characters great amid what we m[ight]t call superstition'.[39]

Forsyth's starting point, after a critical understanding of scripture, was Calvin and the classic Reformed tradition, modified by Kant and the German thinkers who followed him. From Kant he took the emphasis upon the ethical or moral approach to the heart of theology, which he regularly contrasted with an intellectual approach. This view of Kant 'quite definitely interpreted as an anti-metaphysical moralist'[40] may have been due to the teaching of Ritschl. He also adopted Ritschl's anti-Pietism and his emphasis upon the doctrines of Reconciliation and Justification. Forsyth acknowledged his debt to the writings of Wilhelm Herrmann at the beginning of his essay on 'Revelation and the Person of Christ', without citing any particular work, but it was probably *The Communion of the Christian with God*; he must have read the book in German.[41] Bradley suggested that Herrmann's influence on Forsyth was restricted to the early years of his ministry between 1879 and 1884; but that would not account for the similarities with Herrmann's book of 1886.[42] In the debate between Herrmann and Kähler, however, Forsyth had more in common with the latter and his emphasis that the power of God's grace is seen in his redeeming action.[43] Herrmann taught both Barth and Bultmann at Marburg, and the shared influence may explain some of the oft-noted similarities between Forsyth and Barth. The latter described Herrmann as '*the* theological teacher of my student years'[44] and said that he learnt from him the Christocentric impulse, which was decisive.[45] Forsyth also shared with James Denney an emphasis upon holiness in relation to God and the

---

37    Ibid., 21 October 1894.

38    Ibid., 4 and 11 November 1894.

39    Ibid., 23 February 1896.

40    K. Barth, *Protestant Theology in the Nineteenth Century* (London, 1972), p. 655.

41    P.T. Forsyth, 'Revelation and the Person of Christ' in *Faith and Criticism: Essays by Congregationalists* (London, 1893), p. 97. Forsyth very rarely acknowledged sources or used footnotes, so this is particularly valuable. The first edition of Herrmann's book was published in 1886 and extensively revised for the second German edition of 1892; it was not translated into English until 1896.

42    Bradley, *P.T. Forsyth*, p. 106.

43    See R. Voelkel, Introduction to W. Herrmann, *The Communion of the Christian with God* (London, 1971), pp. xxxvii–xli.

44    K. Barth, *Theology and Church* (London, 1962; German edn 1928), p. 238; quoted in E. Busch, *Karl Barth* (London, 1976), p. 44; T.F. Torrance, *Karl Barth: An Introduction to His Early Theology, 1910–1931* (new edn, Edinburgh, 2000), p. 16.

45    Busch, *Karl Barth*, p. 45.

death of Christ.[46] But, however many names one adds to the list of influences, Forsyth's voice was his own, and he produced a distinctive blend of emphases. No one other than Forsyth was speaking in this way in the Cambridge of the 1890s. Nor were there many other similar voices in nonconformity. R.W. Dale said of Forsyth's essay in *Faith and Criticism*, 'Who *is* this P.T. Forsyth? He has recovered for us a word we had all but lost – the word Grace'.[47]

Forsyth's view of revelation, authority, atonement and incarnation has to be considered as a whole; his view of the church can be treated separately. In his essay on Revelation Forsyth wrote, in words which put Hort's Hulsean Lectures in a new light, 'The way is the truth and the life. Revelation, that is to say, is not *through* Christ, but *in* Christ'.[48] If revelation had to be a fact of history, then the fact had to be a person.[49] It was a matter of will, not of thought (a similar emphasis to that of Ward): revelation was not a series of truths:

> The active contents of Revelation ... are not truths, ideas, or even principles. That is the fatal error shared also by the vicious notion of an orthodoxy or saving system. The sole content of Revelation, the power and gift in it, is the love, will, presence and purpose of God for our redemption.[50]

This was more than a declaratory act or a manifestation: 'God does not simply show Himself, He *gives* Himself; and a gift is not a gift (however genuine the giving)

---

46    G.O. Griffith, *The Theology of P.T. Forsyth* (London, 1948), p. 16.
47    Memoir by Jessie Forsyth Andrews in P.T. Forsyth, *The Work of Christ* (London, 1965), p. 17.
48    Forsyth, 'Revelation and the Person of Christ', p. 98.
49    Compare the following quotations from Herrmann: 'God makes Himself known to us, so that we may recognise Him, through *a fact, on the strength of which we are able to believe on Him* ... No doctrine can bring it about that there shall arise in our hearts the full certainty that God actually exists for us; only a fact can inspire such confidence within us. Now we Christians hold that we know only one fact in the whole world which can overcome every doubt of the reality of God, namely, the appearance of Jesus in history. Our certainty of God may be kindled by many other experiences, but has ultimately its firmest basis in the fact that within the realm of history to which we ourselves belong, we encounter the man Jesus as an undoubted reality.' 'It is a fatal error to attempt to establish the basis of faith by means of historical investigation ... Whether faith ... arises in us or not depends on whether this personal spirit wins power over us, or we hold ourselves back from Him.' 'Whenever the Person of Jesus touches on us as a fact that is real to ourselves, then we are hearing the gospel ... We see it only when it pleases God to reveal His Son in us, and this can happen to us only when, with minds intent on exercising our moral judgment and satisfying our religious need, we come in contact with the biblical tradition regarding Jesus Christ.' 'Only when we reserve the name of faith exclusively for the trust which the picture of Christ awakens in us, and the new purpose and courage which are born of that trust, is the notion of the faith given us by God made quite definite and clear.' Herrmann, *The Communion of the Christian with God*, pp. 59–60, 76, 83, 241 (English translation of 2nd German edn of 1892, published in 1896 and revised in 1906).
50    Forsyth, 'Revelation and the Person of Christ', p. 102.

till it is received and realized as such.'[51] It was therefore not the philosophy of the two natures, but 'the benefits of His work' that provided the key to understanding God's revelation.

Consequently various points of doctrine were not directly part of revelation, even though they might be its corollaries: creation, the origin of sin, the constitution of the Godhead before the birth of Christ and the origin of the Redeemer. Although Forsyth could say that 'there is but one Christ, and the Bible is His prophet',[52] he immediately warned against misinterpretation:

> Christianity is not a book religion. It has a book, but the book is not the Revelation. It does not even contain the Revelation any more than the reflecting telescope contains the heavens … All question of a book as a revelation ought to cease when we recall that the Revelation Himself never wrote a word, never ordered a word to be written, and apparently never contemplated any Bible more extended than the Scripture He Himself had used. He thought of the New Testament as little as He thought of the creeds. And so far as His authority goes, there is just as much reason to believe in the infallibility of the one as of the other. If that infallibility be carried beyond Himself, if it be not confined to Himself, and to Himself in His direct equipment for Redemption, there is no logical halting-place till we arrive at the Vatican Decrees.[53]

Personal experience was more important than historical evidence, thus 'Revelation takes effect in us, not as an act of insight, but only as an experience of being redeemed';[54] or again 'Revelation does not tell us what to do or believe'.[55] Christ did not simply prepare forgiveness or declare it, but by his historic personality, his life, death, and resurrection he effected it in us. Faith was the response to revelation

> and what God revealed was neither the Incarnation nor the miraculous birth. It was Jesus Christ, the living God as the living man. We have been going the wrong way to work. We have been beginning to build our church at the spire. These great doctrines are true, but they are the fruit of Christian faith, not its condition.[56]

Not only were the doctrines of scripture and of authority readjusted under the true light of Revelation, but also the doctrine of Redemption itself. The person of Christ could only be understood by his work. In saying this Forsyth meant more

---

51    Ibid., p. 104.
52    Ibid., p. 106.
53    Ibid.
54    Ibid., p. 116; cf. p. 111. Compare this with Herrmann: 'The Gospel not only sets ideas before us, but presents us with a mighty fact, such as, once experienced, gives to our life such height and depth as seems to enable us for the first time to perceive its immensity. This fact, which we must not merely "believe", but ourselves see, is the Person of Jesus Christ': W. Herrmann, 'The Moral Teachings of Jesus' in A. Harnack and W. Herrmann, *Essays on The Social Gospel* (London, 1907), p. 149. (This lecture was given in 1903, so obviously it did not influence Forsyth in 1893.)
55    Forsyth, 'Revelation and the Person of Christ', p. 121.
56    Ibid., p. 136.

than the traditional view that the atonement was the key to the incarnation; it was rather that the moral authority of Christ for us turned upon our experience of 'the actual redeeming effect upon our conscience of the man Jesus'.[57] Above all it was the sense of divine authority that the world after centuries of metaphysical theology needed.[58] Even Hegel's work was regarded by Forsyth as another attempt to scholasticise Christianity.

To contextualise what Forsyth was saying, it is necessary to remember that he was providing an antidote to a liberal understanding of Christ as example, but not by reverting to a traditional evangelicalism. In a little-known address of 1891, as Chairman of the Leicestershire and Rutland Congregational Union, he had criticised the 'new evangelicalism' for ceasing to be evangelical, partly because it was inward, full of moral sympathies but lacking moral sinew, and partly because it was 'over-engrossed in the outward and social questions which monopolise the journalism of the hour'.[59] Indeed the word 'evangelical' lost its meaning 'when the love of God takes the place in religion which is due to His holiness, and when the divine justice is conceived to be more engaged with wrongs than in the war with sin'.[60] The two centres of Christianity were the Cross and the Kingdom, each of which needed to be interpreted in terms of the other. The old faith was too individualistic – note the echoes of Maurice here – but in moving the emphasis to the community it was important not to lose sight of redemption, a theme little emphasised in liberal theology.[61]

Here Forsyth was drawing on Schleiermacher and Ritschl. He later put the same point in *The Person and Place of Jesus Christ* thus: 'The Incarnation, being for a moral and not a metaphysical purpose, must be in its nature moral. Its metaphysic should therefore be a metaphysic of ethics, and not of thought as pure being.'[62] Kenneth Mozley pointed out that Forsyth in his theory of knowledge stood on the side of the voluntarists over against the intellectualists, but his voluntarism was of the Kantian kind.[63] Whereas Hegel argued that the real was the rational, Forsyth argued that Kant brought about a revolution in suggesting that 'the ethical was the real'.[64] This enabled Forsyth to link authority and holiness. Because of the primacy of the ethical, the holy in Christianity was best expressed in ethical terms as the absolute moral Reality: 'We too are holy according to our relation to that power, or rather according to His relation to us.'[65] 'The chief lack of religion to-day is authority; and it must find that in the cross or nowhere, in the

57   Ibid., p. 139.
58   Ibid., p. 142.
59   P.T. Forsyth, *The Old Faith and the New* (Leicester, 1891), p. 3, quoted in Bradley, *P.T. Forsyth*, p. 44.
60   Ibid.
61   Ibid., pp. 4, 8, 12–13, 26, quoted in Bradley, *P.T. Forsyth*, p. 45.
62   P.T. Forsyth, *The Person and Place of Jesus Christ*, ed. D.M. Thompson (London, 1999), p. 219.
63   J.K. Mozley, 'The Theology of Dr Forsyth', *The Heart of the Gospel* (London, 1925), p. 73; also in Forsyth, *Person and Place*, pp. xxiv–xxv.
64   P.T. Forsyth, *The Principle of Authority* (London n.d. [1913]), p. 5.
65   Ibid.

real nature of the cross, in its relation to the holy demand of God.'[66] The same theme was developed in his Boston Sermon, which ultimately became the basis for his lectures on the Principle of Authority in 1913. Echoing Kant he said that authority was to be found in the practical reason, rather than the pure reason: 'There is not truth that we may not criticise; but there is such a person. There is no absolute formal truth, only an absolute person and his act. Science, even theology in so far as it is scientific, owns no truth as final. The absolute is the only final authority, and we touch that by the moral act of personal faith alone.'[67]

Forsyth's view of the incarnation, and indeed the atonement, was different from that of Westcott and other contemporary Cambridge scholars. The difference was most clearly seen in his frequent use of the category of holiness – in a way which was totally different from contemporary Methodist usage and the Keswick 'holiness' movement. In *Faith and Criticism* Forsyth had concluded his essay by describing the work of Christ as 'to realize and transfer to us the experience of God's holy love in the conditions of sin. It was not to give an equivalent for sin, but to effect in man God's own sense of what sin meant for His holiness.'[68] Forsyth related the whole idea of sin to holiness, since sin was a concept outside the natural order: 'Nature includes no holiness; and it is holiness that makes sin sin'.[69]

His sermon of 1896, 'The Holy Father', was a critique of easy notions of the fatherhood of God. 'The new revelation in the cross was more than "God is love". It was this "Holy Father". That is, God at his divinest, as He was *to* Christ, as He was *in* Christ.'[70]

> The Church of to-day has gained greatly in its sense of the *love* of God. There are still greater things waiting when she has moved on as far again, to that *holiness* whose outward movement is love ... You can go behind love to holiness, but behind holiness you cannot go. It is the true consuming fire.[71]

The parable of the prodigal son, therefore, was a marvellous story of God's free grace in forgiveness, but it was not the whole story of the significance of the cross. Nor was the teaching of Christ to be elevated over his redeeming work. 'Christ came not to *say* something, but to *do* something. His revelation was action more than instruction. He revealed by redeeming.'[72] For Forsyth the gospels, which was where the emphasis on Jesus' teaching came from, 'were not meant for a finished portrait of Christ, or a complete manual of His truth'.[73] Nor was the

---

66    P.T. Forsyth, 'The Holy Father', in *God the Holy Father* (London, 1957; first published 1897), pp. 5–6.

67    P.T. Forsyth, 'The Evangelical Principle of Authority', *Proceedings of the Second International Congregational Council* (Boston, 1900), p. 57.

68    Forsyth, 'Revelation and the Person of Christ', p. 142.

69    Forsyth, 'The Holy Father', p. 8.

70    Ibid., p. 3.

71    Ibid., p. 5.

72    Ibid., p. 19.

73    Ibid., p. 16.

'social gospel' an adequate account of the fullness of Christian faith.[74] 'The soul of divine fatherhood is forgiveness by holiness. It is evangelical. It is a matter of grace meeting sin by sacrifice to holiness, more even of love meeting need by service to man.'[75]

Forsyth was more concerned about the fact of atonement than any theory of it. 'Both Christ and the New Testament are disappointingly reticent about the cost of grace, the "plan of salvation", the "theory of Atonement", the precise way and sense in which Christ bore our curse before God, and took away the guilt of the world.'[76] Characteristically he turned the emphases around: 'It is atonement that makes repentance, not repentance that makes atonement.'[77] God's self-giving affected our understanding of revelation itself: so gracious was God with His revelation 'that He actually lets it come home to us as if we had discovered it. That is His fine manner – so to give as if we had found'.[78] Forsyth also mentioned his kenotic understanding of incarnation, which he developed fully in *The Person and Place of Jesus Christ*: 'His self-emptying meant self-limitation in knowledge as in other things. I have already applied to Christ's consciousness the words which Calvin applies to his ubiquity: "The whole Christ was there, but not all that is in Christ was there".'[79] The allusion to the controversy stirred up by Gore in *Lux Mundi* was clear but unexpressed. In his sermon on 'The Divine Self-Emptying' of 1897, he said that limitation was 'a *power* of Godhead, not a curtailment of it ... Incarnation is not impossible to the Infinite; it is necessary'.[80] So for Forsyth the centre of the incarnation was where Christ placed the focus of his work: 'The key to the Incarnation is not in the cradle, but in the cross. The light on Bethlehem falls from Calvary.'[81] Again the virgin birth was subordinated to the cross. Christ sought no equality with God; the godlike glory he had was that of subordination. For 'subordination *is* godlike ... *Subordination is not inferiority*'.[82] Forsyth strongly denied that for human beings it was a mark of inferiority to be subordinate or to obey. Those who asserted their determination to be subordinate to no one, whether men or women, ended up in 'a hard, coarse individualism, a selfishness gradually growing arrogant (if it be not that to begin with), the rupture of family life, filial faith, homely duty, and kindly rule, and the dissolution of all the fine loyalties of the soul for which great men worthily die'.[83] The deepest error of Christianity was to conceive of God as a being 'whose first and Divinest work was to *receive* sacrifice instead of offering it'. With the

---

74    Bradley, *P.T. Forsyth*, pp. 67–71.
75    Forsyth, 'The Holy Father', p. 5.
76    Ibid., p. 13.
77    Ibid., p. 11.
78    Ibid., p. 17.
79    Ibid., p. 22, cf.p. 18.
80    P.T. Forsyth, 'The Divine Self-Emptying' in *God the Holy Father* (London, 1957), p. 33.
81    Ibid., p. 40.
82    Ibid., p. 42.
83    Ibid., pp. 42–3.

faith that 'it is a godlier thing to give than to receive', Christians would 'empty themselves to make room in themselves and the world for the fulness and glory of God in the cross of Christ the Lord'.[84]

Forsyth's distaste for the social gospel did not lead to any underestimate of the significance of the Christian community. In fact, he was constantly affirming the significance of the communal over the individual. At Boston he said that the ethical authority he had described 'cannot be merely individual in its action; it must be social: morality has not meaning except through a society'.[85] His lectures of 1896 in Emmanuel, *The Charter of the Church*, were prompted by the beginning of the Church of England's campaign for rate aid for church schools. Forsyth made a theological case for disestablishment rather than a political one. Just as our Christian life was our due response to God's grace, so our faith was 'simply its human echo; it is God's redeeming grace returning *through* man upon itself – the Holy Spirit returning to Him who gave it'.[86] The only congenial expression of the freedom of faith responding to the freedom of grace was 'a Free Church – free in the sense of autonomous, and not in the sense of comprehensive'.[87] Thus Forsyth distanced himself from the contemporary Anglican church reform movement, based on comprehension. 'If I am asked,' said Forsyth, 'why I do not belong to the Established Church, I reply that my chief reason is because I am such a Churchman – a High Churchman – with such a high ideal of the Church.'[88]

The medieval church had had two principles – unity and autonomy. At the Reformation the unity of the national church had been preserved (though that of the Western Church had been lost), but at a terrible price, namely, the royal supremacy, which led to the supremacy of the state, and thus of parliament. 'And to this there was sacrificed what is the very essence of faith, *its* supremacy, *its* autonomy, *its* independence of any power outside itself, its direct dependence on the Spirit, its Lord.'[89] Nonconformists, rather than the Church of England, had kept continuity in principle with the medieval church through the autonomy of faith, and that had moved the best minds who had left Anglicanism for Rome.[90] Nor did he see much hope of change until people had become more disillusioned with the current social gospel. Indeed he feared that the Labour or socialist party wished to use the church in the same way that previous secular powers had: 'In the spirit of State Socialism it wants to take the religious industry and exploit it in the public interest.'[91]

Characteristically rejecting the individualist tendencies of nonconformity, Forsyth agreed with Henry Scott Holland in saying that faith and a church were

---

84    Ibid., p. 44.

85    Forsyth, 'The Evangelical Principle of Authority', p. 57.

86    P.T. Forsyth, *The Charter of the Church: Six Lectures on the Spiritual Principle of Nonconformity* (London, 1896), pp. iv–v.

87    Ibid., p. v.

88    Ibid., p. 7.

89    Ibid., p. 12.

90    Ibid., p. 13.

91    Ibid., p. 37.

inseparable: 'To believe in Jesus is to have by that very same act believed in the Christian Church.'[92] Such faith was inconceivable as a lonely act of a solitary soul:

> It puts an end to that individualism in religion which, after some precious service, has turned to atomism, political or pietist, and which is apt to become such a curse to us Nonconformists and Independents. A man is saved, not as a unit, but as a member of a community. It was a race that Christ redeemed, and souls as members of it ... The very act of faith in Christ places a man by its ideal nature in a community of believers, *which he must serve, else his faith decays.* No man can believe in Christ who refuses association with some Christian community.[93]

Christ was the unity of his society, since he was 'the member of a manifold and social Godhead – the Trinity. And He is, second, the life, soul, and spirit of a varied and social Kingdom.'[94]

In affirming that freedom was a spiritual principle, Forsyth recognised the disadvantage arising from the fact that 'to the general mind [freedom] is a negative idea. What is thought of is freedom *from* something, and only in a very secondary degree freedom *for* anything, except perhaps individual preference'.[95] He defined the idea of nonconformity as '*the autonomy, supremacy, and ethical quality of the spiritual principle*',[96] and concluded by affirming that

> the saving principle of freedom in the State is the same principle which saves and frees the guilty soul; that the only establishment of religion in a nation is the establishment of its spirit in our common conduct, not of its machinery in a sectional institution; and that churches and nations and all other institutions are alike but the agents, and never the peers, of that mightiest force in action on earth – the Kingdom of God, which is but the social aspect of the Son of God.[97]

B.L. Manning said that Forsyth 'made dogmatic theology attractive even to undergraduates'.[98] Although his Cambridge ministry was relatively short (just over seven years) and it was dogged by the death of his wife soon after it began and by frequent bouts of ill-health, he consolidated his reputation as a national figure within Congregationalism, and left a mark on the Emmanuel congregation. In the summer of 1901 Forsyth moved to Hackney and on to a wider stage, though

---

92    H.S. Holland, *God's City and the Coming of the Kingdom* (London, 1894), p. 18. Scott Holland's remark was directed against the evangelical tendency to separate a decision for Christ from the decision about which church to join.

93    Forsyth, *Charter of the Church*, p. 41; cf. 'It is society that is being saved, and not only a group of individuals, an elect out of society', Forsyth, 'The Evangelical Principle of Authority', p. 63; 'It was a race that Christ redeemed, and not a mere *bouquet* of believers', P.T. Forsyth, *Lectures on the Church and the Sacraments* (London, 1917), p. 40.

94    Forsyth, *Charter of the Church*, p. 41.

95    Ibid., p. 71.

96    Ibid., p. 72.

97    Ibid., p. 102.

98    Manning, *This Latter House*, p. 28.

he continued to visit Emmanuel to preach from time to time and did not transfer his membership from the church until 1917.

T.R. Glover's diaries illustrate the life of the Cambridge nonconformist network, including James Rendel Harris, William Robertson Smith, Agnes Lewis and Margaret Gibson (the twins of Castlebrae, who discovered manuscripts at St Catherine's Monastery on Sinai and the Genizah of the Ben Ezra Synagogue in Cairo), various of the staff of Westminster College after its transfer to Cambridge in 1899, and indeed Glover himself, whose ambitions in the 1890s lay in biblical study but whose career from his time at McGill and then his return to Cambridge was primarily spent in ancient history.

William Robertson Smith became Lord Almoner's Professor of Arabic in 1883. After his expulsion from the Free Church College in Aberdeen for unsound views on the inspiration of scripture in 1881, he was appointed Joint Editor of the *Encyclopaedia Britannica*, and moved to Edinburgh. It was in earlier volumes of the *Encyclopaedia* that some of his controversial articles, such as 'Bible' and 'Hebrew Language and Literature', had been published. During the winters of 1881 and 1882 he delivered two series of popular lectures in Edinburgh and Glasgow setting out the implications of biblical criticism for the understanding of the Old Testament, which were immediately published as *The Old Testament in the Jewish Church* (1881) and *The Prophets of Israel* (1882). At this stage his work was essentially a popularisation of the chronology of the Old Testament books, which placed the final redaction of the Pentateuch in the post-Exilic period, with a consequential reappraisal of the nature of Jewish religion at the time of the prophets. The Preface to the former set out his 'manifesto' clearly:

> The great value of historical criticism is that it makes the Old Testament more real to us. Christianity can never separate itself from its historical basis on the Religion of Israel; the revelation of God in Christ cannot be divorced from the earlier revelation on which our Lord built. In all true religion the new rests upon the old. No one, then, to whom Christianity is a reality can safely acquiesce in an unreal conception of the Old Testament history; and in an age when all are interested in historical research, no apologetic can prevent thoughtful minds from drifting away from faith if the historical study of the Old Covenant is condemned by the Church and left in the hands of unbelievers.[99]

In 1875 Robertson Smith had been invited to join the Old Testament Revision Committee on the death of Principal Fairbairn (of the Free Church College, Glasgow). The meetings of the Committee, like those of the New Testament, generally lasted for sessions of about ten days three or four times a year in the Jerusalem Chamber of Westminster Abbey. This work made Robertson Smith a regular visitor to London, and enabled him to get to know Cambridge scholars such as R.L. Bensly (later one of his successors as Lord Almoner's Professor of Arabic), J.J.S. Perowne (Hulsean Professor, 1875–78, Dean of Peterborough,

---

99   W. Robertson Smith, *The Old Testament in the Jewish Church* (2nd edn, London, 1902), p. xi.

1878–90 and then Bishop of Worcester) and William Wright (Sir Thomas Adams's Professor of Arabic, 1870–89). He also met the Cambridge trio, when there were joint meetings of the Old and New Testament Committees. His first visit to Cambridge was also in 1875, when Perowne invited him to a feast in Trinity.[100] So it was not surprising that, when the Lord Almoner's chair became vacant in 1882, Robertson Smith's Cambridge friends should urge his claims upon the Lord Almoner, who was also Dean of Worcester. Testimonials were received from a variety of foreign scholars including Lagarde, Nöldeke and Wellhausen, and Robertson Smith was appointed on 1 January 1883. Hort predicted that he would be well received everywhere.[101] His first lectures were given in the Easter Term, and Hort suggested to Westcott, that they agree to his use of the large lecture room in the Divinity School: 'I have the strongest feeling that the representatives of "Divinity" in Cambridge should give him a cordial welcome ... He will be a power wherever he is; and there is every reason to help forward his evidently strong and sincere desire to take his stand as a Christian among Christians.'[102] Dr Swainson, the Lady Margaret's Professor from 1879 to 1887 and Master of Christ's, secured Robertson Smith's election to a Fellowship at Christ's in 1885.[103]

When the University Librarian, Henry Bradshaw, died suddenly in 1886, Robertson Smith was elected as his successor by a majority of more than 200 votes in the Senate. In 1887 he was invited to deliver the Burnett Lectures in Aberdeen. The subject was 'The primitive religions of the Semitic peoples, viewed in relation to other ancient religions, and to the spiritual religion of the Old Testament and of Christianity'. Three series of lectures were given in October 1888 and March 1889, March 1890 and December 1891.[104] The first series was published in 1889, but the second and third series remained in manuscript form until rediscovered in the Cambridge University Library in 1991.[105] They broke new ground, not only in providing a systematic comparison between Old Testament religion and that of other Semitic peoples, but in pioneering the study of fundamental religious institutions as such. Robertson Smith noted that the significance of comparative studies for the religion of the Bible had first been brought out by John Spencer, Master of Corpus Christi College, Cambridge, in the seventeenth century. But a new enquiry was opportune because effective comparison of Hebrew religion with that of other Semitic peoples was not possible so long as the historical order of the Old Testament books was unknown or wrongly understood. Thanks to the work

---

100    J.S. Black and G. Chrystal, *The Life of William Robertson Smith* (London, 1912), pp. 167–70.

101    Black and Chrystal, *William Robertson Smith*, pp. 467–71, W. Robertson Smith, *Lectures on the Religion of the Semites, First Series: The Fundamental Institutions* (London, 1894), p. v.

102    Hort to Wescott, 18 April 1883: A.F. Hort, *Life and Letters of Fenton John Anthony Hort* (London, 1896), ii, p. 294.

103    Black and Chrystal, *William Robertson Smith*, pp. 478–80.

104    Ibid., pp. 485–90.

105    W. Robertson Smith, *The Religion of the Semites: Second and Third Series*, ed. J. Day (Sheffield, 1995).

of Kuenen and Wellhausen in particular, it was now possible to trace the growth of Old Testament religion from stage to stage.[106]

By Semites Robertson Smith was referring to the Arabs, Hebrews, Phoenicians, Aramaeans, Babylonians and Assyrians. In his first series he was particularly concerned with 'the fundamental institutions' – holy places, seasons and persons, the sacrificial system and ritual generally, rather than creed and dogma. These were the 'unconscious religious traditions' which lay behind the '*positive* religions' of Judaism, Christianity and Islam, whose origin lay in the teaching of 'great religious innovators'.[107] Chief among these was the whole idea and practice of sacrifice. By making the prophets chronologically prior to the Pentateuch, Robertson Smith was able to argue that before the Exile the mass of the Israelites had the greatest difficulty in keeping their national religion distinct from that of the surrounding nations: 'The whole history of Israel is unintelligible if we suppose that the heathenism against which the prophets contended was a thing altogether alien to the religious traditions of the Hebrews.'[108] The sacred places were those where the priests offered sacrifice; but the rites were not connected with dogmas, but myths. However, there could be different explanations and different stories to account for the same rite, so that it was wrong to attach too much importance to one myth rather than another. Indeed the significance of mythology had probably been exaggerated in the study of religion. 'The conclusion is, that in the study of ancient religions we must begin, not with myth, but with ritual and traditional usage.'[109]

Robertson Smith was pointing the study of religion in a new direction. He was a man at home in two worlds. One of his friends was Sir James Frazer, author of *The Golden Bough* (1890), who popularised the study of primitive religions; but the conclusion to the First Series betrayed his Presbyterian background:

> Redemption, substitution, purification, atoning blood, the garment of righteousness, are all terms which in some sense go back to antique ritual. But in ancient religion all these terms are very vaguely defined; ... and the attempt to find in them anything as precise and definite as the notions attached to the same words by Christian theologians is altogether illegitimate ... In primitive life, all spiritual and ethical ideas are still wrapped up in the husk of a material embodiment. To free the spiritual truth from the husk was the great task that lay before the ancient religions, if they were to maintain the right to continue to rule the minds of men. That some progress in this direction was made, especially in Israel, appears from our examination. But on the whole it is manifest that none of the ritual systems of antiquity was able by mere natural development to shake itself free from the congenital defect in material forms. A ritual system must always remain materialistic, even if its materialism is disguised under the cloak of mysticism.[110]

---

106 Smith, *Religion of the Semites*, pp. vi–vii.
107 Ibid., p. 1; Black and Chrystal, *William Robertson Smith*, pp. 511–20.
108 Smith, *Religion of the Semites*, p. 4.
109 Ibid., p. 18.
110 Ibid., pp. 439–40.

Stanley Cook (Regius Professor of Hebrew, 1932–38) wrote a new Introduction to the third edition in 1927, in which he suggested that Robertson Smith was better regarded as the founder of 'the Science and Theory of Religion' than of Comparative Religion. Whereas theologians had discussed questions of ritual, theology and myth, sin and atonement, sacramentalism, immanence and transcendence within the limits of Christian theology, Robertson Smith had gone to the most essential ideas, 'and those not of Christianity alone'. He had 'an insight into the fundamental theories of Religion which ... has never been surpassed'.[111] Robertson Smith's health was beginning to fail by 1892, when tuberculosis was diagnosed, and he died on 31 March 1894.

The other group of nonconformists were concerned with new sources for the study of early Christianity. James Rendel Harris (1852–1941) was a scholar of Clare College and third wrangler in 1874; he became a Fellow of Clare in 1875 and lecturer in Mathematics. In June 1875 he was admitted to membership of Emmanuel Congregational Church by transfer from Plymouth. In the dispute between the minister, Matthew Robertson, and the deacons in 1877, Harris seconded the motion requesting three of the leading deacons (including William Bond) to resign. This failed by three votes and a motion asking the minister to resign passed by five votes. Harris requested a ballot in view of the close vote, but when that was rejected he said he had no alternative but to resign and left the meeting.[112] He became a member of the Society of Friends in 1880, and left Cambridge in 1882 to teach New Testament Greek at Johns Hopkins University in Baltimore, Maryland. In 1885 he moved to the Quaker University of Haverford College, Pennsylvania, as professor of biblical languages and literature. That was the year of his first book, *The Teaching of the Apostles and the Sybilline Books*, the title of which illustrates a similar comparative approach to that of Robertson Smith. In 1893 Harris returned to Cambridge to a Lectureship in Palaeography, established in connexion with the Special Board for Divinity.[113]

Harris's visit to St Catherine's, Mount Sinai, in 1889, when he discovered a Syriac version of the *Apology of Aristides*, inspired the Lewis and Gibson twins to make a similar trip. In preparation for the journey they learnt Syriac from R.H. Kennett, but neither Harris, F.C. Burkitt nor Bensly was available to accompany them in 1892. In Sinai they discovered a Syriac palimpsest of the gospels, which they photographed. On their return to England they consulted various friends, who were too busy to look at their pictures. Several suggested that it might be the same text as the Cureton Syriac version, published in 1858. Bensly identified it as being of the same type in July 1892 and insisted on complete secrecy. The twins, together with Burkitt and Rendel Harris, agreed that it was

---

111   W. Robertson Smith, *Lectures on the Religion of the Semites*, ed. S.A. Cook (3rd edn, London, 1927), pp. x–xi.

112   Emmanuel Church Meeting Minutes 1868–92, 6 June and 28 November 1877, Cambridgeshire County Record Office.

113   Tanner, *Historical Register*, p. 123. This lectureship was held by F.C. Burkitt after Harris's resignation in 1903.

necessary to visit Sinai again, in order to make a proper transcription of the text.[114] This was done in January–March 1893. The publication in the *British Weekly* of a letter from Harris, sent from Suez on 30 March, announcing the discovery of the manuscript, caused conflict between him and the others, partly because it was done without consultation and partly because it was felt by Bensly and Burkitt to be a claim that the credit for the discovery lay with Harris.[115] The breakdown in relationships was intensified by Bensly's death three days after returning to Cambridge, as a result of a chill caught in Rome. Glover remarked in his diary in March 1896 that he had been surprised to discover from the Burkitts how violent the row between Rendel Harris and Bensly had been.[116]

Burkitt described the significance of the discovery at the Church Congress in Norwich in October 1895, saying that it was 'a very faithful representative of the earliest Syriac translation of the Gospels'.[117] It therefore had implications for the longstanding discussion over the best Greek versions of the New Testament, and particularly the argument about the relative merits of the Received Text and the new version produced by Westcott and Hort. Burkitt (who had been a pupil of Hort) noted that the Syriac palimpsest confirmed Hort's theory of an Antiochene revision of the Greek text of the New Testament, adding that it was sad that Hort should have died only a few months before the transcription of the manuscript.[118] Subsequently discussion turned to the question of whether the Syriac version of the gospels was made after Tatian's *Diatesseron*, or whether it

---

114   M.D. Gibson, *How the Codex was found* (Cambridge, 1893), pp. 1–8, 70–81, 124–5; A.S. Lewis, *In the Shadow of Sinai* (Cambridge, 1898), pp. ii–xii. It is not clear why Bethune-Baker, in his Obituary Notice of Burkitt, should have said that Mrs Lewis 'had brought back photographs the year before without knowing their importance, until it was pointed out by Burkitt' (*Proceedings of the British Academy*, (1936): 464), unless he based his statement on Mrs Bensly's account alone: R.L. Bensly, *Our Journey to Sinai* (London, 1896), pp. 12–13. Mrs Lewis's own account made it clear that her father had explained to her what a palimpsest was, and the point of their trip was to examine the manuscripts which Harris had not had time to look at in 1889; hence his provision of a camera for their use.

115   *British Weekly* (13 April 1883): 400. The Harris–Nestlé Letters in Westminster College show Harris trying to correct the wrong impression created by a similar note published in Germany, and also contain letters from Mrs Bensly and Burkitt to Nestlé, putting their side of the story.

116   Glover Diaries, 6 March 1896; cf. D. Cornick and C. Binfield, *From Cambridge to Sinai: The worlds of Agnes Smith Lewis and Margaret Dunlop Gibson* (London, 2006), p. 18. The situation was made worse by the fact that Harris and the twins had gone ahead of the others on the last part of the return journey from Suez, because the twins needed to catch the boat in Alexandria in order to be back for the Presbyterian Synod in April, when the question of the move of the theological college to Cambridge was to be discussed.

117   F.C. Burkitt, 'Recently Discovered MSS' in C. Dunkley, *Offical Report of the Church Congress held at Norwich, 8 to 11 October 1895* (London, 1895), pp. 200–206; cf. Bensly, *Our Journey to Sinai*, pp. 175–85.

118   Burkitt, 'Recently Discovered MSS', p. 202.

represents an earlier, independent version. Here Burkitt argued for the former position, and Agnes Lewis and Rendel Harris took the latter.[119]

In 1903 Harris was invited to become Professor of Early Christian Literature and New Testament Exegesis at the University of Leiden, but declined in favour of becoming the first Director of Studies at the new Quaker house for religious and social study at Woodbrooke in Selly Oak, Birmingham. He became an Honorary Fellow of Clare in 1909, a Fellow of the British Academy in 1927, and died in 1941. Burkitt succeeded to his Lectureship in Palaeography. Harris's interest in the New Testament apocryphal books has perhaps left him on the margins, so far as assessment as a scholar is concerned. Hort was sceptical about his study of the *Codex Bezae* in 1891.[120]

Finally a word should be said about T.R. Glover (1869–1943). His diaries offer a fascinating insight into the problems of nonconformists making their way in the University, academically and financially. Glover secured first class honours in Part I and II of the Classical Tripos in 1891 and 1892, but the question of what he would do next became a pressing one. A diary entry in September 1892 suggests that he had considered the possibility of going to Mansfield College, Oxford to train for ministry.[121] As an undergraduate and subsequently he went to St Columba's as well as Emmanuel, depending on the preacher; in February 1896 while staying with Rendel Harris at Hitchin he went to the Friends' Meeting for the first time and found it 'pleasant and thoughtful'.[122] As a graduate he broadened his interests to include theology, discussing *The Shepherd of Hermas* with the Master of St John's (Charles Taylor), the Apostolic Fathers with Armitage Robinson, and palaeography with Rendel Harris (whom he met through the Nonconformist Union), as well as J.E.B. Mayor's lectures on Tertullian, and H.M. Gwatkin's on Church History.[123] Whilst at dinner in Christ's as the guest of Armitage Robinson, Robertson Smith urged him to learn Syriac (which he did).[124] In the summer of 1893 Glover read Edwin Hatch's Hibbert Lectures ('one of the best books I have ever read'), following it up with his Bampton Lectures ('Rarely does one man write two such good books'), and Harnack on the Apostles' Creed in German.[125] In October A.M. Fairbairn urged him to go to Germany to study with Harnack, whilst Robinson suggested Zahn at Erlangen.[126] In November Glover was elected to a Fellowship at St John's. In the following year he broadened his study into the Old Testament, reading Wellhausen – he was already familiar with Robertson

---

119  B.M. Metzger, *The Early Versions of the New Testament* (Oxford, 1977), pp. 45–6; A.S. Lewis, *Light on the Four Gospels from the Sinai Palimpsest* (London, 1913), pp. 8–11. Characteristically the late Professor J.S. O'Neill in his last contribution to New Testament studies supported Agnes Lewis: Cornick and Binfield, *From Cambridge to Sinai*, pp. 39–63, especially pp. 42–3.

120  Hort, *Life of Hort*, ii, pp. 382–3.

121  Glover Diaries, 22 September 1892.

122  Ibid., 16 February 1895.

123  Wood, *Glover*, pp. 27–8.

124  Glover Diaries, 14 February 1893.

125  Ibid., 7 June, 21 August, 22 August, 6 September and 7 September 1893.

126  Ibid., 12 October 1893.

Smith.[127] On 6 November his guest at a College Feast was Burkitt, which Glover very much enjoyed.[128]

Nevertheless by 1895 Glover was starting to look for opportunities elsewhere. He wondered about the Greek chair in Cork, a Classical chair in Adelaide, or even the possibility of Semitic studies. In March he applied unsuccessfully for a chair at Cornell, after being urged to do so by Whibley of Pembroke, who ran the Castle End Mission.[129] Meanwhile he secured some additional cash by taking work as an examiner for the Local Examinations Syndicate at Keynes's invitation.[130] In October he was offered a post at Cheshunt College (then still in London), which he turned down on Heitland's advice.[131] Finally in June he received a letter from Principal Grant of Queen's University, Kingston, Ontario, inviting him to be a candidate for the Chair of Latin at a salary of $2,000 a year – a sum of greater importance following his engagement. Fairbairn had suggested Glover's name to Grant, while he was staying at Mansfield, and urged Glover to take it seriously, since it would offer the opportunity 'to cultivate not only Classics but Theology'. A meeting in London with Grant and the Chancellor of the University followed; he applied and at the end of August heard that he was successful. On 11 September he travelled to Bristol, noting in his diary 'So ends my Cambridge life'; he sailed from Liverpool on 17 September, and landed in Canada on 26 September.[132] In fact, it was not the end. In March 1901 Glover received a letter from St John's inviting him to return as Fellow and Classical Tutor, which he accepted with great joy and thankfulness to God. A similarly decisive diary entry to that five years earlier read 'Landed in England to settle.'[133]

Although Glover retained strong theological interests, his future at Cambridge lay in Classics. He failed to secure a University Lectureship in Ancient History immediately upon his return, but was successful in 1911. After failing to get either the Latin or the Greek chair at Glasgow in 1906–7, he ceased to apply elsewhere; but he was always uncomfortable as a dissenter in Cambridge.[134] Heitland's remark to him in the Combination Room at St John's in 1896, that Baptists were not very much in themselves, but very good as an antidote, summed up the half-joking half-serious view of dissent in late nineteenth-century Cambridge.[135] Until very recently that ambiguity has remained true of many Anglican voices, and Glover's own share in the ambiguity is illustrated by his description of the remark as 'very

127 Ibid., 26 May 1894.
128 Ibid., 6 November 1894.
129 Ibid., 16 January, 5 March, 8 March, 14 April 1895. Whibley had also resigned as a member of Emmanuel as a result of the dismissal of Robertson.
130 Ibid., 25 March, 6 April 1895.
131 Ibid., 10 and 11 October 1895, cf. 14 and 19 September 1895.
132 Ibid., 26 June, 1 July, 29 August, 11 September, 17 September and 26 September 1896; Wood, *Glover*, p. 35.
133 Glover Diaries, 18 March, 15 May 1901.
134 Ibid., 15 May 1901; Wood, *Glover*, 61–2. Rendel Harris proposed him as a member of the Special Board for Theology in December 1901; Swete, the Regius Professor, said it was a good name; but he came second: Diaries, 1 December 1901.
135 Glover Diaries, 16 May 1896.

amusing'. Only in Canada did he realise quite how stifling Cambridge was to someone like him.

In 1905 Glover was invited to give the Dale Lectures at Mansfield College, Oxford; and he decided to write a description of Jesus and his early followers 'as they appeared among their contemporaries'.[136] This was set primarily in the Roman context, though Glover showed himself aware of the diversity of worlds in Alexandria, Asia Minor and beyond. The eight lectures at Mansfield became ten chapters in the published book. The first three chapters were on Roman religion, with a more detailed treatment of the Stoics and Plutarch. Chapter 4 was on Jesus and chapter 5 on his followers. The remaining chapters began with one on the conflict between Christian and Jew, continued with one on the third century, beginning with Marcus Aurelius, and another on Celsus; and the final two chapters were on Clement of Alexandria and Tertullian.

The straightforward description of the teaching and beliefs of particular individuals in the opening chapters was continued in that on Jesus of Nazareth. But it was more than a life of Jesus in miniature. The centre in the new religion, wrote Glover, was not 'an idea, nor a ritual act, but a personality'.[137] Glover emphasised the charm and ease of Jesus' language, his peculiar tenderness for children, his outdoor life, which was reflected in his parables. Jesus was a realist, lacking the sentimentalism that Glover observed in some lovers of nature; this explained his words about poverty and the Kingdom of God, and 'the advantage of disadvantages, for they at least make a man in earnest with himself'.[138] 'No other teacher dreamed that common men could possess a tenth part of the moral grandeur and spiritual power which Jesus elicited from them – chiefly by believing in them.'[139] In his teaching about God Jesus' central thought was the Fatherhood of God; and although parallels in phraseology might be found in the Old Testament or Homer, Glover asserted that 'the meaning which Jesus gave to it is his own'.[140] There were two related terms, the Kingdom or Kingship of God and Messiah: in Glover's view the understanding of both terms had to be subordinated to the 'master-thought of God's fatherhood'. Thus Glover believed that the idea of Jesus as a mediator in the Pauline sense was foreign to the gospels, and 'the later conception of a purchase of mankind from the devil, or from the justice of God, by the blood of a victim is still more alien to Jesus' mind'.[141] But, concluded Glover, it was not the teaching of Jesus which won the world, but his death on the cross: that gave certainty to everything that Jesus taught about God.

---

136  T.R. Glover, *The Conflict of Religions in the Early Roman Empire* (London, 1909), p. v.

137  Ibid., p. 116.

138  Ibid., p. 125.

139  Ibid., p. 130.

140  Ibid., p. 134.

141  Ibid., p. 138.

The Gospels neither were, nor are, the source of the Christian movement ... Jesus lives for us in the pages of the Gospels, but we are not his followers on that account, nor were the Christians of the first century ... The Church was a nexus of quickened and redeemed personalities, – men and women in whom Christ lived.[142]

Such an emphasis is similar to that of Forsyth, and indeed of Westcott and Hort, but it came by a rather different route.

The chapter on the followers of Jesus focused on the missionary expansion of the church. Here Glover emphasised the key role played by those reared in the atmosphere of Hellenistic Judaism in making Christianity a faith with universal appeal. Paul on the one hand and the author of the fourth gospel on the other represented different ways of explaining the significance of Jesus in such a universal way. For Glover neither was completely satisfactory, since Columbus, Copernicus and Darwin, without being philosophers or theologians, had changed the perspectives of philosophy and theology. The idea of the Messiah was strange to the Greeks, but the Logos was as strange to people today:

We have really at present no terms in which to express what we feel to be the permanent significance of Jesus, and the old expressions may repel us until we realize, first, that they are not of the original essence of the Gospel, and second, that they represent the best language which Greek and Jew could find for a conviction which we share – that Jesus of Nazareth does stand at the centre of human history, that he has brought God and man into a new relation, that he is the personal concern of everyone of us, and that there is more in him than we have yet accounted for.[143]

Glover did not pursue the history of the church as an organisation or the sacraments very far, since he believed that the force of the Christian movement lay in neither, but rather in people. The characteristic of those people, in Glover's view, was a strong hope and essential happiness. 'The holy spirit was a glad spirit, and gladness – joy in the holy spirit – was the secret of Christian morality.'[144]

Despite the brevity of this account, it will be clear that Glover's emphasis was not on the development of Christology or trinitarian theology, although these topics did appear in his later discussion of Clement and Tertullian. It is not surprising that some critics should have described Glover's views as Arian, though more discerning reviewers saw his affinities with Ritschl and Harnack. Some of his closest friends did not care for the chapter on Jesus: his father preferred the one on 'The Followers of Jesus'; and John Skinner, John Oman and Kirsopp Lake thought that chapter 4 was too western and too modern. Nevertheless H.G. Wood rightly said that the book established Glover's reputation as a writer and a scholar.[145] *The Conflict of Religions* was in its third edition within six months; and in many ways Glover's later best-selling *The Jesus of History*, commended by the Archbishop of Canterbury in 1917, was an expansion of his basic thesis.

---

142  Ibid., pp. 139–40.
143  Ibid., p. 157.
144  Ibid., p. 166.
145  Wood, *Glover*, pp. 78–81.

It is also fascinating that in his final chapter on Tertullian, Glover gave a scathing criticism of chapter 15 of Gibbon's *Decline and Fall*, noting that Gibbon's description of Tertullian was more useful 'as an index to the mind of Gibbon than to that of Tertullian'. The translation was abridged; Gibbon had missed Tertullian's points in one or two clauses; and he had ended his quotation 'exactly when he knew there was little or nothing more to be quoted that would serve his purpose'. 'He has made no attempt to understand the man he quotes, nor the mood in which he spoke, nor the circumstances which gave rise to that mood.' On the evidence of that, and a sonnet of Matthew Arnold, English readers had passed a swift judgment on Tertullian. Yet, in Glover's view, Tertullian was the first Latin churchman: 'He, too, was the first great Puritan of the West, precursor alike of Augustine and the Reformation.'[146] Thus the story returns to the apologetic task first embarked upon by Richard Watson 150 years earlier, when he sought to combat the influence of Gibbon.

These nonconformist voices, varied as they were, showed that Cambridge theology was changing. It is unfair to end the century by referring to the nonconformists without mentioning Anglicans like Swete and Handley Moule, or the *Cambridge Theological Essays* of 1909. Burkitt has been referred to in passing. But, for whatever reason, the nonconformists in Cambridge were more easily able to pick up the new ideas and run with them; for them the apologetic task was not a response to scepticism but the revision of evangelicalism. Just before the outbreak of the First World War, the Lecture List in Divinity for the year 1913–14 included John Oman on 'The Philosophy of Religion', W.A.L. Elmslie on '2 Samuel and Isaiah in Hebrew', and Charles Anderson Scott on 'The Epistle to the Galatians'. That reflected the arrival of Westminster College. This development was enhanced after 1918.

---

146  Glover, *Conflict of Religions*, pp. 305–6.

# Chapter 8

# Conclusion

'Here therefore the language of enquiry is deliberately employed, ... because it is by contemplating the controversy under the form of a problem that truth, whatever that truth may be, seems most likely to be attained.'[1] Hort's words in the Introduction to his Hulsean Lectures provide one answer to the question of whether there is a 'Cambridge tradition' in theology in the long nineteenth century. He was commenting on the appropriate way of presenting Christian doctrine. John Hulse's benefaction had originally required the Lecturer to show the truth and excellence of Christianity, especially by collateral arguments, and to explain the more difficult or obscure parts of the holy scriptures. When Hort gave the lectures, the regulations had recently been amended so as to remove those specific requirements, but he felt that their original character as sermons should be honoured. He sympathised with Hulse's intentions concerning the true view of Christian evidences, and believed that it was only in speaking to Christians that a Christian could set out the weightier grounds of faith. Yet he was equally sensitive to the fact that apologetic treatises could be counter-productive, and that someone unable to accept some of the widely held views of Christian doctrine might be a reluctant public champion of a dominant and popular religion.

Even if those problems could be resolved, others remained. There was no simple way to verify Christian dogma independently. In the area of first principles tradition and evidence were so intertwined that it was hard to separate them; and any deeply held personal conviction was both absolutely and relatively inexpressible. All that could be done was to offer 'a tentative exhibition' of some of the leading lines of such a position. This was why he used the language of inquiry, believing that the presentation of a controversy in the form of a problem was most likely to lead to truth; and to speak in any other way would misrepresent the way in which the subject appeared to him. 'Beliefs worth calling beliefs must be purchased with the sweat of the brow', he wrote; and Hort was not prepared to supply 'ready nourishment to the credulity which is truly said to be a dangerous disease of the time'.[2] Anything less likely from Hort is difficult to imagine! But would Newman or Pusey have been so cautious in tackling such a theme? It is absolutely typical that the first point which Hort makes in the first lecture is that Jesus' words in John 14:5–6 'belong more to dialogue than to discourse' – thus

---

1    F.J.A. Hort, Introduction to *The Way, the Truth and the Life* (London, 1893), p. xxxiii.

2    Ibid., pp. xxxiv–xxxv.

he includes Thomas's question as well as Jesus' response, 'I am the Way and the Truth and the Life: no one cometh unto the Father save through me'.[3]

If there is a thread running through the account which has been given, it is the willingness to consider theology as a series of open questions rather than already determined conclusions. To be sure, this was not true of all those who have been discussed – Rose and Simeon immediately come to mind; nor was Cambridge the only place in which such openness was to be found – Arnold, Jowett and Stanley might be mentioned. But Arnold and Stanley spent relatively little time teaching at Oxford, and arguably Jowett's mind was not as open to such a variety of possibilities as Hort's. In many ways the positions affirmed by Cambridge men were entirely traditional; the emphases on scripture, the Fathers and the Reformation, for example. Such openness in theology in Richard Watson's time was considered to be verging on heresy, but it survived – probably because several of those who posed such questions, including Watson himself, but also Herbert Marsh, had impeccably anti-revolutionary political credentials.

In 1904 *The Church Quarterly Review* published an article entitled, 'Religion in Cambridge', which was ostensibly a review of the biographies of Benson, Westcott and Hort, together with some articles in the *Nineteenth Century* and a history of the Cambridge Mission to South London in the previous twenty years. The author regarded Westcott as the greatest influence on Cambridge, and regretted that the current professors lacked his influence in the University. He felt that the majority of devotedly Christian undergraduates were probably evangelical in their views and there were no centres of influence for high churchmen comparable to those in Oxford. The author's main criticism was that there was no obvious teaching in the principles of the Church of England.[4] But he also drew attention to the power of the increasing number of scientists in the University and of the number of agnostic philosophers, who though courteous to those in holy orders were nevertheless anti-clerical. Their influence on young men, who easily laid aside the religious impressions received at their public schools, seemed to be growing.[5]

The reviewer acknowledged that not all natural scientists were against Christianity and that it was wiser for the religious teachers in the University to maintain a neutral position. In fact, despite the understandable attention given to Charles Darwin, natural science in itself did not pose any kind of threat to Christianity for many Cambridge scientists in the nineteenth century. In the earlier period men like Adam Sedgwick and William Whewell were more concerned to broaden the curriculum than to train theologians to answer the questions raised

---

3     Ibid., pp. 2–3. Note that Hort uses his own translation, not the Authorised Version; nor did the Revisers translate the verse this way.

4     There was a slight irony here, since a comparable article on 'Religion in Oxford' in 1902 (probably by the same author) criticised Oxford for not adequately providing coverage of dogmatic theology and philosophy, and said that it needed to abandon the demand that Christianity is only to be taught in the form of 'definite Church teaching': 'Religion in Oxford', *Church Quarterly Review*, lv, 109 (October 1902): 23.

5     'Religion in Cambridge', *Church Quarterly Review*, lix, 117 (October 1904): 1–28.

by scientific discoveries. Whewell, even while writing his natural theology, was preaching orthodox sermons on justification by faith in Trinity College Chapel.[6] In the second half of the century James Clerk Maxwell, who as the first Professor of Experimental Physics from 1871 supervised the building of the Cavendish Laboratory, was one of those who petitioned the Presbytery of London in 1879 for the establishment of what became St Columba's Presbyterian Church.[7] Second Wrangler in 1854 and a Fellow of Trinity in 1855, he had subscribed to the tests, but in 1856 he moved back to Scotland to a chair at Aberdeen. He was an Apostle and a close friend of Hort, whose own interest in the Natural Sciences has already been noted. When Maxwell died in 1879 at the early age of 48, Hort wrote to his daughter that 'he was one of the greatest men living, and ... one of the best'.[8] Maxwell had approved both of Hare's sermons and of Maurice.[9] Hort contributed an account of Maxwell's religious opinions to his *Memoir*, which included these words: 'in his eyes every subject had its affinities with the rest of the universal truth'.[10] This fits Hort's strongly held view that 'the Divinity Professors are the natural guardians of what one may call the comprehensiveness of the Divinity School'.[11] He also referred to Maxwell's membership of the Apostles, saying that 'it is likely that his mind was at least invigorated and consolidated by an influence which others have found reason to count among the strongest and also on the whole most salutary that they have known'.[12]

The reasonableness of Christianity, and particularly the moral objections to some of the aspects of God depicted in the Old Testament, together with the doctrines of hell and everlasting punishment, remained much more problematic for many than evolution by natural selection. Utilitarians like John Stuart Mill were felt to need answers; and this is the significance of Henry Sidgwick and an erstwhile nonconformist like James Ward. Several Cambridge men, including Sidgwick and Ward, towards the end of the century were involved in the Society for Psychical Research. To modern eyes this may seem to have been a curious and fringe activity; but it was an attempt to verify by scientific methods the existence of a life beyond death, and of a different kind of world from that which was the

---

6    J.H. Brooke, 'Indications of a Creator: Whewell as Apologist and Priest' in M. Fisch and S. Schaffer (eds), *William Whewell: A Composite Portrait* (Oxford, 1991), pp. 160–62.

7    R.B. Knox, *St Columba's Church, Cambridge, 1879–1979* [Cambridge, n.d.], p. 3.

8    Hort to his eldest daughter, 9 November 1879: A.F. Hort, *Life and letters of Fenton John Anthony Hort* (London, 1896), ii, p. 276. Clerk Maxwell died the day before the new Divinity School was opened.

9    L. Campbell and W. Garnett, *Life of James Clerk Maxwell* (London, 1882), p. 171.

10   Quoted in Hort, *Life of Hort*, ii, p. 231; cf. Campbell and Garnett, *Life of Clerk Maxwell*, p. 419.

11   Hort to Mr S. Sandars, 21 April 1891, Hort, *Life of Hort*, ii, p. 430. Sandars was the donor of the statues on the front of the old Divinity School in Saint John's Street.

12   Campbell and Garnett, *Life of Clerk Maxwell*, p. 417.

subject of experience on earth. From an agnostic and scientific perspective it was an entirely natural track to follow.

The alternative route was to rethink the harshness of evangelicalism and indeed questions associated with the interpretation of scripture. Maurice's reflections on the difference between 'everlasting' and 'eternal' punishment in his *Theological Essays* (1853) resulted in his dismissal from King's College, London; but his dismissal did not end the speculation. Hort was influenced by Maurice; Westcott reached a similar position by a different route.[13] A Presbyterian like Robertson Smith or a Congregationalist like Forsyth was also articulating a rather different theology from the 'Calvinism' of Jonathan Edwards. The important point was that such modified views were not precluded by the teaching of the Church of England (though for Robertson Smith and Forsyth the position on justification set out in chapter 11 of the Westminster Confession and the Savoy Declaration was in principle more problematic). Nevertheless, as the *Church Quarterly Review* article noted, undergraduate evangelical religion thrived in the later nineteenth century. This was the time of the 'Cambridge Seven', the Student Volunteer Movement for Foreign Missions and the founding of the Cambridge Inter-Collegiate Christian Union.

History and historical criticism provided the core and strength of the way in which the Cambridge theological tradition evolved during the century. The scientific tradition in Cambridge from at least Newton's time had convinced people that facts, whether in physics or history, were sacred. So the results of historical research, or even speculation, had to be verified or challenged. This applied as much to biblical studies as to any other field; in fact, work in biblical studies could be argued to have led the way, or at least to have followed hard on the heels of work in Greek and Roman literature. There was no point in denying anything which could be established as fact, however inconvenient the consequences might be for established opinions. This was the enduring effect of Locke, as well as Newton. Julius Hare's interest in philological investigation offered the opportunity of a new way of establishing historical facts. His view of the potential of philology was broader than the modern restricted meaning of it. 'Philology in the highest sense,' he wrote, 'ought to be only another name for Philosophy. Its aim should be to seek after wisdom in the whole series of its historical manifestations. As it is, the former usually mumbles the husk, the other paws the kernel.'[14] Despite, or because of, his Platonism, Hare attached importance to 'historical manifestations'. Westcott's approach was similar. In a pair of very revealing articles on 'The Myths of Plato', printed in the *Contemporary Review* in the late 1860s, Westcott defended the Platonic myths as 'an unfailing testimony to the religious wants of man'.[15] Indeed he regarded them as 'the shape which a revelation for men might be expected to take'. 'The doctrine is conveyed in an historic form: the ideas are offered as facts; the myth itself is the message.'[16] Furthermore, he saw Plato as

---

13    For a more general discussion see G. Rowell, *Hell and the Victorians* (Oxford, 1974), especially pp. 76–89.

14    *Guesses at Truth by Two Brothers*, p. 525.

15    B.F. Westcott, *Religious Thought in the West* (London, 1891), p. 48.

16    Ibid., p. 49.

'an unconscious prophet of the Gospel': 'The Life of Christ is, *in form no less than in substance*, the Divine reality of which the Myths were an instructive foreshadowing'.[17] He concluded his essay with a quotation from Simmias in the *Phaedo*, about the necessity, if it were impossible to learn or discover the truth about ultimate questions, to trust in 'some Divine Word', and added, 'The Word for which the wavering faith of Simmias thus longed, has, we believe, been given to us; and once again Plato points us to St John'.[18] Ultimately the readiness to follow the approach of Hare and Westcott led to deeper critical questions about the framework of understanding, within which scriptural and ecclesiastical history fitted, but such questions were delayed so long as the primary emphasis lay upon establishing the authenticity of the scriptural documents.

Underlying these investigations in the first two-thirds of the nineteenth century was a deep and abiding commitment to the Church of England. Hare was a conscientious archdeacon, more so than Paley, reviving the practice of regular visitations; Marsh and Kaye, Lightfoot and Westcott became bishops; the first two were involved in the reforms of the early nineteenth century, the latter two became almost paradigms for the rare ideal of the pastorally involved scholar-bishop. In the long run the exclusion of dissenters from the University was abandoned; but this would have been inconceivable to Marsh and probably Kaye; Lightfoot and Westcott accepted change as academically expedient, but were to the fore in seeking to ensure the survival of an exclusive Anglican tradition in the form of Selwyn College. It was Thirlwall who put his academic head on the block for this cause in the 1830s, though at the time he could not have anticipated the relatively speedy Whig reward in his appointment as Bishop of St David's.

In 1890 Hort agreed to a request from Dr William Moulton to discover whether Westcott would be prepared to speak at one of the functions arranged to mark the centenary of John Wesley's death; Moulton was President of the Wesleyan Conference in that year. Westcott declined, partly because of the cool Wesleyan response to the Lambeth Quadrilateral of 1888. Hort agreed with Westcott that 'we must not recognise Separatism as a normal and permanent state of things'; but he also felt that it was impossible to expect that Wesleyans would simply cry *peccavimus* and go back over a century. Nevertheless he was equally disappointed by Moulton's belief that 'a plurality of independent Christian communities in the same country is the ideal state of things, not merely a present necessity'. Having said that, he added, 'who can wonder if Dissenters shrink from being merged in a body which they fear is on the way to taking its doctrine of the Church from the Oxford Tracts? *That natural fear* is surely the deadliest hindrance to reunion'.[19] In the event the Anglican address was given by Archdeacon Farrar. The reactions on

---

17    Ibid. (emphasis added).

18    Ibid., p. 50.

19    Hort to Westcott, 2 Oct, 7 October and 11 October 1890: Hort, *Life of Hort*, ii, pp. 426–9 (emphasis added); cf. W.F. Moulton, *William F. Moulton: A Memoir* (London, 1899), p. 248–52. The drift of Westcott's response, which was affected by the reactions to his address on Socialism at the Hull Church Congress in 1890, has been inferred from Hort's side of the correspondence.

all sides are significant in indicating the limited extent of Anglican-Nonconformist rapprochement at this time, despite the cooperation in the Revision of the Old and New Testaments, in which all three men had been involved. Yet the question would not have been worth asking at Oxford.

The apologetic agenda behind the pursuit of theology has been repeatedly emphasised. It is seen in the stress placed upon the evidences of Christianity. In biblical studies it is seen in the vigorous defence of the authenticity of the New Testament documents against the criticisms, first of Gibbon and later of the Tübingen School. Watson and Paley represent different versions of the former; Lightfoot and Hort represent the latter. Evidence for the significance of this apologetic is seen in the *Heads of Lectures* of John Hollingworth, Norrisian Professor from 1824 to 1838.

Candidates for ordination were expected to attend the lectures of the Norrisian Professor. Hollingworth's text does not survive; but there was a series of headings for each lecture and a book list – an early example of a lecture hand-out! The fifty lectures were based, as was customary, on Bishop Pearson's book on the Apostles' Creed. It is perhaps a relief that the subject was not the Nicene Creed. However, their scope was broader than Pearson's book might suggest. Each article of the Creed was considered in detail, but there were also lectures on prophecy, canon, variant readings of the New Testament text, miracles, and the harmony of the gospels; there were also several lectures refuting contrary views – on ancient heretics, the objections of ancient heathens, Jews, Mahometans, deists and atheists. The lectures on original sin and baptism included discussion of free will, conversion and predestination, justification and sanctification, with the clear intention of refuting the Calvinism of the Synod of Dort. So the book list included Gibbon, Samuel Clarke, Newton, Locke, Watson's *Apology for Christianity*, and *Apology for the Bible*, all Paley's major works, Hey, Marsh, Kaye, and even Henry Martyn. Interestingly the German works listed, such as Semler and Michaelis, were listed in Latin; perhaps it was when German theology was written only in German that it became more inaccessible, until it was translated into English as with Michaelis or Mosheim's *History*.[20]

Lightfoot pursued the same apologetic agenda, both in his Commentaries on the Epistles and his attacks on *Supernatural Religion*. Hort's lectures on *Judaistic Christianity*, like many of his works, were published posthumously. The editor, J.O.F. Murray, wrote in the preface of Hort's admiration for the genius of F.C. Baur and his appreciation of modern theology's debt to him 'for leading the way in the effort to interpret Christian documents in the light of the historical situation out of which they sprang'. Nevertheless Hort's ultimate verdict 'was entirely in favour of the genuineness and the historical accuracy of all the leading Christian documents'.[21] That Murray should have considered this the primary significance of Hort's work is an illustration of the hold, which that particular apologetic had even in the closing decade of the nineteenth century.

20    J.B. Hollingworth, *Heads of Lectures in Divinity* (3rd edn, Cambridge, 1835).
21    F.J.A. Hort, *Judaistic Christianity* (Cambridge, 1894), pp. vi–vii.

How then is the achievement of the Cambridge trio to be assessed? John Riches has suggested that biblical criticism in England until relatively late in the twentieth century was largely reactive, often defensively, to developments in Germany 'rather than exploring of its own accord the more fundamental, searching, historical questions'; and it was more concerned with upholding its religious traditions against attack from historical criticism, 'at most attempting to strengthen and revivify such traditions by providing a more contemporary interpretation as well as an historical justification for them'. Whilst he did not wish 'to decry the great works of Westcott, Lightfoot and Hort' or to suggest that they were illiberal in their scholarly, political or social attitudes, they nevertheless belonged to an established church which was fundamentally conservative.[22] He did not, however, make it clear how he was evaluating the Cambridge trio, and, although they did belong to an established church, that raises the question of why German scholars, who belonged to churches which were just as established in the German sense as the Church of England, were capable of raising fundamental, searching historical questions. It is more relevant that university teachers in Germany were state employees rather than office-holders in the Church. Is that why so many backed the German government in the First World War, to the horror of Karl Barth? (Yet most British theologians backed the British government, but that does not gain the same attention – in Britain.) In truth, the range of German scholarly opinion was as diverse as in England. In the history of theology generally heretics have always attracted more interest from scholars than the orthodox; and this says more about the retrospective preoccupations of historians than it does about the nature of the contemporary scholarship.

Professor Riches identified a wider theological context for the development of New Testament scholarship in England after 1890 in the collection of Oxford essays, *Lux Mundi* (1889), edited by Charles Gore, particularly in Gore's understanding of progressive revelation. Gore was taught by Westcott at Harrow and Henry Scott Holland, another leading member of the group, read with Westcott at Peterborough in the 1870s. Both had been involved in the formation of the Christian Social Union, of which Westcott was invited to be President – an invitation issued on the basis of Westcott's preaching as a Canon of Westminster before he was nominated as Bishop of Durham. It is true that Gore emphasised the idea of progressive revelation in order to take account of new views about the inspiration and authorship of the Old Testament, just as he invoked a kenotic understanding of the incarnation in order to get round Liddon's argument in his Bampton Lectures against such views, that Jesus endorsed some of the allegedly mistaken attributions of Old Testament authorship. But this was not very different from the way in which the trio understood the Old Testament: and on the understanding of the Old Testament 'as a preparation in history for Christ' (the title of E.S. Talbot's essay), Gore was at one with Lightfoot, Westcott and Hort; and Gore's openness to critical scholarship stopped with the end of the Old Testament. The point at which Gore most obviously distanced himself from the Cambridge tradition was when he said in the Introduction that he and his

---

22    J. Riches, *A Century of New Testament Study* (Cambridge, 1993), pp. 4–5.

colleagues attempted to put the Catholic faith into its right relation to modern
intellectual and moral problems 'not as "guessers at truth", but as servants of the
Catholic Creed and Church', which for those with eyes to see was a clear allusion
to the title of Julius Hare's book, *Guesses at Truth*.[23]

A more telling criticism of Cambridge generally in the trio's time is that
expressed by J.M. Creed in his inaugural lecture of 1927. Creed argued that a deep-
seated weakness of the Westcott-Hort-Lightfoot tradition was their neglect of Old
Testament criticism. Thereby they ignored the challenge of the *Religionsgeschichte*
school of critics, and two questions in particular: first the extent to which the Old
Testament could still 'provide a setting of universal history, both religious and
secular, for the Incarnation and the Redemption', and secondly the whole question
of 'the syncretic tendency of religions in the Roman Empire', or even Persian and
Egyptian influences. Thus their work was useless for the succeeding generation.[24]
Certainly Westcott, Lightfoot and Hort did not work on the Old Testament; they
were primarily classical scholars by training. In 1864 Hort had written to Lightfoot
saying that he had only a smattering of Hebrew grammar and no Syriac.[25] When
J.W. Colenso's book on the Pentateuch appeared in 1862, Hort wrote to Lightfoot
that he supposed they would all 'now be obliged to study the O.T. a little more'
and that 'we shall sooner or later be driven to take some such ground as that of
Ewald and Bunsen, however little satisfied with their special criticisms'. After
Colenso's death in 1883, he remarked that Colenso had damaged the cause of
progressive Old Testament criticism in England.[26] Hort welcomed Robertson
Smith to Cambridge in 1883, and encouraged Herbert Ryle, by supporting his
candidacy for the Hulsean chair in 1887, explicitly on the ground of work on the
Old Testament and the great problems raised by recent criticism.[27]

Thomas Jarrett, Regius Professor of Hebrew, 1854–82, spent much of his
time transliterating a variety of oriental languages into roman characters in his
own way, and contributed nothing to biblical criticism. A.F. Kirkpatrick, Regius
Professor of Hebrew, 1882–1932, did more, with books on *The Divine Library
of the Old Testament* (1891), *The Doctrine of the Prophets* (1892) and popular
lectures on higher criticism in the early 1900s. The weakness of Cambridge was
due to the lack of any established theological chair dedicated to Old Testament
study – which is still true in 2007.[28] Although Hort knew no Syriac in 1858, he did
learn it, and applied it fruitfully. Westcott wrote to Archdeacon Farrar in 1883,

23    C. Gore (ed.), *Lux Mundi* (15th edn, London, 1904), p. viii.
24    J.M. Creed, 'The Study of the New Testament', *Journal of Theological Studies*,
xlii (1941): 3–9; Hort to Westcott, 10 May 1890: Hort, *Life of Hort*, ii, p. 416.
25    Hort to Lightfoot, 26 April 1864: Hort, *Lifeof Hort*, ii, p. 7.
26    Hort to Lightfoot, 3 November 1862, and to Mr Westlake, 7 December 1884:
Hort, *Life of Hort*, i, p. 469; ii, p. 312.
27    Hort to Westcott, 18 April 1883: Hort, *Life of Hort*, ii, p. 294; M.H. Fitzgerald,
*A Memoir of Herbert Edward Ryle* (London, 1928), p. 84.
28    In recent years certain personal chairs have been established, which have
recognised Old Testament scholars; technically none of the established chairs is attached
to any particular theological discipline, though certain traditions have emerged.

'For the last few years I have been thrown a good deal among Rabbinic fragments, and the more I can understand the more I value them: but then I understand very little'.[29] However, it should not be assumed that pre-critical views were still in vogue. Hort in his series of sermons on the Bible at St Ippolyt's in 1868 said that he did not pretend to understand everything in the opening chapters of Genesis, but he did emphasise that the Bible begins with goodness rather than sin; and similarly, when speaking of the terrible events in the conquest of Canaan, he said that 'God speaks to men according as they are able to receive His teaching'.[30] Even if the phrase 'progressive revelation' was not used here (and that was hardly to be expected in a village congregation), the essence of the principle is clear.

Robertson Smith was the real innovator here; but his time at Cambridge was brief and by the time he arrived he had moved beyond the initial questions of historical criticism to more fundamental ones about the nature of the origins of the Semitic religions. He did not use the word 'Religionsgeschichte', but that was where he was leading. Thus he gave scarcely any lectures in Cambridge on staple problems of Old Testament criticism, and was more concerned with the examination of the non-Jewish Semitic traditions, as indicated through their literatures and other remains. This is why Herbert Ryle regarded Old Testament criticism as such an important issue when presenting himself for the Hulsean chair in 1887. His lectures were crowded – 150 twice a week on 'The monarchy of Israel' in the Lent Term 1891, and over 200 in a class in January 1893.[31] He published books on *The Early Narratives of Genesis* (1892), based on his lectures, *The Canon of the Old Testament* (1892) and *Philo and Holy Scripture* (1895). But after his election as President of Queens' in 1896 he published little, apart from articles in Hastings' *Dictionary of the Bible*, and various other publishing projects were abandoned. His appointment as Bishop of Exeter in 1900 virtually ended his scholarly career, apart from the commentary on Genesis in the Cambridge Bible in 1914. Although he expounded the work of Wellhausen effectively, Ryle's emphasis on the fact that criticism left the spiritual truths of the Old Testament intact tended to evade some of the more awkward theological and historical questions.

The concentration on the authenticity of the New Testament documents as the means to discredit the Tübingen school obscured the question of the significance of Jesus and his teaching. Here it is easy to be misled by general talk about 'the quest for the historical Jesus'. J.R. Seeley's *Ecce Homo* (1865) achieved popularity, if not notoriety. But in so far as lives of Jesus questioned the doctrine of the incarnation, Cambridge theology came down hard against them. The Cambridge classical tradition, with its recurrent inclinations towards neo-Platonism, did not equip Cambridge scholars to wrestle with the more alien notions of the Kingdom of God, and eschatology was more difficult still.

---

29    Westcott to Farrar, St Mark's Day (25 April) 1883; A. Westcott, *Life and Letters of Brooke Foss Westcott* (London, 1903), i, p. 441. He added, 'As for reading, I can read nothing, except a little Greek Testament. But that is enough.'

30    F.J.A. Hort, *Village Sermons* (London, 1897), pp. 154, 156, 177.

31    Fitzgerald, *Herbert Edward Ryle*, p. 92.

Both crucially involved questions about the significance of historical time in an understanding of the incarnation.

F.C. Burkitt (1864–1935) represented in some senses a coming together of the legacy of Hort and Robertson Smith. In the Theological Tripos he obtained a first in the Hebrew section; but he also won University Prizes in Hebrew, the Septuagint, New Testament and Church History. Initially he was a member of William Wright's seminar (Sir Thomas Adams' Professor of Arabic, 1872–89). His interest in Syriac explains why he was involved with Robert Bensly and Rendel Harris in the Sinai expedition with Mrs Lewis and Mrs Gibson. He was also a man of independent means, and therefore not subject to the same financial pressures as Glover; indeed having had his proposal for a Fellowship dissertation on the Synoptic Problem rejected as too slight, he was not a Fellow of any College until after the New Statutes of 1926.[32]

The difference between Burkitt and the trio was this: whereas Westcott, Lightfoot and Hort were satisfied to demonstrate the authenticity of the New Testament, Burkitt pressed on to understand the documents, not in terms of what the church taught, but of what the historical evidence said. Bethune-Baker said of him: 'His interest was always in facts, what people said and did, what actually happened or was going to happen'. Thus his closest affinities were with Lightfoot and Hort, rather than Westcott, whose mysticism he did not like.[33] In his major lecture series on *The Gospel History and its Transmission* (1906) he argued that there was more genuine history in the canonical gospels than many had supposed. He doubted whether the same pattern of source criticism as had been applied to the Pentateuch could so easily be applied to the gospels, not so much because the method was wrong but because it was not so easy to reconstruct the sources. Quite apart from those problems, there was clearly not enough information to write a modern biography of Jesus. But that was not all loss: 'The real question is not whether we have as much as we should like, but whether we have as much as we need'.[34] Burkitt cheerfully acknowledged that the evangelists had altered the sources they used, by change, addition or omission. Was that disastrous? His answer was interesting:

> Put very shortly, I think we may say that a true impression is on the whole and for most people better conveyed by a friend than by an observer wholly dispassionate. What is the real reason for the modern demand for documents? Is it not because we believe in our hearts that we, the modern historian, have a better right than those who have gone before us to sit in judgement on the evidence?[35]

---

32    Obituary Notice in *Proceedings of the British Academy* (1936): p. 451.

33    Ibid., p. 449.

34    F.C. Burkitt, *The Gospel History and its Transmission* (Edinburgh, 1906), p. 20.

35    Ibid., p. 22.

What really mattered in the gospels was 'the moral impression produced by Jesus Christ upon His followers'.[36] Historical criticism did not provide vital truth but the removal of errors. So the rise of Christianity was more complex and confused than could be gathered from the 'epic selectiveness of the Creeds and the theological manuals'.[37] And there was a recurrent tendency for each age to ignore the aspects of the gospels that did not fit the prevailing ideas and to regard its own interpretation of Christ as final; thus there was a recurrent task for the historian.

Burkitt's world was clearly very different from that of the trio. It enabled him to cope with the questions raised by the new emphasis on eschatology, coming from Germany. Thus it was natural for him to write a Preface to the English translation of Albert Schweitzer's survey of the German Lives of Jesus in the nineteenth century. This Preface is not often read. In it he contrasted the unflinching scepticism of the most extreme German critics with the unconsciously constructed Harmony of the Four Gospels of most English readers: 'This kind of "Harmony" is not a very convincing picture when looked into, if only because it almost always conflicts with inconvenient statements of the Gospels themselves.' Burkitt believed there was more history in the gospels than Schweitzer, but in any case the true view was that which explained the course of events in the first and second centuries, rather than that which had spiritual and imaginative value for the twentieth century. Nevertheless

> We have to learn, as the Church in the second century had to learn, that the End is not yet, that New Jerusalem, like all other objects of sense, is an image of the truth rather than the truth itself. But at least we are beginning to see that the apocalyptic vision, the New Age which God is to bring in, is no mere embroidery of Christianity, but the heart of its enthusiasm. And therefore the expectations of vindication and judgment to come, the imagery of the Messianic Feast, the 'other-worldliness' against which so many eloquent words were said in the nineteenth cenntury, are not to be regarded as regrettable accretions foisted on by superstition to the pure morality of the original Gospel. These ideas are the Christian Hope, to be allegorised and 'spiritualised' by us for our own use whenever necessary, but not to be given up so long as we remain Christians at all.[38]

Burkitt was outlining a new agenda for New Testament study, which has dominated much of the period since. But at the heart of those comments about the significance of Schweitzer were the tell-tale phrases that had lain at the heart of the Cambridge apologetic in theology for the previous century – 'no mere embroidery', 'regrettable accretions foisted on by superstition'. Eschatology nevertheless made it necessary to rethink how Christianity was presented to a modern world; in particular it involved the awkward question, Was Jesus wrong? Burkitt did not offer a solution here. One way forward was that represented by

36   Ibid., p. 27.
37   Ibid., p. 29.
38   A. Schweitzer, *The Quest of the Historical Jesus* (3rd edn, London, 1954), pp. xviii–xix.

what became the Modern Churchmen's Union, which involved Cambridge figures like Bethune-Baker. Another way forward was represented by Edwyn Hoskyns and C.H. Dodd.

The real significance of the apologetic agenda is the emphasis that so long as Christianity looks inwards it will cut no ice. It has to look outwards. In one of his last letters to Hare in September 1842 Sterling wrote that the translation of Strauss would mean the fate of all moral obligation:

> The accounts I hear from very competent persons, of the utter absence of any religious feeling and any kind of thought among huge masses of the manufacturing poor, daily amaze me; and my own knowledge of the state of some of the peasantry ... goes far to satisfy me that all our institutions have been almost entirely worthless for humanizing the poor as a class.[39]

The comment was undoubtedly exaggerated, but the perception of the issues is spot on. It is necessary relentlessly to ask why the synoptic problem is important, why the chronology of the Old Testament is important, why eschatology is important? These are questions to which Forsyth might provide more effective answers than Hort. Similarly it was necessary to ask whether, even if the New Testament documents were authentic, they were credible; and, if credible, whether and how they were relevant for the twentieth century. It was perhaps too easy to rest in the assurance that the apologetic task was complete, when in reality it was just beginning. This book has offered only a selection of the Cambridge figures who could be examined, particularly at the end of the century, to shed light on these problems.

There was a final key idea in Burkitt's Preface: the difference between 'an image of truth' and truth itself. Here the echo of Hort is most strong. At the end of his second Hulsean lecture Hort said:

> The pursuit of truth begins in a sense of freedom. We almost make truth itself the symbol of freedom for the workings of our minds. We are slow to learn that truth is never that which we choose to believe, but always that which we are under a necessity to believe. In proportion to the earnestness of the pursuit we discover that we must needs be servants where we thought to be masters. A life devoted to truth is a life of vanities abased and ambitions forsworn. We have to advance far in the willing servitude before we recognise that it is creating for us a new and another freedom. The early dream was not false: only freedom comes last, not first. The order of experience corresponds with the order of the Lord's promises which He offered to those who had begun to believe Him: 'If ye abide in my word, ye are truly disciples of mine', and then 'ye shall know the truth', and then 'the truth shall make you free'.[40]

This is complemented by two observations from men, who in other ways were very different. In a University Sermon of 1860 Connop Thirlwall remarked

39   J.C. Hare, 'Memoir of the Author' in J. Sterling, *Essays and Tales, with a Memoir of his Life by Julius Charles Hare* (London, 1848), pp. cxcviii–cxcix.
40   Hort, *The Way, the Truth and the Life*, pp. 93–4.

that 'Truth received only is in the degree to which it is felt, loved and lived'; and Westcott wrote to Benson in 1883, 'I distrust all verbal arguments. The life, that is all, and it is enough, if it can be lived'.[41]

---

41   C. Thirlwall, 'The Spirit of Truth, the Holy Spirit', University Sermon, 16 May 1860, in J.J.S. Perowne (ed.), *Remains Literary and Theological of Connop Thirlwall* (London, 1878), iii, p. 398; Westcott to Benson, 16 April 1883: Westcott, *Life of Westcott*, i, p. 440.

# Epilogue

After the Second World War the Cambridge Faculty of Divinity put on a series of Open Lectures for all members of the University each year. In 1962 the Faculty Board decided to run a course entitled, 'Objections to Christian Belief', with lectures by Professor Donald Mackinnon, Harry Williams, Dr Alec Vidler and J.S. Bezzant. They were given in February 1963 in the depths of the iciest winter of the later twentieth century in the Large Hall of the Examination Schools (since converted for other uses). The hall was packed on each occasion: Alec Vidler reckoned that the attendance was about 1,500 each week; Harry Williams noted that there was not even standing room five minutes before the lectures began.[1] They were published by Constable in April 1963 and were reprinted three times in two weeks.[2] (It should be noted that this was the term *before* the publication of John Robinson's *Honest to God*, which happened in the following Easter Vacation.) The four types of objection discussed were moral, psychological, historical and intellectual. The initiative almost certainly came from Alec Vidler, who had himself delivered a series of open lectures in 1949 on 'Christian Belief' and in 1961 edited the volume, *Soundings*, by a group of members of the Cambridge Faculty.[3] As an undergraduate at the time I attended each lecture with several friends, making sure each week that we were there in time to get a seat. Assuming that the same people were there each week (which is not likely) those involved would have been nearly 20 per cent of the total number of undergraduates in Cambridge at the time, or around 12.5 per cent of the number of undergraduates and graduates combined. It is no exaggeration to say that people were talking about them in remarkably unexpected places.

Alec Vidler explained in the Introduction to the published lectures that the intention was not to provide answers to the objections, for which 'a spate of books' was available. Rather it was to explore the depths of those objections without assuming that answers were readily available: 'in a university Christians must understand the fundamental doubts to which their faith is exposed in this age of the world'. They were intended to be disturbing rather than reassuring.[4] Ronald Gregor Smith, reviewing the book in the *Glasgow Herald*, noted that the lecturers did not attempt what Reinhold Niebuhr once said of theological students, 'that when they were faced with intractable problems they straightaway took an elevator

---

1    A.R. Vidler, *Scenes from a Clerical Life* (London, 1977), p. 181; H.A. Williams, *Some Day I'll Find You* (London, 1984), p. 217.

2    A.R. Vidler (ed.), *Objections to Christian Belief* (London, 1963).

3    A.R. Vidler, *Christian Belief* (London, 1950); A.R. Vidler (ed.), *Soundings* (Cambridge, 1961).

4    Vidler, *Objections to Christian Belief*, pp. 6–7.

for the eternal'.[5] Vidler himself was reluctant to accept the branding of this as 'Cambridge theology', since many Cambridge theologians did not share these points of view and in any case there was no new theological synthesis or system behind them. Nevertheless it is not easy to imagine the Oxford Faculty putting on a similar series at that time; and the readiness to examine the possible objections to and questions about Christianity seriously and respectfully was characteristic of both the objectives and the methods described in this study.

---

5    *Glasgow Herald* (22 May 1963), quoted in Vidler, *Scenes from a Clerical Life*, p. 182.

# Bibliography

**Manuscript Sources**

*Cambridge University Library*

J.N. Keynes, Diary, Additional Manuscripts 7832(1); Theological Correspondence of F.J.A. Hort, Additional Manuscripts 6597.

*Cambridgeshire County Record Office*

Emmanuel Congregational [United Reformed] Church records 1868–1892.

*St Andrew's Street Baptist Church, Cambridge*

St Andrew's Street Church Book, 1832–96

*St John's College, Cambridge*

T.R. Glover Papers

*Trinity College, Cambridge*

E.W. Benson Papers

*Westcott House, Cambridge*

B.F. Westcott Papers (including material on permanent loan from Selwyn College, Cambridge).

*Westminster College, Cambridge*

Harris–Nestlé Correspondence.


**Unpublished Dissertations**

Braine, R.K., 'The life and writings of Herbert Marsh', unpublished Cambridge PhD dissertation, 1989.
Lethaby, J.I., '"A less perfect reflection": perceptions of Luther in the nineteenth-century Church of England', unpublished Cambridge PhD dissertation, 2001.

Yule, J.D., 'The impact of science on British religious thought in the second quarter of the nineteenth century', unpublished Cambridge PhD dissertation, 1976.


**Periodicals**

*British Critic.*
*Church Quarterly Review.*
*Congregational Year Book.*
*Critical Review.*
*Eclectic Review.*
*Edinburgh Review.*
*English Review.*
*The Expository Times.*
*Monthly Review.*
*Politics for the People* (London, 1848; reprinted New York, 1971).
*Proceedings of the British Academy.*
*Quarterly Review.*
*Theologische Literaturzeitung.*
*Universal Magazine.*


**Printed Primary Sources**

Abbott, E. and Campbell, L., *Life and Letters of Benjamin Jowett* (2 vols, London, 1897).
Barlow, N. (ed.), *Autobiography of Charles Darwin* (London, 1958).
Benson, A.C., *The Life of Edward White Benson* (2 vols, London, 1900).
Black, J.S. and Chrystal, G., *The Life of William Robertson Smith* (London, 1912).
Blunt, J.J., *Essays contributed to the Quarterly Review* (London, 1860).
Blunt, J.J., *Two Introductory Lectures on the Study of the Early Fathers* (2nd edn, Cambridge, 1856).
Blunt, J.J., *Undesigned Coincidences* (London, 1847).
Blunt, J.J., *The Veracity of the Historical Books of the Old Testament* (London, 1832).
Burkitt, F.C., 'Recently Discovered MSS', in C. Dunkley, *Official Report of the Church Congress held at Norwich, 8 to 11 October 1895* (London, 1895).
Bury, J.P.T. (ed.), *Romilly's Cambridge Diary, 1832–42* (Cambridge, 1967).
Bury, M.E. and Pickles, J.D. (eds), *Romilly's Cambridge Diary 1848–1864* (Cambridge, 2000).
Butler, J., *The Analogy of Religion* (London, 1788).
Campbell, I. and Chrisianson, A. (eds.), *The Collected Letters of Thomas and Jane Welsh Carlyle* (Durham, North Carolina, 1995).
Carus, W., *Memoirs of the Life of the Rev Charles Simeon, MA* (London, 1847).

[Cassels, W.R.], *Supernatural Religion*, 6th edn (London, 1879).

Clark, J.W., *Endowments of the University of Cambridge* (Cambridge, 1904).

Coleridge, S.T., *Aids to Reflection*, ed. J. Beer, The Collected Works of Samuel Taylor Coleridge VII (Princeton, 1993).

Coleridge, S.T., *Confessions of an Inquiring Spirit*, ed. H.StJ. Hart (London, 1956).

Coleridge, S.T., *The Friend*, ed. B.E. Rooke, The Collected Works of Samuel Taylor Coleridge IV (2 vols, Princeton 1969).

Coleridge, S.T., *Lay Sermons*, ed. R.J. White, The Collected Works of Samuel Taylor Coleridge VI (Princeton, 1972).

Coleridge, S.T., *Lectures 1795 on Politics and Revealed Religion*, ed. L. Patton and P. Mann, The Collected Works of Samuel Taylor Coleridge I (Princeton, 1971).

Coleridge, S.T., *On the Constitution of the Church and State*, ed. J. Colmer, The Collected Works of Samuel Taylor Coleridge X (Princeton, 1976).

Coleridge, S.T., *Table Talk*, ed. C. Woodring, The Collected Works of Samuel Taylor Coleridge XIV (2 vols, Princeton, 1990).

Conybeare, J.J., *Bampton Lectures for the year MDCCCXXIV* (Oxford, 1824).

Doddridge, P., *The Works of Philip Doddridge, DD*, ix (Leeds, 1805).

Forsyth, P.T., *The Charter of the Church: Six Lectures on the Spiritual Principle of Nonconformity* (London, 1896).

Forsyth, P.T., 'The Divine Self-Emptying' (1897), reprinted in Forsyth, P.T., *God the Holy Father* (London, 1957).

Forsyth, P.T., 'The Evangelical Principle of Authority', *Proceedings of the Second International Congregational Council* (Boston, 1900).

Forsyth, P.T., 'The Holy Father' (1896), reprinted in Forsyth, P.T., *God the Holy Father* (London, 1957).

Forsyth, P.T., *Lectures on the Church and the Sacraments* (London, 1917).

Forsyth, P.T., *The Old Faith and the New* (Leicester 1891).

Forsyth, P.T. *The Person and Place of Jesus Christ*, ed. D.M. Thompson (London, 1999).

Forsyth, P.T., *The Principle of Authority* (London, n.d. [1913]).

Forsyth, P.T., 'Revelation and the Person of Christ' in *Faith and Criticism: Essays by Congregationalists* (London, 1893).

Forsyth, P.T., *The Work of Christ* (London, 1965).

Gibbon, E., *The History of the Decline and Fall of the Roman Empire*, ed. H.H. Milman, M. Guizot and W. Smith (London, 1908).

Goodman, N., 'How we may best avail ourselves of the Universities of Oxford and Cambridge for the education of our ministers', *Congregational Year Book* (1870).

Gore, C. (ed.), *Lux Mundi* (15th edn, London, 1904).

*Guesses at Truth, by Two Brothers* [A.W. and J.C. Hare] (London, 1867).

Hare, J.C., *The Children of Light* (Cambridge, 1828).

Hare, J.C., *The Mission of the Comforter*, ed. E.H. Plumptre (London, 1886).

Hare, J.C., *The Victory of Faith* (3rd edn, London, 1874).

Hare, J.C., *Vindication of Luther against his recent assailants* (London, 1855).

Hare, J.C., *Vindication of Niebuhr's History of Rome from the Charges of the Quarterly Review* (Cambridge, 1829).

Hollingworth, J.B., *Heads of Lectures in Divinity* (3rd edn, Cambridge, 1835).

Holroyd, M., *Memoirs of the Life of George Elwes Corrie* (Cambridge, 1890).

Hort, A.F., *Life and Letters of Fenton John Anthony Hort* (2 vols, London, 1896).

Hort, F.J.A., *The Apocalypse of St John* (London, 1908).

Hort, F.J.A, *The Christian Ecclesia* (London, 1897).

Hort, F.J.A., 'Coleridge', *Cambridge Essays 1856* (London, 1856).

Hort, F.J.A., *Judaistic Christianity* (Cambridge, 1894).

Hort, F.J.A., *Two Dissertations* (London, 1876).

Hort, F.J.A., *Village Sermons* (London, 1897).

Hort, F.J.A., *The Way, the Truth and the Life* (London, 1893).

Jowett, B., *The Epistles of St Paul to the Thessalonians, Galatians, Romans* (2 vols, London, 1855).

Kaye, B.N. and Treloar, G.R., 'J.B. Lightfoot and New Testament Interpretation: An Unpublished Manuscript of 1855', *Durham University Journal*, lxxxii, 2 (July 1990).

Kaye, W.J.J. (ed.), *The Works of John Kaye* (8 vols, London, n.d.).

Lardner, N., *The Works of Nathaniel Lardner, DD in eleven volumes* (London, 1788).

Lessing, G.E., 'Editorial Commentary on the "Fragments" of Reimarus', *Philosophical and Theological Writings*, ed. H.B. Nisbet (Cambridge, 2005).

Lessing, G.E., *Gottwald Ephraim Lessing Werke*, vii (Munich, 1976).

Lightfoot, J.B., *The Apostolic Fathers* (2 vols in 3 pts, London, 1885).

Lightfoot, J.B., *Essays on the Work Entitled Supernatural Religion* (London, 1889).

Lightfoot, J.B., *Notes on Epistles of St Paul from Unpublished Commentaries* (London, 1895).

Lightfoot, J.B., *Primary Charge: Two Addresses delivered to the Clergy of the Diocese of Durham in December 1882* (London, n.d.).

Lightfoot, J.B., 'Recent Editions of St Paul's Epistles', *Journal of Classical and Sacred Philology*, iii (March 1856).

Lightfoot, J.B., *St Paul's Epistle to the Galatians* (3rd edn, London, 1869).

Lightfoot, J.B., *Saint Paul's Epistle to the Philippians* (4th edn, London, 1879).

Lightfoot, J.B., *Sermons preached on special occasions* (London, 1891).

Locke, J., *A Collection of Several Pieces of Mr John Locke never before printed or not extant in his Works* (London, 1720).

Locke, J., *The Works of John Locke* (7th edn, London, 1768).

Marsh, H., *An Address to the Members of the Senate of the University of Cambridge, occasioned by the Proposal to introduce into this Place an Auxiliary Bible Society* (Cambridge, 1811).

Marsh, H., *The Authenticity of the Five Books of Moses considered* (Cambridge, 1792).

Marsh, H., *A Comparative View of the Churches of England and Rome* (2nd edn, London, 1816).

Marsh, H., *A Course of Lectures, containing a Description and Systematic Arrangement of the Several Branches of Divinity* (Cambridge, 1809).

Marsh, H., *An Essay on the Usefulness and Necessity of Theological Learning to those who are designed for Holy Orders* (Cambridge, 1792).

Marsh, H., *The History of the Politicks of Great Britain and France* (London, 1800).

Marsh, H., *Lectures on the Criticism and Interpretation of the Bible* (London, 1842).

Marsh, H., *A Letter to the Rev Charles Simeon, MA, in answer to his Pretended Congratulatory Address, in Confutation of his various Mis-Statements, and in Vindication of the Efficacy ascribed by our Church to the Sacrament of Baptism* (Cambridge, 1813).

Marsh, H., *The National Religion the Foundation of National Education* (London, 1811).

Marsh, H., *A Reply to the Strictures of the Rev Isaac Milner* (Cambridge, 1813).

Marsh, H., *A Vindication of Dr Bell's System of Tuition* (London, 1811).

Maurice, F., *The Life of Frederick Denison Maurice* (2 vols, London 1884).

Maurice, F.D., *The Epistle to the Hebrews* (London, 1846).

Maurice, F.D., *The Patriarchs and Lawgivers of the Old Testament* (5th edn, London, 1878).

Meadley, G.W., *Memoirs of William Paley, DD* (2nd edn, Edinburgh, 1810).

Merivale, J.B., *Autobiography and Letters of Charles Merivale* (Oxford, 1898).

Michaelis, J.D., *Introduction to the New Testament*, trans. H. Marsh (4th edn, 4 vols in 8 parts, London, 1823).

Middleston, Conyers, *A free inquiry into the miraculous powers, which are supposed to have subsisted in the Christian church, from the earliest ages through several successive centuries* (London, 1749).

Milner, I., *Strictures on some of the Publications of the Rev. Herbert Marsh, DD, intended as a Reply to his Objections against the British and Foreign Bible Society* (London, 1813).

Niebuhr, B.G., *History of Rome*, trans. J.C. Hare and C. Thirlwall (2 vols, Cambridge, 1828).

Oman, J.W., *Grace and Personality* (Cambridge, 1917).

Overton, J., *The true churchmen ascertained, or, An apology for those of the regular clergy of the establishment who are sometimes called evangelical ministers* (London, 1801).

Paley, W., *Defence of the Considerations on the Propriety of requiring a Subscription to Articles of Faith*, in R. Lynam (ed.), *Works of William Paley*, iv, *Sermons and Tracts* (5 vols, London, 1825).

Paley, W., *Evidences of Christianity*, ed. T.R. Birks (new edn, London, n.d.).

Paley, W., *Horae Paulinae, or The Truth of the Scripture History of St Paul Evinced*. ed. T.R. Birks (London, 1850).

Paley, W., *Natural Theology; or Evidences of the Existence and Attributes of the Deity* (London, 1802; 15th edn, 1815).

Paley, W., *The Principles of Moral and Political Philosophy* (London, 1824).

Pearson, E., *Cautions to the hearers and readers of the Rev Mr Simeon's Sermon* (London, n.d.).

Pearson, E., *Remarks on the Revd Mr Simeon's 'Fresh Cautions to the Public'* (London, n.d.).

Perowne, J.J.S. (ed.), *Remains Literary and Theological of Connop Thirlwall* (London, 1878).

Perowne, J.J.S., and Stokes, L. (eds), *Letters Literary and Theological of Connop Thirlwall* (London, 1881).

*Reimarus: Fragments*, ed. C.H. Talbert (London, 1971).

Robertson Smith, W., *The Prophets of Israel* (London, 1882).

Robertson Smith, W., *Lectures on the Religion of the Semites: First Series: The Fundamental Institutions* (London, 1894).

Robertson Smith, W., *Lectures on the Religion of the Semites*, ed. S.A. Cook (3rd edn, London, 1927).

Robertson Smith, W., *The Old Testament in the Jewish Church* (2nd edn, London, 1902).

Robertson Smith, W., *The Religion of the Semites: Second and Third Series*, ed. J. Day (Sheffield, 1995).

Rose, H.J., *The Commission and consequent Duties of the Clergy* (Cambridge, 1828).

Rose, H.J., *The Duty of Maintaining the Truth* (Cambridge, 1834).

Rose, H.J., *The state of the Protestant religion in Germany; in a series of discourses preached before the University of Cambridge* (Cambridge, 1825).

Rose, H.J., *The Study of Church History Recommended* (London, 1834).

Simeon, C., *Dr Marsh's Fact; or A Congratulatory Address to the Church-Members of the British and Foreign Bible Society* (Cambridge, 1813).

Simeon, C., *Fresh Cautions to the Public* (2nd edn, London, n.d).

Schleiermacher, F., *A Critical Essay on the Gospel of St Luke* (London, 1825).

Stair Douglas, Mrs, *The Life and Selections from the Correspondence of William Whewell* (London, 1881).

Sterling, J., *Essays and Tales, with a Memoir of his Life by Julius Charles Hare* (2 vols, London, 1848).

Strauss, D.F., *Die christliche Glaubenslehre in ihrer geschichtlictlichen Entwicklung und im Kampf mit der modernene Wissenschaft dargestellt* (Tübingen, 1840–41).

Strauss, D.F., *The Life of Jesus Critically Examined*, ed. P.C. Hodgson (London, 1973).

Tanner, J.R. (ed.), *Historical Register of the University of Cambridge* (Cambridge, 1917).

Tennyson, A., *In Memoriam A.H.H.*, in Tennyson, A., *Poetical Works*, Oxford 1953.

Thirlwall, C., 'The Spirit of Truth, the Holy Spirit', University Sermon, 16 May 1860, in J.J.S. Perowne (ed.), *Remains Literary and Theological of Connop Thirlwall* (London, 1878).

Treloar, G.R., and Kaye, B.N., 'J.B. Lightfoot On Strauss and Christian Origins: An Unpublished Manuscript', *Durham University Journal*, lxxix, 2 (June 1987).

Turton, T., *Natural Theology considered with reference to Lord Brougham's Discourse on that Subject* (Cambridge, 1836).

Turton, T., *Thoughts on the admission of persons without Regard to their Religious Opinions, to certain Degrees in the Universities of England* (Cambridge, 1834).

Vaughan, D.J. (ed.), *Official Report of the Leicester Church Congress held at Leicester, 1880* (London, 1881).

Venn, J.A. *Alumni Cantabrigienses:* a biographical list of all known students, graduates and holders of office at the University of Cambridge pt. 2. From 1752 to 1900 (6 vols, Cambridge, 1922–54).

Warburton, W., *The Doctrine of Grace; or the Office and Operations of the Holy Spirit* (2nd edn, London, 1763).

Watson, R., *Anecdotes of the Life of Richard Watson* (2nd edn, 2 vols, London, 1818).

Watson, R., *An Apology for the Bible* (7th edn, London, 1797).

Watson, R., *An Apology for Christianity* (Cambridge, 1776).

Watson, R., *A Collection of Theological Tracts* (2nd edn, 6 vols, London, 1791).

Westcott, A., *Life and Letters of Brooke Foss Westcott* (2 vols, London, 1903).

Westcott, B.F., *An Address to the University Church Society* (Cambridge, [1873]).

Westcott, B.F., *Characteristics of the Gospel Miracles* (Cambridge, 1859; first cheap edn, London, 1913).

Westcott, B.F., *Elements of the Gospel Harmony* (Cambridge, 1851).

Westcott, B.F., *The Epistle to the Hebrews* (London, 1889).

Westcott, B.F., *The Epistles of St John* (Cambridge, 1886).

Westcott, B.F., *A General Survey of the History of the Canon of the New Testament* (6th edn, Cambridge, 1889).

Westcott, B.F., *The Gospel according to St John* (London, 1890).

Westcott, B.F., *The Gospel of the Resurrection* (5th edn, London, 1884).

Westcott, B.F., *An Introduction to the Study of the Gospels* (5th edn, London, 1875).

Westcott, B.F., 'On a Form of Confraternity suited to the Present Work of the English Church', *Contemporary Review*, xiv (April 1870).

Westcott, B.F., *Religious Thought in the West* (London 1891).

Westcott, B.F., *Social Aspects of Christianity* (London, 1887).

Westcott, B.F. and Hort, F.J.A., Introduction to *The New Testament in the original Greek* (Cambridge, 1882).

Wilberforce, R.I. and Wilberforce, S., *Life of William Wilberforce* (5 vols, London, 1838).

Wordsworth, W., *'The Prelude'*, ed. E. de Selincourt (Oxford, 1926).

**Secondary Sources**

Addinall, P., *Philosophy and Biblical Interpretation* (Cambridge, 1991).

Allchin, A.M., *The Joy of all Creation* (London, 1984).

Allen, P., *The Cambridge Apostles: The Early Years* (Cambridge, 1978).

Annan, N., *Leslie Stephen* (London, 1951).

Annan, N., *Leslie Stephen: The Godless Victorian* (London, 1984).

Barrett, C.K., 'Joseph Barber Lightfoot', *Durham University Journal*, lxiv, 3 (June 1972).

Barrett, C.K., *Westcott as Commentator* (Cambridge 1958).

Barrett, C.K., 'J.B. Lightfoot as Biblical Commentator', Lightfoot Centenary Lectures, *Durham University Journal* (January 1992).

Barth, K., *Protestant Theology in the Nineteenth Century* (London, 1972).

Barth, K., *Theology and Church* (London, 1962; German edn, 1928).

Bensly, R.L., *Our Journey to Sinai* (London, 1896).

Bradley, W.L., *P.T. Forsyth: the Man and his Work* (London, 1952).

Brooke, C.N.L., *A History of the University of Cambridge*, iv (Cambridge, 1993).

Brooke, J.H., 'Indications of a Creator: Whewell as Apologist and Priest' in M. Fisch and S. Schaffer (eds), *William Whewell: A Composite Portrait* (Oxford, 1991).

Brown, F.K., *Fathers of the Victorians* (Cambridge, 1961).

Burgon, J.W., *Lives of Twelve Good Men* (2 vols, London, 1888).

Burkitt, F.C., *The Gospel History and its Transmission* (Edinburgh, 1906).

'F.C. Burkitt', *Proceedings of the British Academy* (1936).

Busch, E., *Karl Barth* (London, 1976).

Campbell, L and Garnett, W., *The Life of James Clerk Maxwell* (London, 1882).

Carlyle, T., *The Life of John Sterling* (London, 1897).

Chadwick, H., *The Vindication of Christianity in Westcott's Thought* (Cambridge, 1961).

Chadwick, O., *The Victorian Church* (2 vols, London, 1966, 1970).

Clark, J., *English Society 1688–1832* (Cambridge, 1985).

Clarke, M.L., *Paley: Evidences for the Man* (London, 1974).

Conder, E.R., *Josiah Conder: A Memoir* (London, 1857).

Cornick, D. and Binfield, C., *From Cambridge to Sinai: The worlds of Agnes Smith Lewis and Margaret Dunlop Gibson* (London, 2006).

Creed, J.M., 'The Study of the New Testament', *Journal of Theological Studies*, xlii (1941).

Cunich P., Hoyle, D., Duffy, E. and Hyam, R., *A History of Magdalene College, Cambridge, 1428–1988* (Cambridge, 1994).

*Dictionary of National Biography*, ed Sir L. Stephen and Sir S. Lee (63 vols, London, 1908).

Distad, N.M., *Guessing at Truth* (Shepherdstown, West Virginia, 1979).

Dunn, J.D.G., 'Lightfoot in Retrospect', Lightfoot Centenary Lectures, *Durham University Journal* (January 1992).

Eden, G.R. and Macdonald, F.C., *Lightfoot of Durham* (Cambridge, 1933).

Fairbairn, A.M., 'Some Recent English Theologians', *Contemporary Review*, lxxi (March 1897).

Fitzgerald M.H., *A Memoir of Herbert Edward Ryle* (London, 1928).

Forbes, D., *The Liberal Anglican Idea of History* (Cambridge, 1952).

Froude, J.A., *Short Studies on Great Subjects*, iv (London 1893).

Fuller, T., *The History of the University of Cambridge,* ed., J. Nichols (Cambridge, 1840).

Furneaux, R., *William Wilberforce* (London, 1974).

Gascoigne, J., *Cambridge in the Age of the Enlightenment* (Cambridge, 1989).

Gibson, M.D., *How the Codex Was Found* (Cambridge, 1893).

Glover, T.R., *The Conflict of Religions in the Early Roman Empire* (London, 1909).

Griffith, G.O., *The Theology of P.T. Forsyth* (London, 1948).

Gunning, H., *Reminiscences of the University, Town and County of Cambridge* (2 vols, London, 1854).

Gunton, C., 'The Real as the Redemptive: Forsyth on Authority and Freedom' in T. Hart (ed.), *Justice the True and Only Mercy*: *Essays on the Life and Theology of Peter Taylor Forsyth* (Edinburgh, 1995).

Harnack, A., Review of Edwin Hatch, *Essays in Biblical Greek*, in *Theologische Literaturzeitung*, 14 June 1890.

Harnack, A and Herrmann, W., *Essays on The Social Gospel* (London, 1907).

Harris, H., *David Friedrich Strauss and his Theology* (Cambridge, 1973).

Hedley, D., *Coleridge, Philosophy and Religion* (Cambridge, 2000).

Hengel, M., 'Bishop Lightfoot and the Tübingen School on the Gospel of John and the Second Century', Lightfoot Centenary Lectures, *Durham University Journal* (January 1992).

Herrmann, W., *The Communion of the Christian with God*, ed. R, Voelkel (London, 1971).

Hinchliff, P., *Benjamin Jowett and the Christian Religion* (Oxford, 1987).

Hinchliff, P., *God and History: Aspects of British Theology, 1875–1914* (Oxford, 1992).

Headlam, A.C., 'Hugh James Rose and the Oxford Movement', *Church Quarterly Review*, xciii (October 1921).

Hilton, B., *The Age of Atonement* (Oxford, 1988).

Hilton, B., *A Mad, Bad, and Dangerous People: England 1783–1846* (Oxford, 2006).

Hole, R., *Pulpits, Politics and Public Order, 1760–1832* (Cambridge, 1989).

Holland, H.S., *God's City and the Coming of the Kingdom* (London, 1894).

Holland, H.S., *Brooke Foss Westcott, Bishop of Durham* (London, 1910).

Hort, A.F., 'Fenton John Anthony Hort', *The Modern Churchman*, xvii (October 1927).

Johnston, J.O., *Life and Letters of Henry Parry Liddon* (London, 1904).

Knight, F., *University Rebel: The Life of William Frend (1757–1841)* (London, 1971).

Knox, R.B., *St Columba's Church, Cambridge, 1879–1979* [Cambridge, n.d.].

Kümmel, W.G., *The New Testament: The History of the Investigation of its Problems* (London, 1973).

LeMahieu, D.L., *The Mind of William Paley* (Lincoln, Nebraska, 1976).

Lewis, A.S., *In the Shadow of Sinai* (Cambridge, 1898).

Lewis, A.S., *Light on the Four Gospels from the Sinai Palimpsest* (London, 1913).

Lubenow, W.C., *The Cambridge Apostles, 1820–1914* (Cambridge, 1998).

Maitland, F.W., *The Life and Letters of Leslie Stephen* (London, 1906).

Manning, B.L., *This Latter House* (Cambridge, 1924).

Metzger, B.M., *The Early Versions of the New Testament* (Oxford, 1977).

Morgan, R.C., '"Non Angli sed Angeli": Some Anglican Reactions to German Gospel Criticism' in S. Sykes and D. Holmes (eds), *New Studies in Theology 1* (London, 1980).

Morris, J.N., *F.D. Maurice and the Crisis of Christian Authority* (London, 2005).

Moule, H.C.G., *My Cambridge Classical Teachers* (Durham, n.d. [1913]).

Moulton, W.F., *William F. Moulton: A Memoir* (London, 1899).

Mozley, J.K., 'The Theology of Dr Forsyth', *The Heart of the Gospel* (London, 1925).

Murray, J.O.F., *The Goodness and the Severity of God* (London, 1924).

Neill, S.C., *The Interpretation of the New Testament, 1861–1961* (London, 1964).

Newman, J.H., *An Essay on the Development of Christian Doctrine* (London, 1845).

Newman, J.H., *The Idea of a University*, ed. I.T. Ker (Oxford, 1976).

Newsome, D., *Two Classes of Men: Platonism and English Romantic Thought* (London, 1974).

Nicoll, W. Robertson, *Princes of the Church* (3rd edn, London, [1922])

Nockles, P., *The Oxford Movement in Context* (Cambridge, 1994).

Overton, J.H., *The English Church in the Nineteenth Century* (London, 1894).

*Oxford Dictionary of National Biography* (Oxford, 2004).

Parsons, K.A. (ed.), *St Andrew's Street Baptist Church 250th Anniversary* (Cambridge, 1971).

Patrick, G.A., *F.J.A. Hort: Eminent Victorian* (Sheffield, 1988).

Patrick, G.A., *The Miners' Bishop* (2nd edn, Peterborough, 2004).

Pattison, M., 'Tendencies of Religious Thought in England, 1688–1750' in *Essays and Reviews* (London, 1860).

Perowne, J.J.S., 'Dr Pusey on Daniel the Prophet', *Contemporary Review*, i (Jan 1866).

Reynolds, D. (ed.), *Christ's: A Cambridge College over Five Centuries* (London, 2004).

Riches, J., *A Century of New Testament Study* (Cambridge, 1993).

Robinson, J.A., 'The late Professor Hort', *The Expositor*, 4th series, vii (1893).

Rowell, G., *Hell and the Victorians* (Oxford, 1974).

Rupp, G., 'Hort and the Cambridge Tradition' in *Just Men* (London, 1977).

Sanday, W., 'The Future of English Theology', *The Contemporary Review*, lvi (July 1889).

Sanday, W., 'The Life and Letters of F.J.A. Hort', *American Journal of Theology*, i (January 1897).

Sanders, C.R., *Coleridge and the Broad Church Movement* (Durham, NC, 1942).

Schultz, B., *Henry Sidgwick: Eye of the Universe* (Cambridge, 2004).

Schweitzer, A., *The Quest of the Historical Jesus* (3rd edn, London, 1954).

Searby, P., *A History of the University of Cambridge, iii 1750–1870* (Cambridge, 1997).

Sidgwick, A., and Sidgwick, E.M., *Henry Sidgwick: A Memoir* (London, 1906).

Smith, W., *Dictionary of the Bible* (2 vols, London, 1863).

Smith, W., *A Concise Dictionary of the Bible* (London, 1865).

Smyth, C., *Simeon and Church Order* (Cambridge, 1940).

Stanley, A.P., *Life and Correspondence of Thomas Arnold* (London, n.d.).

Stell, C.F., *Nonconformist Chapels and Meeting-Houses in Eastern England* (London, 2002).

Stephen, L., *History of English Thought in the Eighteenth Century*, ed. Crane Brinton (2 vols, London, 1962).

Stephen, L., 'Jowett's Life', in Jowett, B., *The Interpretation of Scripture and other Essays* (London n.d.; originally published in *The National Review*, May 1897).

Sutherland, L.S. and Mitchell, L.G., *The History of the University of Oxford: v The Eighteenth Century* (Oxford, 1986).

Sykes, N., *Church and State in England in the Eighteenth Century* (Cambridge, 1934).

Taylor, T.F., *J. Armitage Robinson* (Cambridge, 1991).

Thirlwall, J.C., *Connop Thirlwall* (London, 1936).

Thompson, D.M., *Baptism, Church and Society in Modern Britain* (Bletchley, 2005).

Thompson, D.M., 'Lightfoot as Victorian Churchman' in J.D.G. Dunn (ed.), 'The Lightfoot Centenary Lectures', *Durham University Journal*, special issue (January 1992).

Thompson, D.M., 'Nonconformists at Cambridge before the First World War' in D.W. Bebbington and T. Larson (eds), *Modern Christianity and Cultural Aspirations* (London, 2003).

Tice, F., *The History of Methodism in Cambridge* (London, 1966)

Torrance, T.F., *Karl Barth: An Introduction to His Early Theology, 1910–1931* (new edn, Edinburgh, 2000).

Treloar, G.R., *Lightfoot the Historian* (Tübingen, 1998).

Tuckwell, W., *Reminiscences of Oxford* (London, 1900).

Twigg, J., *A History of Queens' College, Cambridge, 1448–1986* (Woodbridge, 1987).

Vidler, A.R., *Christian Belief* (London, 1950).

Vidler, A.R. (ed.), *Objections to Christian Belief* (London, 1963).

Vidler, A.R., *Scenes from a Clerical Life* (London, 1977).

Vidler, A.R. (ed.), *Soundings* (Cambridge, 1961).

Ward, J., *Essays in Philosophy* (Cambridge, 1927).

Ward, M., 'The New Reformation', *The Nineteenth Century*, xiv (March, 1889).

Waterman, A.M.C., 'A Cambridge "Via Media" in Late Georgian Anglicanism', *Journal of Ecclesiastical History*, xlii, 3 (July 1991).

Webster, A.B., *Joshua Watson* (London, 1954).

White, J.F., *The Cambridge Movement: The Ecclesiologists and the Gothic Revival* (Cambridge, 1962).

Williams, H.A., *Some Day I'll Find You* (London, 1984).

Wilson, R., 'Lightfoot, Savage and Eden – Sidelights on a Great Episcopate', *Theology*, lv, 386 (August 1952).

Winstanley, D., *Early Victorian Cambridge* (Cambridge 1940).

Winstanley, D., *Unreformed Cambridge* (Cambridge, 1935).

Wood, H.G., *Terrot Reaveley Glover* (Cambridge, 1953).

# Index

James I 59
Jarrett, Thomas 180
Jebb, John 17, 21
Jeremie, J.A. 7
Jerusalem 77, 104, 183
Jerusalem bishopric 88, 89
Jesus Christ 6, 14, 19, 53, 65, 77, 78, 87,
    102, 106, 116, 118, 120, 142, 152, 153,
    156, 157, 158, 159, 160, 162, 170–71,
    173–4, 179, 181, 182, 183, 191, 194,
    199
Johnson, W.H.F. 147
Jones, T. 27, 199
Jowett, Benjamin 1, 2, 3, 110, 112, 116,
    130–31, 133–4, 174, 190, 192, 197
Jowett, Henry 49
Jowett, Joseph 45
Justin Martyr 55, 56

Kähler, Martin 155
Kant, Immanuel 143, 155, 158, 159
Kaye, John (Bishop of Lincoln) 7, 53–6,
    63, 65, 66, 177, 178, 192
Keble, John 57, 99
Ken, Thomas 65
Kennett, R.H. 166
Keynes, J. Neville 150, 152, 154, 169, 189
King's College, London 56, 130, 176
Kingsley, Charles 5, 6, 93, 94
Kipling, Thomas 17, 33, 41, 43
Kirkpatrick, A.F. 124, 180
Knox, E.A. (Bishop of Manchester) 1, 2
Kuenen, A. 165

Lachmann, C. 108
Lagarde, A.P. de 164
Lake, Kirsopp 191
Lancaster, Joseph 44
Lardner, Nathaniel 13, 18, 29, 32, 33, 35,
    55, 192
La Salette 117, 118
Latimer, Hugh 62, 83
Law, Edmund 14, 26, 27
Law, John 26
Law, William 66
Lecky, William 117
Le Clerc, J. 39
Lee, James Prince 73, 96, 99, 103
Lee, Samuel 6
Less, G. 35

Lessing, G.E. 89, 102
Lewis, A.S. 6, 148, 149, 163, 166–7, 168,
    182, 196, 198
Leys School 148
Liddon, H.P. 120, 140, 154, 179, 197
Lightfoot, J.B. i, ix, 2, 4, 6, 7, 10, 29, 63, 74,
    95, 96–7, 98, 104, 105, 106–8, 109–11,
    112–13, 114, 115, 116, 117, 120, 121,
    124, 125, 127–8, 130–31, 133, 135, 136,
    137–41, 143, 145, 150, 177, 178, 179,
    180, 182, 192, 195, 196, 197, 199, 200
Lincoln 7, 53, 54, 98, 108
Lindsay, Theophilus 24
Liverpool 1, 96, 150, 169
Livy 36, 79
Lloyd, Charles 54
Locke, John 3, 13, 14, 21, 22, 24, 25, 26,
    30, 55, 65, 69, 82, 90, 133, 176, 178,
    192
Lotze, Hermann 150
Louis XVI 43
Lubernow, W.C. 73, 152, 198
Ludlow, J.M. 92, 94
Luther, Martin 10, 79, 83, 84, 85, 99, 128,
    189, 191
Lutheranism 38
*Lux Mundi* 4, 125, 126, 139, 143, 160, 179,
    191

Mackinnon, Donald 187
Macmillan, Alexander 109, 115, 145
Macmillan, Daniel 92, 93, 94, 101
Mainwaring, John 46
Manning, B.L. 150, 162, 198
Manning, Henry 92, 141
Mansel, H.L. 134
Mansel, William 45
Marsh, Herbert 5, 10, 30, 31–2, 33–5, 36,
    37–8, 39–42, 43–5, 46–7, 49, 52–3, 54,
    56, 66, 69, 72, 76, 114, 174, 177, 178,
    189, 192–3, 194
Martyn, Henry 53, 178
Mary, mother of Jesus 117
Maurice, Esther 74
Maurice, J.F.D. 2, 5, 6, 7, 9, 10, 71, 73, 86,
    89, 91–4, 98–9, 100, 114, 116, 124, 125,
    127, 128–30, 131, 132, 135, 136, 141,
    143, 145, 147, 158, 175, 176, 193, 198
*Theological Essays* 94, 130, 176
Maurice, Priscilla 2, 74